Madness and Blake's Myth

MADNESS & BLAKE'S MYTH

Paul Youngquist

The Pennsylvania State University Press
University Park and London

Library of Congress Cataloging-in-Publication Data

Youngquist, Paul.
Madness and Blake's myth/Paul Youngquist.

p. cm.
Includes index.
ISBN 0-271-00669-2
1. Blake, William, 1757–1827—Knowledge—Psychology.
2. Mental illness in literature. 3. Myth in literature.
4. Literature and mental illness—Great Britain. I. Title.
PR4148.M45Y6   88-43441   1989
821'.7—dc20

Copyright© 1989 The Pennsylvania State University
All rights reserved
Printed in the United States of America

Contents

Preface	vii
Acknowledgments	xiii
Introduction	1
1 Refuge from Unbelief	17
2 Lyric into Myth	45
3 King, Creator, Madman	71
4 Schizophrenia and the Ancient Man	101
5 Trial and Defense	137
Notes	169
Index	189

Preface

When I first became interested in Blake and started to wrestle with the formidable body of scholarship his poetry has inspired, I noticed that most of his best critics went out of their way to defend him against the charge of madness. Why this worry? I wondered. If it were so obvious that Blake was as sane as these critics ardently claimed, then why bother? No one considers Wordsworth in need of such defense. The very fact that critics of high standing felt obliged to endorse Blake's mental health made me suspicious, and all the more so since such endorsements usually grew tendentious or effusive. It occurred to me that there might be reason to consider Blake mad, or at least possessed of a mentality atypical of the human norm. Genius, of course, is similarly atypical, and there is no question that Blake was a literary genius of the highest order. But the "flavor" of his genius includes something extraordinarily piquant, a tendency toward the irrational that gives the impression of mental eccentricity. Could it be that an artistic achievement as great as William Blake's was born in the collision between a sound mind and its pathology?

We must not discount this possibility if we hope to reach a deep understanding of Blake's visionary art. Unlike the Romantic poets with whom he is usually grouped, Blake made madness a central subject of his poetry. To be sure, other Romantic poems also approach this subject. In "Resolution and Independence," Wordsworth frets over poets whose lives end in madness. At the end of "Kubla Khan," Coleridge depicts the potential madness of the inspired artist. And in the disturbing poem "Julian and Maddalo," Shelley, in some ways closest to Blake in spirit, examines the mad demise of one whose political and libidinal desires never reach fulfillment. What these poems by the other Romantic poets have in common is the tendency to mediate their representations of madness. Wordsworth contemplates the possibility of a mad despair, but finds new strength in the apt admonishment of the Leech-Gatherer. Coleridge imagines the fury of inspiration, but his vatic description remains conditional, a mere possibility. And Shelley keeps his madman at a safe distance, shutting him in a tower. Only Blake allows the dynamics of mental distress to become a main preoccupation of his poetry. In this he betrays his kinship to those close literary cousins, the sensibility bards, for whom madness became a personal threat that eventually crippled their poetic talents. Precisely because Blake made madness into myth, he avoided the fate of the sensibility bards, but without resorting to the extreme mediations of later Romantic poets.

Such an argument presumes that Blake understood the nature of mental suffering and that he used his artistic activity to give it a form. If this is true, then we must reevaluate the way we approach Blake's poetry. The accepted approach, conceived by Northrop Frye and consolidated by his followers, treats Blake's engraved works as a definitive canon supported by a permanent system of ideas. Accordingly, any poem that Blake saw fit to engrave necessarily partakes of this system and its ideological assumptions. This approach is an effective way to begin the study of Blake, but blinds us to important discontinuities and schisms in his artistic life. If Blake always meant for his engraved work to comprise a single canon, then why did he censor it later in life by suppressing the sale of *The Marriage of Heaven and Hell?* This interesting question usually goes unanswered because it implies a discontinuity in Blake's "system." Recent studies of Blake's thought have begun to take such discontinuities honestly into account. It is part of my aim to continue this reassessment by examining the psychological uses to which Blake put his poetry. Only by attending closely to Blake's changes of mind can we appreciate fully the character of his myth.

What often gets lost in discussions of Blake's "system" is a sense of the individual who built it. In his late poem *Jerusalem*, Blake describes his prophetic labors as "Striving with Systems to deliver Individuals from those Systems" (*J*, 11:5). It is an indication of how far criticism of Blake's poetry has advanced in recent years that Blake himself needs to be delivered from his own system. Our sense of the individual behind that system has been obscured by the very impressiveness of his thought. But Blake's poetry everywhere bears the stamp of the highly individual mind that conceived it. By honoring that individuality and examining the mental eccentricity to which it was subject, we get a clear picture of the psychological purposes that poetry served Blake. Such an insight is indeed significant, since an artist bases his expectations of how others will benefit from his activity upon how he does himself. This approach to Blake's poetry justifies alertness to its biographical implications, but not that naive sort of criticism which finds evidence for interpretation in the length of a man's nose. Blake's visionary experience shaped his life *and* his work; we falsify both when we fail to investigate the character of Blake's mentality and its manifestation in his myth. When art originates in an unusual mentality, as a visionary art must, it communicates a kind of experience that, to paraphrase Blake, some suffer so the rest of us need not.

Besides, contemporary criticism is in danger of losing sight of the individual as creator. Certain post-structural and Marxist methods of interpretation have so diminished the role of the artist in the act of creation that art seems to arise without the intervention of individual will or desire. To many critics, politics or history now appears to be the great demiurge, fabricating poems and paintings that materialize, somehow, in the libraries and studios of various surrogate creators. The strange notion has occurred to some that there is no such thing as an author, that language speaks without a mouthpiece, or that when poets compose, history really does all the work. While it is unquestionably true that history shapes an author's aims and ought therefore to be studied, the extent to which history *determines* literary activity is a question that requires the greatest critical tact even to raise. We must not discount, for reasons of fashion or convenience, the role that the individual plays in producing a work of art. By restoring Blake to Blake studies we restore the individual to the act of creation, but with the awareness that the biography of the mind cannot be reduced to historical circumstance. And to restore Blake to Blake studies is to consider inevitably the character of Blake's own mental life.

For this reason I rely upon a primarily empirical method for examining Blake's visionary poetry and experience. Although throughout this study literary analysis takes priority over biographical analysis, I believe the latter has a role to play in critical discourse that we too easily discount, and where appropriate I shall employ it. An empirical as opposed to a psychoanalytical approach emphasizes observed experience rather than an inferred psychodynamic. Poems do not reduce to hypothetical antecedents such as Oedipal rivalry but simply manifest a particular way of experiencing the world. The danger of applying psychoanalytic hypotheses and methods to a highly psychological poetry like Blake's is that the results simply compare one interpretation of the mind with another. In a sense, a psychoanalytical approach is too literary to yield conclusive results. I prefer therefore a more empirical approach and draw upon evidence from Blake's biography to provide a solid context for literary analysis, a "stubborn structure" on which to build a credible discussion of madness and Blake's myth.

In the interest of making that myth contemporary with modern experience, I occasionally use clinical insights to substantiate critical ones, though in full awareness of their provisionality. After all, Blake himself imagined a time when man would awaken to that "sweet Science" which unites intellectual rigor with human feeling. Clinical insights can improve our understanding of certain unusual qualities of Blake's mind and the visionary art it produced. Blake claimed, for instance, that when he looked at the sun, he saw not a round disk of fire somewhat like a guinea, but an innumerable company of the heavenly host singing holy, holy, holy. This claim is usually interpreted as an example of the extraordinary power of Blake's imagination. But to what extent, we might ask, is such power evidence of mental eccentricity, particularly in a world where the heavenly host appears so rarely? Clinical insights come to the aid of criticism here by providing a contemporary context for interpretation. Blake's beatific vision of the sun might be more than an imaginative metaphor; it might be symptomatic of a mentality which, however conducive to artistic activity, poses a real threat to health and happiness.

Finally, a word about the occasional use of the term "schizophrenia" in this study. By "schizophrenia" I do not have in mind the very narrow range of mental illness described by the latest genetic and neuro-chemical research. Poems have no genes, and it would be futile, not to say silly, to impose upon them a scientific description of madness that presumes a genetic motivation. I use the term in a more generic sense, meaning by "schizophrenia" the fundamental experience of madness in our modern world. Clinicians will quibble with this description, finding it scientifically naive. But what follows is a critical study of a poet and his poetry, not a scientific inquiry into one man's mental illness. My purpose is to interpret Blake's myth in a way that enhances its contemporaneity and explains, to the extent possible, why madness is so central a thematic preoccupation.

As we travel the darker roads of Blake's artistic development, we will be discussing madness in a variety of contexts: philosophical, thematic, and clinical. This flexibility does not undermine but rather invigorates our undertaking, since it enhances the relevance of madness to Blake's myth and, ultimately, to ourselves. Through some supremely subtle intuition, Blake understood that madness defines our humanity—*by negating it.* In making madness the subject of his myth, he lays claim to the distinction of being an epic poet of the modern mind and a physician of the modern spirit.

Acknowledgments

"He who has sufferd you to impose on him knows you": if in this instance Blake speaks truly, as so often he does, then I fear I have been the cause of much suffering. Those who know me know too how very much I owe them. Paul Cantor and Robert Langbaum have been constant tutors of the critic's craft, practiced not merely as a professional habit, but more rewardingly as an art of discovery. David V. Erdman and Martin Bidney scrupulously read drafts of my manuscript, saving me from a variety of gaffes, grammatical, historical, and hermeneutic. Philip Winsor, Sue Lewis, and the staff at the Penn State Press guided the book patiently through the many stages of its revision and production. And finally, inexpressibly, my lasting gratitude goes to Megan, without whom what I do would not be worth the doing.

Behold, this dreamer cometh.
—Genesis 37:19

Introduction

In what sense and how far is the genius master of his madness? For it goes without saying that to a certain degree he is master of it, since otherwise he would be actually a madman. For such observations, however, ingenuity in a high degree is requisite, and love; for to make observation upon a superior mind is very difficult.
—Kierkegaard, *Fear and Trembling*

I

What is madness? How is it to be understood critically? Such questions present formidable barriers to a criticism that would make madness the subject of interpretation. Seeking a suitable method, one soon realizes that madness, more than most human problems, exists relative to its definition. This insight has led some investigators, most notably Michel Foucault, to conclude that madness is primarily a social phenomenon with a history that reveals significant variations across the centuries in what it means to be mad.[1] But the madman is not merely a historical curiosity. He suffers real anguish, in our own age as in any other. The alternative to historical relativism as a method for investigating madness appears to be the clinical determinism practiced by today's psychiatrists and psychologists, who classify mental afflictions and diagnose the individual accordingly. Science differs from social history in construing madness as primarily a physiological problem.

Neither the historical nor the clinical method, however, provides the literary critic with a satisfying approach to madness. The first reduces a suffering individual to a historical epi-phenomenon, the second, to a quantifiable object. Neither method regards madness as an existential problem, a disturbance, that is, in the human experience of the world. And yet madness does not exist except embodied in the madman. The trouble with historical relativism is that it disregards an individual's experience of the social conditions that structure madness. Should this experience find its way into literature, the historical method explains it as the effect of social forces, not of personal suffering.

Clinical determinism, on the other hand, too often regards the human being as an appendage of its physiology. Under the gaze of the diagnostician, the individual becomes a specimen ("proband" in contemporary jargon) and his or her suffering becomes a physiological disorder. As suffering thus acquires a classification, experience ceases to belong to the individual. But what clinicians rarely admit is that diagnosis is an act of interpretation, even though clinical psychology has in common with literary criticism reliance upon interpretation to draw conclusions. An individual is not a schizophrenic, for instance, until a diagnostician interprets his symptoms according to professional standards such as those advanced in the most recent edition of the *Diagnostic and Statistical Manual*. Since these standards change with each new edition of the manual, however, their validity is clearly provisional. They assist in the interpretation of mental suffering, but do not provide an objective standard of reference. The critic investigating madness through a clinical method must support his or her own interpretations by means of others which, however illuminating, lack an assured validity. This chance is worth taking if it gives new life to old literature, but not if it distorts the experience of a particular author. After all, literature lives on in ways that authors do not.

What is needed is a method that combines historical integrity with clinical insight without reducing a human artifact—literature—to either a social or a psychological object. A phenomenology of mental life answers these requirements rather nicely. Such a method gives full credence to an author's experience of the world. The facts of his life take on importance, not as biographical clues to literary meaning, but as indices of the mind's life, substantial tokens of one being's relationship with the world it inhabits. History, both personal and public, becomes the context for experience, but neither conditions it in an absolute sense nor isolates it from what precedes and follows. On the contrary, experience of the world binds one generation to the next and allows human beings to gaze in recognition across the centuries. Given this existential continuity it becomes possible and even important to describe and interpret variations in the way individuals experience the world. In the arena of mental life, anomalies bear special significance for the norm, since they establish a boundary beyond which the whole character of human experience changes. Madness makes visible this change in an individual's experience of the world, this aberration of the mind's life. Such an anomaly, as experienced in life or expressed in literature, demands our attention, for it challenges our common humanity.

William Blake was a poet for whom madness became a major subject. He wrote about it abundantly, and in his own lifetime was accused of being mad. For a time the charge of madness tainted his reputation as a poet; the great achievement of modern criticism has been to press beyond this indictment to the poetry itself, saving it from being dismissed as foolishness and confusion. But in doing so criticism has overlooked—or neglected—the eccentricity of Blake's mental life, from which his poetry flowers like a strange orchid from exotic soil. Critics hesitate to say that Blake's experience deviated from the human norm, as if such a statement would discredit serious consideration of his poems. But a deviation, if there were one, demands all the more attention, since the norm acquires meaning primarily by being compromised. Put another way, "You never know what is enough unless you know what is more than enough." A criticism fully awake to the claims of Blake's mental life would compare them with the norm of human experience and consider the implications of any deviation.

But the norm of human experience is a slippery item. Historical relativism teaches that experience develops in accordance with the conditions of history; the attempt to normalize it is therefore an exercise in bad faith. This belief can only be true, however, if time alters us absolutely. In fact history plays variations on the persistent theme of being human. Experience produces history, not history experience, and human experience consists in the relation of men and women to the world. This being the case, it indeed becomes possible to make a few valid remarks about the norm of human experience.[2]

First of all, because experience involves a *relation* between the human being and the world, both parties in that relation, individual *and* world, contribute something to it. Men and women act upon the world, but are acted upon as well. Every breath is an exchange between a being and its environment. Every sight a being sees is the world's spontaneous unveiling.

This relation between I and Other is fundamental to human experience. To cancel either half of the equation is to reduce lived experience to dead abstraction.

A second point. Because this relation is continuous, sensation organizes and guides it. This does not mean that the senses build up, as in Locke's psychology, a mental image of the outside world. Such a notion presupposes severing the relation between I and Other fundamental to human experience. On the contrary, sensation establishes this relation and facilitates a creative engagement with the world. The words of a friend are not experienced as a subjective construct of external stimuli, but as a portion of the world come alive through the sensation of hearing. This sensation can be shared, and must be to maintain an active relation between I and Other. Sensation thus reinforces the relation of man and world precisely because it is shareable. Were it not, the experiencing being would drift into a prison of sensory solipsism.

Finally, a third remark. Experience is pre-reflective. It does not come to us by thought but by immersion in the world. As I sit here in my study busied with these ideas, my experience dwindles to nil. Reflection shuts it out. But stepping outdoors I confront a world rich in possibility. The pre-reflective character of experience means that any retreat into pure thought turns it off. So the Cartesian consciousness that knows the world through doubt no longer experiences the world in human terms. *Res cogitans* equals *mens solitaria*, and under these conditions human being turns against the world—and itself.

Such is the norm of human experience, characterized by a mutual relation between individual and world, shareable sensation, and pre-reflective awareness. One must confess, however, that this human norm is not always identical with the historical. What passes for human experience changes with the times, and since Descartes, many have held that human beings know the world primarily through reflection. Such a bias does not compromise the norm, since most men and women simply do not *live* this way. But in comparing the experience of one being to that norm, one must be wary of the degree to which deviation occurs in historical terms. Blake's eccentricities, for instance, arose in part because of his strong objection to a historical norm that favored reflection. Even so, a close look at the facts of his life—physical and mental—shows that Blake's experience of the world differed from the *human* norm as well. It is this difference that encouraged his contemporaries to dismiss him as mad. An important question in approaching his work critically therefore becomes whether or not their charge is at all credible.

II

A brief biographical sketch that attends to the strange character of Blake's experience best opens the question of madness and its significance for his myth. Very little is known about Blake's early years. He was born on November 27, 1757, to James and Catherine Blake, who had him baptized in St. James Church, Picadilly. James Blake was a hosier by trade and fathered a total of seven children, six boys of whom two died early, and one girl, the poet's younger sister Catherine. Though it is known that William was the third, his boyhood remains obscure. He was raised in quarters above his father's shop at 28 Broad Street, near the pleasant green called Golden Square and not far from the woods and fields surrounding London. As a boy Blake appears to have been remarkable for his refractory temperament, which even then showed traces of eccentricity. Stories were told of how, when only four, Blake saw God for the first time: the Almighty put His head to a window and set the child to screaming. On another occasion, while walking the fields one summer morning, the boy saw angels among the haymakers. These anecdotes and others like them suggest that even in childhood Blake's experience of the world differed in significant ways from the human norm. Blake experienced visions literally and valued them as if they were part of the world at large. That such visionary experience became a large part of his life is confirmed by a rather querulous remark made by his wife many years later: "I have very little of Mr. Blake's company; he is always in Paradise."[3]

James Blake was particularly sensitive to his son's unusual nature and spared him the ordeal of attending school, where he would have bridled against the usually strict discipline. William was educated mostly at home, and his father encouraged his artistic interests. When he reached the age of fourteen, he was engaged as an apprentice to an engraver. Circumstance helped make his choice of craft, for although painting was his first love, the cost of studying with a master would have overburdened the family. Blake chose engraving as a related craft by which he could be sure to make a living. Indentures were exchanged with James Basire, a distinguished if somewhat old-fashioned topographical and antiquarian engraver. The term was the traditional seven years, during which time Blake studied at his master's behest and probably lived with him as well.

Blake worked at Basire's side for two years, until the arrival of new apprentices made him the butt of much foolery. To reduce tensions

Basire sent him to Westminster Abbey to sketch sculptures and monuments that would be engraved for the Society of Antiquarians. There Blake acquired a lasting taste for Gothic architecture and design and also cultivated his visionary gift. He saw Christ and his apostles among the tombs and once witnessed a procession of monks, priests, cloisterers, and censer-bearers while hearing their uncanny chant—accompanied by organ. Blake made steady progress in the study of his craft, and by the end of his apprenticeship he was qualified to set up shop as a journeyman engraver. His artistic interests never left him, however, and he planned to distinguish himself also as a designer.

Throughout his youth Blake was testing the wings of another talent, a talent for poetry. In 1783, with the help of friends, he published a collection of juvenilia entitled *Poetical Sketches,* which shows a startlingly precocious sensibility in hard pursuit of its own idiom. Blake was at the time part of a circle of dilettantes that met regularly at the home of Reverend and Mrs. Anthony Steven Mathew, where he often sang his poems to tunes he composed himself. He eventually lost interest in these literary evenings, perhaps as a result of his own contentiousness.

Blake seems to have preferred more intimate relationships than those he found among the Mathews set. The great event of his early manhood was his marriage to Catherine Boucher, a girl he met in 1781 while on the rebound from an unrequited crush. If tradition can be trusted, Blake's courtship progressed with impressive speed. Soon after meeting Catherine he confessed his heartache and won her sympathy. "Do you pity me?" he asked his new acquaintance. "Yes I do," was her response. "Then I love you," he replied and left her company resolved to marry. He worked for a year before he had money enough to support a wife, finally marrying Catherine on August 18, 1782, in St. Mary's Church at Battersea. Theirs was a tense but abiding relationship that endured prosperity and penury, in that order.

The other significant relationship in Blake's life was that with his younger brother Robert, the one member of Blake's family who shared his artistic and visionary interests. By 1782 both brothers had been admitted to the Royal Academy as students of engraving, a membership Blake had held since the completion of his apprenticeship. During the early years of his marriage Blake continued to teach Robert the rudiments of art. Their drawings prove them kindred spirits, men who experienced the world as an enchanted place. Early in 1787 Robert fell gravely ill, and Blake tended him to the last, watching continuously for a fortnight until his brother gave up the ghost. "At the last solemn moment," according to Blake's best biographer, "the visionary eyes beheld the released spirit ascend heavenward through the matter-of-fact ceiling, 'clapping its hands for joy.' "[4] Robert's loss was the deepest Blake ever suffered, though he asserted on several occasions that he conversed daily with his dead brother in spirit and even owed the secret of his unique printing method to Robert's apparition. Robert lived on for Blake in vision and remained actively part of his experience.

Visionary experience such as this added something extra to Blake's world. Blake came to respect this something extra and allowed it to shape his activity, though never absolutely. The idea, for instance, of using carpenter's glue as a binding agent for water colors came to him, he liked to insist, in a vision of Joseph, "the sacred carpenter." Such visions were a real part of the world Blake experienced and must not be discounted as insignificant or inessential.

About 1789 Blake moved with his wife into quarters at 13 Hercules Buildings, Lambeth. He remained there ten years and for five of them enjoyed greater prosperity than at any other time in his life. Blake flourished as an artisan and flowered as an artist. His graver was in demand and his muse was at his call. Between 1789 and 1794 he engraved more plates of verse than he would for the remainder of his career as a poet, which was a long one by any standard, lasting at least until 1822. The works of this short period at Lambeth include most of those commonly associated with the name William Blake: *Songs of Innocence and of Experience, The Book of Thel, The Marriage of Heaven and Hell, Visions of the Daughters of Albion, The Book of Urizen, America,* and *Europe.* Among the somewhat less familiar works that were also produced in this creative outburst are *The French Revolution, The Song of Los, The Book of Ahania, The Book of Los,* and *The Gates of Paradise.* A slew of notebook lyrics date as well from the Lambeth years. Blake clearly hit his stride as a poet, found both what he had to say and the right way of saying it. Such eras in an artist's development assume special prominence. Blake later looked back on the Lambeth years as a kind of Golden Age in his career.

But he was not alone in the conviction that the early nineties were a special time. It was shared by those of his peers who had caught the revolutionary fever emanating from France. London had become a center of republican unrest; Thomas Paine published *The Rights of Man,* and Horne Tooke was tried for treason. Always an advocate of liberty, Blake fell in with a republican crowd at the home of Joseph Johnson, the publisher, for whom Blake occasionally did engravings. Johnson published many of the day's republican authors and regaled them with weekly dinners, which on any given Tuesday might have been attended by Joseph Priestly, Henry Fuseli, Mary Wollstonecraft, William Godwin, Joel Barlow, or Tom Paine. Blake probably attended at least some of these dinners as well, and certainly endorsed their revolutionary spirit, though there is little reason to believe the old story that after one at which Paine delivered a particularly stirring speech, Blake took him aside and told him to flee the country, thus saving his life. Blake's poem entitled *The French Revolution* (1791) makes his political sympathies clear, however, so clear that "Book the First" was withheld from publication after having been set in type. Johnson was to be the publisher, but either he or Blake suppressed the poem, probably because Blake himself feared the consequences of openly declaring his allegiance to revolutionary France.

His growing preference for symbolic poetry and a personal means of publication were motivated in part by a desire to mask republican sympathies during an era of extreme tension between England and France. The poems of the mid-nineties, especially *America* (1793) and *Europe* (1794), are highly topical creations, but celebrate the cause of rebellion only obliquely, since their symbolic method somewhat obscures their revolutionary message. They are the productions of a prophet either unable or unwilling to proclaim himself openly. The supersaturated symbolism of a poem like *Europe* owes its difficulty to the hostility toward republicanism that Blake sensed all around him. For reasons of security as much as preference, he wrapped his prophecy of one humanity in a thick garment of symbols.

Then, quite abruptly, Blake stopped engraving his poems, falling publicly silent for ten years after 1795. He continued to write, sometimes furiously, but not to illuminate and publish new compositions. This era of silence marks the start of a new phase in Blake's career as a poet in which he turned from lyric and short prophecy to the larger task of epic, or more precisely, epic-prophecy. This swerve away from his earlier style came first, however, in the service of the visual arts. In 1795 Blake produced a magnificent series of colored drawings, printed in a unique method of his own devising and finished individually. These included some of his most recognized visual images: "God Creating Adam," "Newton," and the haunting "Nebuchadnezzar."

The next year, 1796, presented Blake with an opportunity he felt would make his name as a designer and engraver. Richard Edwards, a bookseller impressed with Blake's genius, commissioned him to illustrate and engrave "an embellished edition of an english classick," Edward Young's *Night Thoughts*, a poem then very much in vogue. Blake worked on the project single-mindedly for over a year, producing 543 watercolor sketches. When Book One appeared in June of 1797, Blake believed it would rank among the finest engraved works of the age. But the public felt otherwise. Poor sales were in part the result of a financial crisis that depressed all markets. It must be admitted, however, that the 43 engravings Blake executed for *Night Thoughts* are not his best. Sublimity lapses frequently into the comic or the grotesque, though one might argue that Young's poem suffers similarly. The later reaction of Bulwer Lytton is probably representative of the public's response: "the whole makes one of the most astonishing and curious productions which ever balanced between the conception of genius and the raving of insanity" (*Blake Records*, 59). The poem's remaining books never appeared.

The failure of *Night Thoughts* dealt a blow to Blake's reputation as an artisan. Orders for engravings dwindled to a trickle and even friends like Johnson and Fuseli passed him over. Though in his forties and at the height of his abilities, Blake fell into neglect. So he turned again to poetry and painting, composing verse for a long poem and producing cabinet paintings on Biblical subjects. "I live by Miracle," Blake wrote in a letter of this period, and the miracle-worker was his faithful patron Thomas Butts. How Blake came to know Butts remains unclear, but this loyal friend kept him afloat at a time when destitution was a real possibility. Butts was muster-master general in the Office of the Commission of Musters; it seems somewhat odd that an army recruiter should take an interest in Blake's visionary productions. He was a charitable and generous patron, however, allowing Blake to follow his inclinations wherever they led. Without Butts's support the last years of the eighteenth century would have been dark ones indeed for William Blake.

In the spring of 1800 another friend, the sculptor John Flaxman, recommended Blake to William Hayley, popular versifier and patron of the arts, as a sure hand to engrave a medallion of Hayley's dying natural son Thomas. Hayley must have known about Blake since the early 1780s, when Flaxman presented him with a copy of *Poetical Sketches*. But it was not until Blake visited him at his Felpham estate in July of 1800 that a relationship grew up between them which shaped the course of Blake's life and poetry for years to come. Hayley was a well-intentioned man who unfortunately confused material assistance and spiritual guidance. He had nursed William Cowper through despair and madness, and in

Blake he saw another artist fallen on hard times but worthy of patronage. The deal was struck for Blake and his wife to move to Felpham, where Hayley would work on their behalf to secure commissions for engravings and such paintings as he deemed worthy of Blake's talent. Blake, he believed, must learn to paint miniatures. That was where the money was. Full of the promise of renewed prosperity, Blake packed his wife, his sister, and all their belongings into a cart and on September 18, 1800, moved to Felpham, some sixty miles south of London.

    Blake took a three-year lease on a plain thatched cottage, which he proclaimed a "Spontaneous Effusion of Humanity" for its simplicity and usefulness. He began working assiduously at Hayley's side, dedicating himself to the tasks his patron assigned him: a series of heads of great poets to ornament Hayley's library, an engraving of Cowper to stand at the front of Hayley's biography of the poet, an illustration to accompany Hayley's ballad, *Little Tom the Sailor*. For the first time in several years Blake had steady employment in the craft he had been trained to, but it soon became apparent that he was a subordinate, perpetrating another man's intentions. Blake began to chafe beneath the bridle of Hayley's generosity. His position was an uncomfortable one, caught as he was between the claims of material security and artistic integrity. He needed the work and the money that Hayley's patronage could provide him. But he had no interest in putting up with the petty tyrannies of a philistine and a literary hack. After the first few happy months at Felpham, Blake found himself under enormous psychological pressure. The artistic rivalry that developed between him and Hayley was all the more intense for being hidden. Blake endured Hayley's guidance in his company, but in his absence pursued his own designs. This civilized hypocrisy proved painful for a man who believed that openness and liberty were fundamental to human happiness. By 1803 Blake was nearing the breaking point, as the shrill quality of his letters of that year attests. He was looking forward to his return to London and a life free from his patron's fetters.

    But an incident occurred that cast a shadow over Blake's hopes. On August 12 Blake discovered a trespasser in the garden of his cottage, a soldier who, as far as Blake knew, had entered uninvited. John Schofield, a private in the First Regiment of His Majesty's Dragoons, claimed that he had been asked in to aid the gardener. Blake and Schofield exchanged words, and in his passion the poet grabbed his adversary by the elbows, pushing him out of the gate and down the road to the inn where he was quartered. Words continued along the way until a little crowd gathered and Schofield retreated to confer with a crony. Charges were brought against Blake the next day, charges of seditious utterance against the King. In the heat of the brawl, Schofield attested, Blake shouted "Damn the King of England—his country and his subjects—his soldiers are all bound for slaves and all the poor people in general."[5] In the tense political atmosphere of 1803, with invasion from France a possibility, such utterance could indeed be found seditious and its speaker punished accordingly. Blake was faced with the ordeal of a public trial and the threat, if convicted, of imprisonment.

It is probably no coincidence that the words Schofield charged Blake with saying possess a curiously Blakean ring. If he didn't speak these words he at least felt them, as anyone acquainted with his poems will agree. Luckily for him, the judges hearing his case on January 11, 1804, had no idea even that Blake was a poet. Thanks to a spirited defense by Samuel Rose, whom Hayley had retained on Blake's behalf, the poet of revolution was acquitted of sedition. But once again Blake was forced to contradict publicly what he felt privately. Poetry and not reality was the arena in which he gave full vent to his ideas and feelings. The poems begun in this period, *Milton* and the monumental *Jerusalem*, both make this tension between personal and public experience a central concern.

Blake returned to London in 1803 and remained there the rest of his life, slipping gradually into obscurity. He supported himself and his wife with what work he could find, engraving for whoever would hire him or painting for Butts. Out of a sense of gratitude and responsibility, he at first acted as Hayley's agent in town, making inquiries and running errands. His notebook shows how he felt about *that* engagement. In 1807 he executed a series of designs for Thomas Blair's popular poem *The Grave*, only to see them given to another man to engrave. At this time too the idea of painting a tableau of the Canterbury pilgrims was suggested by the same shady agent to both Blake and the fashionable painter Thomas Stothard, the latter of whom more readily catered to the public taste and realized a handsome profit for his pains. Blake sought to even the score for these and other artistic snubs in 1809 by holding a private exhibition at his brother's house. The show was a failure, but to accompany it Blake composed a descriptive catalogue containing not only instructive literary criticism but also descriptions of his visionary experience. From his visions he derived ideas of great public monuments that would establish England's reputation as a bastion of the arts. He imagined covering Westminster Hall with movable frescoes and erecting huge statues to English heroes.

With the failure of his exhibition Blake lapsed into oblivion for almost ten years. How he earned a living during this period is a mystery. In 1812 he exhibited four works with the Water Color Society, and in 1814 a friend who called upon him recorded in a diary that Blake was "still poor and Dirty" (*Blake Records,* 232). Records indicate that he did some routine engravings for Josiah Wedgewood, probably at Flaxman's recommendation. But these years of penury show most pathetically that Blake could not win regular employment as an engraver. For whatever reason he was forced to live on what little came his way and probably owed his subsistence to the generosity of friends.

In 1818 Blake emerged from the shadows with a new set of admirers and brighter prospects. The aspiring artist John Linnell befriended him and looked after him until the poet's death, securing employment, largely in the form of personal commissions. Under Linnell's patronage Blake produced his greatest work of engraving, the illuminations of *The Book of Job,* which rank among the best engravings ever. Blake also made the acquaintance of a number of young artists, whose minds he nourished and whose abilities he nurtured. They called him "the Interpreter" after Bunyan's character of that name, and went on to become some of the leading artists of their generation. Samuel Palmer was among them, as was Edward Calvert, George Richmond, and Frederick Tatham. With some others they styled themselves "the ancients" and identified strongly with Blake's visionary Gothicism. It seems fitting that Blake, champion of youthful energy, should have his largest influence as a living artist upon the young. But he had older friends too, among whom John Varley was the most unusual. Varley was an astrologer and a landscape painter in whose company late in 1819 Blake drew, as if from life, the strange sketches that have become known collectively as the "visionary heads." These drawings of historical and legendary celebrities attest to Blake's extraordinary ability to see literally what he imagined, even late in life. Varley claimed that when Blake drew these heads, he behaved as if a living model were before him—except that none was! Blake's visionary experience was so mundane a feature of his life that he could easily persuade companions that spirits stood before him.

Blake died on August 12, 1827, a painter of very little repute and a poet of even less. Like so much else about him, the manner of his death was remarkable. George Richmond, who stood with Catherine at the poet's bedside to the end, described Blake's passing as an awakening to bliss:

> He died ... in a most glorious manner. He said He was going to
> that Country he had all His life wished to see & expressed Him-
> self Happy, hoping for Salvation through Jesus Christ—Just before
> he died His Countenance became fair. His eyes Brighten'd and
> He burst out into Singing of the things he saw in Heaven. In truth
> He Died like a Saint. (*Letters*, 171)

Though Blake entered finally into that other world he had envisioned all his life, he left behind his poems and paintings to inspire the rest of us to follow.

III

History has been kind to Blake. He now possesses a reputation far greater than any he enjoyed during his lifetime. As a poet he is lauded and as a man he is revered. All ages need their heroes, and William Blake, unsung prophet, is as good a choice for ours as any. But the tendency among Blake's critics has been to sing his praises uncritically. In 1947 Northrop Frye published a book that once and for all put Blake on the literary map: *Fearful Symmetry* remains today an astonishing achievement in criticism. All students of Blake owe thanks to Frye for making sense of a great but unusually difficult body of work. Having said this, however, one should admit also certain facts that condition Frye's approach. As he states in his preface, Frye wrote his book during the "hideous" years of World War II. In Blake he found a spokesman for human value and divine vision—a sane prophet, in other words, for an insane world. Frye's Blake enters the world stripped of cantankerousness and eccentricity, a great artist of cosmology and philosopher of the human spirit.

While Blake was without question both, he was also this: an individual whose unusual experience of the world decisively shaped the character of his artistic activity. The preceding biographical sketch, brief as it is, should be enough to indicate the eccentricity of that experience, which was strange enough to elicit the charge of madness from a number of his contemporaries. The question we must ask of that experience is whether it deviated from the human norm. Such a question does not incriminate the quality of Blake's poetry. On the contrary, it opens new possibilities for criticism by reevaluating what that poetry is about.

Blake's experience differed from the human norm in its persistent visionary quality. From childhood to old age Blake had visions and valued them as facts of life. This is not to say that visions *alone* distinguished Blake from the norm. Many men and women at one time or another have visions, but unlike Blake, do not value them as literal facts. By holding them sacred Blake behaved in a manner that suggests a disturbance in the way he experienced the world. Contemporary clinical practice might diagnose that disturbance in any number of ways, but such a diagnosis would fail to appreciate the human experience behind the symptoms. For Blake the world contained something unacknowledged by most people. Admitting as much will return to his poetry the strange richness of vision.

Recall the three characteristics that define the norm of human experience: mutual relation between individual and world, shareable sensation, and pre-reflective awareness. Although Blake's respect for his visions testifies that his awareness of the world was pre-reflective (a reflective man would dismiss them as mere fantasy), in the other two areas his experience differed from that of most men and women. In the relation between individual and world, Blake valued the former over the latter. Visionary experience, though part of the world, was not necessarily reducible to it. Blake possessed the remarkable ability of inhabiting a world of vision, and when he could not, as in his relations with Hayley or his trial for sedition, he split experience in two, public and private, and sought compensation in artistic activity. For Blake the world lacked the persistent and resistant qualities that it possesses for most people, leading one critic to conclude that, in his poetry at least, the Other has no substantial existence.[6] Moreover, sensation, as Blake experienced it, did not always possess the characteristic of shareability. Visionary experience in particular tended to be a private matter, so that Blake could lead others to believe that he communed with a spiritual world. In fact he communed only with this world, but in unfamiliar terms. Blake was aware that his sensory experience differed from that of others, but in his opinion the deficiency was theirs and not his, evidence of their entrapment in a material hell.

It might be objected here that Blake in fact saw and heard no more than others, that the power of his imagination was simply far superior to that of the average impoverished faculty. After all, in *The Marriage of Heaven and Hell,* when Blake himself challenges the prophet Isaiah's sensory experience of God, Isaiah replies, "I saw no God, nor heard any, in a finite organical perception; but my senses discovered the infinite in every thing."[7] Clearly Blake treats his visions as metaphors, not existential facts but heuristic fictions. But does he? It is Isaiah, not Blake, who speaks these lines, and they come in the midst of a brief visionary tableau that makes no sense if not experienced *through* the senses. Seeing the infinite in all things must begin by seeing all things, Isaiah as much as the world around him. Throughout *The Marriage of Heaven and Hell* Blake treats visionary experience as if it were that of the world at large, and his reader must be ready to do the same. Otherwise Blake's poetry remains invisible to the senses, not vision at all but empty fantasy.

In a sense, then, reading Blake's poetry is a little like participating in a hallucination. Critics generally balk at associating the concept of hallucination with any part of Blake's work or life. But it is precisely in its deviation from the norm that Blake's experience can be described as hallucinatory. Only a vulgar and critically inadequate definition holds that hallucination is sensation in the absence of external stimuli. In fact it is a disturbance in the way an individual experiences the world.[8] Blake's hallucinatory experience, which I will continue to call visionary, involved relations with a world that inspired visual and auditory sensation not shareable with others *except through art*. Art became Blake's vehicle for expressing visionary experience and as such functioned as a kind of therapy for it. The compensation gained through artistic activity prevented a disturbed experience of the world from turning pathological. For Blake never swerved in his conviction that visionary experience was a literal fact. Rather he authorized that experience by making it the stuff of visionary poetry.

Blake's historical situation helped in allowing him to honor hallucinatory experience as literal fact. Visions have traditionally been taken to be true in the arena of religion. Blake was heir to a radical Protestantism that gave full credence to the dictates of the inner life. Bunyan is only the most obvious instance of a religious individual who took literally experiences that were in some sense hallucinatory. By the early nineteenth century, such literalism was seen as pathological, the mark of real mental suffering. For some, visions remained a real part of experience, of course, but it became possible to interpret them in metaphorical terms without recourse to a religious meaning. Percy Shelley, for instance, is a poet for whom such experience is wholly metaphorical. In *A Defence of Poetry* he asserts that "the mind in creation is as a fading coal which some invisible influence, like an inconstant wind, awakens to transitory brightness."[9] Put bluntly, poets are visionaries and experience things hidden from the senses of most men and women. For Shelley visionary experience is metaphorical, evidence of a boundless power that inspires poetry. Blake, on the other hand, never endorses the metaphoricity of vision, although he often alludes to its mental origin. For him it remains a literal experience, but without explicitly religious connotations. Blake inhabits a rare moment in history that allows him to take visionary experience literally without recourse to religious or metaphorical meaning. His endorsement of such experience may strike our modern minds as unenlightened, but from his own historical vantage he saw no reason why he could not have his visions and believe them too.

Such devotion to an experience that we must consider hallucinatory explains why Blake's contemporaries dismissed him as mad. But if Blake's biography reveals a potential for madness, nothing suggests that he ever lapsed into it, even for a time. What this background should alert us to, however, is the possibility that Blake made poetry out of pathology. An examination of his major works with this possibility in mind proves illuminating, for it reveals that Blake displaced much of his own psychological ordeal onto the drama of his myth. Madness emerges in his poetry as a thematic preoccupation that eventually takes on larger implications as Blake examines its dynamic in the drama of his myth. As we pursue the development of Blake's mythology we will discover how impressively much of it concerns madness.

1

Refuge from Unbelief

> *How now? Is madness perhaps not necessarily the symptom of degeneration, decline, and the final stage of culture? Are there perhaps—a question for psychiatrists—neuroses of health?*
> —Nietzsche, *The Birth of Tragedy*

I

William Blake was a visionary. In maturity, his visions inspired poems and paintings of rare intensity. Even in youth, they shaped his experience and expression of the world. The story is told how the young Blake, while walking on Peckham Rye by Dulwich Hill, chanced to see a tree full of angels whose wings twinkled like stars. Eager to share the sight, he ran home and told his parents. His father, though not a hard man, took umbrage at his son's fancy, and only through his mother's intercession did William escape a thrashing for telling a lie.[1] That was not the last time that Blake became the victim of unbelief. Throughout his life, his visionary gift provoked skepticism if not denial as the fruits of his artistic labors went unnoticed by an indifferent public. In his father's reaction to his amazing tale, we get a glimpse of the visionary's treatment in a bourgeois world where there is no real place for unsubstantial sights or immaterial perceptions.[2]

In such a world, vision is evidence not of health but of sickness. Blake's works were frequently dismissed as the scrawls and dawbings of a madman. Wordsworth, for instance, reacted to *Songs of Innocence and of Experience* with a mixture of sympathy and censure for their author: "There is no doubt this poor man was mad, but there is something in the madness of this man which interests me more than the Sanity of Lord Byron & Walter Scott!"[3] It is easy to ridicule this judgment and the like, pointing to Blake's artistic achievements to prove the superiority of his mind. But before doing so, we should ask just what part the visionary plays in the modern world. If vision is *not* a mark of mental illness, then what is its value for society? This is a tough question to answer because those for whom visionary experience is a fundamental fact of life, as it was for Blake, are relatively few. Although we all dream, most of us draw a hard line between our dreams and the world we inhabit. Blake possessed the rare mental ability of uniting these two realms in vision.

The modern world has only three arenas in which such a visionary can play a meaningful role. In religion, he can indulge in vision so long as it conforms to a structure of dogma, which usually includes subordination to a transcendent deity. In art, he can give original form to vision, but with the stipulation that its authority be limited to the aesthetic. Blake fits comfortably into neither of these arenas, although the latter has defined most discussions of his achievement. His vision, though potentially religious, resists dogmatic formulation and yet cannot be confined to the aesthetic without violating its social urgency.

Only in the third arena, that of psychology, does Blake's vision take on its fullest meaning, for as a human science, psychology minimizes the limits imposed upon mental phenomena. To admit the visionary into this arena, however, is to place him in the company of the mentally ill, since psychology treats all aberrant mentalities as equally worth investigating. If an affinity between the poet and the madman (which is by no means a new idea) should do some damage to our cherished notions of an artist's sanctity, then so be it: we must take that chance in the hope of learning something new about visionary poetry. As we shall see, madness is a thematic preoccupation throughout Blake's myth, which, as a powerful symbolism of psychic dissociation, defends against the aberration it dramatizes. By hammering madness into myth, Blake secures health in the face of illness. For him, art becomes a kind of therapy, and vision, since it inspires this healing, a "neurosis of health."

When interpreting Blake's poetry, however, it has become almost customary to dismiss the issue of madness as philistine and naive. Harold Bloom takes the typical stand on behalf of Blake's sanity: "The legends of Blake's 'madness' never seem to cease, despite all scholarly rebuttal.... The people who still think Blake to have been mad are merely defending themselves from the keenest diagnostician of their own maladies."[4] Bloom dogmatically declares certain questions off limits to the critic. In this he resembles Northrop Frye: "The complaints that Blake was 'mad' are no longer of any importance, not because anybody has proved him sane, but because critical theory has realized that madness, like obscenity, is a word with no critical meaning."[5] If madness were a meaningless term, then the critic would have little to say about a large portion of *King Lear*. Frye clearly overstates his case. Besides, much energy in the past hundred years has been devoted to the task of making madness critically meaningful. The efforts of Nietzsche and Foucault in philosophy, and in psychology, Bleuler and other clinicians, have contributed to a critical understanding of madness in both philosophical and clinical terms. As our investigation of the relation between madness and Blake's myth proceeds, we shall call upon these thinkers to establish a meaningful context for discussion.

We should not feel that the charge of madness against an author somehow degrades the importance of a work of literature. In the visual arts, Van Gogh offers a parallel to Blake as a student of his own distress. No one doubts that after 1888 Van Gogh was intermittently mad, yet no one thinks his work of that period less valuable. Nor does anyone claim that his achievement rests solely on psychosis. But certain elements of his work, the disturbing brilliance of the yellows and oranges, for example, seem to grow out of his mental crisis. These colors move us because they appeal to something within that goes unnoticed except through Van Gogh's psychosis. Madness leads him through the untraveled passages of the human mind, and in his painting we see into its silent deeps. Van Gogh did not finally, like Blake, conquer his distress. When madness gained the upper hand, he took his own life, a victim of despair. Blake himself was no stranger to despair, but he found a security against it in artistic activity, making mental distress his subject instead of passively becoming its victim.

The psychological honesty of Blake's work gives it, in T. S. Eliot's phrase, "the unpleasantness of great poetry," a quality intensely human, and not merely historical:

> Nothing that can be called morbid or abnormal or perverse, none of the things which exemplify the sickness of an epoch or a fashion have this quality; only those things which, by some extraordinary labor of simplification, exhibit the essential sickness or strength of the human soul.[6]

Could it be, then, that the vulgar "legends" of Blake's madness embody a profound truth about his life and work? Through them we glimpse both the "essential sickness" Blake diagnoses in his myth and the proximity of the visionary to madness.

II

Blake's intellectual eccentricities, in particular his visions, marked him a madman in his own day.[7] Anecdotes about them range in significance from the ridiculous to the uncanny. The detailed notes that Henry Crabb Robinson kept of his conversation with Blake give the best glimpse we possess of the visionary's habits of thought and speech. Blake confessed, for instance, that he came to his profession more by command than by choice: "The spirit said to him 'Blake be an artist & nothing else. In this there is felicity.'"[8] Such references to spiritual command were commonplace for Blake, of a piece with his apparent indifference to the facts of his visionary life: "when he said *my visions* it was in the ordinary unemphatic tone in which we speak of trivial matters that every one understands and cares nothing about—In the same tone he said—repeatedly 'the Spirit told me' " (310). When Robinson, understandably curious, inquired about the relation between Blake's loquacious "Spirit" and Socrates's daemon, Blake disarmingly answered, "I was Socrates. And then as if correcting himself: a sort of brother—I must have had conversations with him—So I had with Jesus Christ—I have an obscure recollection of having been with both of them' " (310).

After several meetings Robinson concluded, in a letter to Dorothy Wordsworth, that Blake enjoyed "constant intercourse with the world of Spirits," receiving visits from Shakespeare, Milton, Dante, Voltaire, "&c, &c, &c" (324). Blake put his visions to good use, basing paintings and poems squarely upon them: "His paintings are copies of what he sees in his Visions—his books—(& his MSS are immense in quantity) are dictations from the Spirits" (324). If Robinson is to be trusted, Blake's visionary experience was the source for much of his artistic production, not of course in the slavish sense implied, but as an inexhaustible fund of images—seen and heard! Blake did not, however, consider this ability as exclusively his own. "Of the faculty of Vision he spoke as One he had had from early infancy," Robinson wrote in his diary. "He thinks all men partake of it—but it is lost by not being cult[i]v[ate]d" (317). The general loss of this faculty was for Blake evidence of a fall from former glory, and his visionary art was an attempt to cultivate it anew and to revive the vision now dormant in all men and women.

The tales of Blake's visionary experiences are too many to rehearse in full, though they include a visitation by the Virgin Mary, a conversation with the Spiritual Sun on Primrose Hill, a disputation with the angel Gabriel, and an encounter with the ghost of a flea.[9] By all biographical accounts, however, Blake was never incapacitated by his visions. Although they gave spice to his conversation, he by no means became their slave. For the critic, private anecdotes therefore possess less interest than public statements, for in the latter Blake openly declares his allegiance to a kind of experience unfamiliar to most of us. His late prose work, the *Descriptive Catalogue* (1809), contains accounts of a visionary experience that far outstrips the average capacity for dream. Blake tells of being taken in vision "into the ancient republics, monarchies, and patriarchies of Asia" (531), where he saw those monumental sculptures, the Cherubim, the grand originals that all classical art merely imitates. "The Artist," Blake writes, "has endeavored to emulate the grandeur of those seen in vision, and to apply it to modern Heroes, on a smaller scale" (531).

By his own witness, then, visionary experience provides the basis for artistic production. The result is a visionary art that possesses the originality and the grandeur of antiquity: "He knows that what he does is not inferior to the grandest Antiques" (544). Vision guarantees that Blake's works are original, not because they are his own but, paradoxically, because they are not. They rise out of a deeper origin, the same that produced the ancient Cherubim. Blake was fond of telling others that he was merely the secretary of his many works.[10] His visionary art evades the burden of literary and pictorial history because in his view it antedates all historical performances ("Egypt and Greece, good-bye, and good-bye Rome"!). It is in this sense that Blake could consider himself an "inhabitant of that happy country," Eden (543): vision revives in him a world as old as antiquity—and as new.

Lest we think such claims are simply metaphors for poetry, rhetorical gestures that conceal belatedness, we should notice that Blake frequently confessed the visionary origin of some of his most beguiling achievements. As we have seen, his secret method of engraving poetry and illumination together came to him, he claimed, in a vision of his dear dead brother Robert.[11] We need not harbor a faith in spiritual visitation to agree that Blake relied upon his visionary experience to supplement his daily life.

In a letter to his future patron William Hayley (6 May 1800), he offered comfort for a recent loss by sharing his conviction of the community of spirits:

> I know that our deceased friends are more really with us than when they were apparent to our mortal part. Thirteen years ago I lost a brother & with his spirit I converse daily & hourly in the Spirit & See him in my remembrance in the regions of my Imagination. I hear his advice & even now write from his Dictate. Forgive me for Expressing to you my Enthusiasm which I wish all to partake of Since it is to me a Source of Immortal Joy: even in this world by it I am the companion of Angels. (*Letters,* 15-16)

Robert's posthumous relations with his brother indicate that Blake took refuge in visionary experience during times of trial. That he should derive the secret of his artistic practice from vision proves how intimately it influenced his creative activity.[12]

An even more literal instance of the way vision underwrote Blake's art appears in the famous frontispiece to his poem *Europe,* in which the Ancient of Days, whom most critics identify with the character of Blake's myth called Urizen, stoops from his own sphere to measure the abyss with compasses for creation. The design was reportedly inspired by a vision that hovered over Blake's head at the top of his staircase at Lambeth. One of his favorite paintings, it shows clear signs of its visionary origin, for it pays no heed to the verisimilitude that naturalistic *mimesis* would require. The old god's hair and beard stream to the left, as if blown that way by a strong wind, but the surrounding clouds show no evidence of such a force. The large vertical leg that supports the leaning deity is anatomically incorrect and seems bolted on to the side of his body. Even so, the overall effect of the design is incontestably powerful. It presents a vision that parodies normal perception, for the orb of the Ancient of Days is also an eye looking out on the world, sizing it up and creating a memory that accords with its dimensions. If we demand verisimilitude from this work, we become its victim, for the eye that accepts nature's limits will never see a vision of the Ancient of Days. A design like this one forces us to admit that vision plays a substantive part in the production of Blake's art.

Having reached this conclusion, however, does not relieve us from the need to examine the question of madness and its relation to Blake's myth.

Most critics, with Frye at their forefront, feel that by proclaiming Blake a visionary they have settled the matter.[13] "The visionary and the artist are allied," Frye asserts, arguing that both achieve a higher spiritual world that is really this one transfigured by a new symbolism.[14] But by thus associating the artist and the visionary, Frye undervalues the force of Blake's experience of vision. If the visionary is like the artist, then he perceives visions at will, and Blake was undoubtedly capable of doing so.[15] But as the biographical evidence suggests, and as Blake's poetry confirms, vision is not an experience wholly accessible to the will. "Now I a fourfold vision see / And a fourfold vision is given to me": if these lines describe vision literally, Blake's visionary experience is in large part unwilled—a perception *and* a reception. The visionary far exceeds the artist in the strength and authority of his visions. Morton Paley's cursory application of "eidetic images" and "autistic thinking" to Blake's visionary experience therefore does not do justice to its power and persistence.[16] Paley offers no explanation of how eidetic imagery could acquire such preponderance over Blake's mind. William Blake was a visionary who also happened to be an artist, and this fortunate circumstance gave him the opportunity to direct his unusual sensibility toward productive ends.[17]

Once again we run into the trouble of finding a place for the visionary in the modern world. Blake's next of literary kin, William Langland, lived in an age that honored the visionary and even allowed him some eminence.[18] Langland found close at hand a structure of dogma that rendered his visions meaningful and in a sense visible to the less gifted run of humanity. Even when vision contradicted dogma, as was occasionally the case for the dreamer Piers, the orderly cosmos of the Middle Ages assimilated it to the prevailing norm of human experience. The visionary was not the stranger in a strange land that he became with the advent of the modern era. Blake's first serious biographer, Alexander Gilchrist (1863), sensed that the modern world was at least in part to blame for Blake's apparent eccentricities: "It is *only* within the last century and a half, the faculty of seeing visions could have been one to bring a man's sanity into question" (1:370).

Blake may indeed have been happier in an earlier age, but the startling correlative of Gilchrist's statement is that a psychological investigation of Blake's visionary art is the only way of approaching it meaningfully in the modern world. For what was true in Blake's day remains true in ours: society has no structure of dogma that can authorize vision and make it intelligible, visible. If psychology can do so better than art or religion, that is because it is the one arena in our world where abnormal experience acquires a meaning. As we examine the thematic and structural function of madness in Blake's myth we must keep one eye on his visionary experience, not because biography influences poetry, but because poetry, as the product of vision, influences biography. To vary De Quincey's well-known phrase, "The man who dreams of oxen, speaks of oxen." Indeed, visionary experience inspired the kind of poetry Blake wrote and the purposes it served him. As he claimed later in life, "Inspiration & Vision was then & now is & I hope will always Remain my Element my Eternal Dwelling place. how can I then hear it Condemnd without returning Scorn for Scorn" (660–1).

III

But condemned it was by his contemporaries, largely with the imputation that Blake himself was mad. An absolute commitment to a profitless art only reinforced this judgment. At one point, Blake felt so beleaguered that he read a popular book about madness, a sort of phenomenology of the abnormal mind. *Observations on the Deranged Manifestations of the Mind, or Insanity*, by the renowned phrenologist Johann Spurzheim, catalogues the causes and possible cures of mental disease. Among the strong causes, Spurzheim places religion. "The primitive feelings of religion," he argues, "may be misled to produce insanity" (663). Blake's rebuttal of this claim in the margin of Spurzheim's book is as strange as it is instructive. Like so much of his poetry, it takes the form of a vision:

> Cowper came to me & said: 'O that I were insane always I will never rest. Can you not make me truly insane' I will never rest till I am so. O that in the bosom of God I was hid. You retain health & yet are mad as any of us all—over us all—mad as a refuge from unbelief—from Bacon Newton & Locke. (663)

It would be easy to laugh off this vision, with Bloom, as a bit of gallows humor.[19] But to do so overlooks what it reveals about Blake's attitude toward madness. As an advocate of mental health, Cowper is a strange choice. His intermittent madness was a well-known fact, and at its worst he wrote some of his finest lyrics. Yet he appears to bear witness to the integrity of Blake's mind, and the authority he invokes is *sanitas*, bodily health. Where the body is healthy, the mind is too; Cowper's bodily illness testifies to his own *insania*.

But more is at stake here than physical fitness. Cowper wants to be, like Blake, "truly insane." Blake's "madness" builds a psychic defense against empiricist philosophy, a "refuge from unbelief—from Bacon Newton and Locke." The truly religious man is truly insane, for he takes refuge in "primitive feelings" of vision irreducible to empirical order. The form this polemic takes, a visionary encounter between two poets, adds substance to the assertion. Vision resembles madness because it baffles reason: both proclaim the unity of desire and truth. If the effect of this union is bodily health, then madness might be evidence of a truth unfathomable by reason and therefore excluded from its ranks. Such thinking lies behind Blake's pronouncement, perhaps apocryphal, upon Bedlam: "that possibly the madmen outside have shut up the sane people."[20]

This remark betrays the insight that madness, though a mental affliction, has social implications. If the difference between the mad and the sane is in part an institutional one, then those possessing the keys to Bethlehem determine its population. In Blake's day, the rationalist played the warden while the enthusiast often played the prisoner. "There are States," Blake writes on the Laocoön engraving, "in which all Visionary Men are accounted Mad men: Such are Greece and Rome: such is Empire or Tax" (274). Christopher Smart fell into such a state when his religious fervor delivered him up to the madhouse. No lesser authority than Samuel Johnson endorsed the sincerity of Smart's enthusiasm with the famous observation that "he insisted on people praying with him; and I'd lief as pray with Kit Smart as any one else."[21] But in society's judgment, Smart's religious enthusiasm was a clear symptom of madness, even if it did make the impression of a close proximity to the deity.

Michel Foucault seconds Blake's assessment of those oppressive states when he argues in *Madness and Civilization* that the opposition of reason and madness is one of the defining features of Western culture. According to Foucault, social power establishes its validity by means of a privileged language of reason and various structures of exclusion that support the crystal walls of reason's castle. These structures confine the unruly and silence the unreasonable, and become visible in the great institutions of confinement that were first established in the Age of Reason: the poorhouse, where an ethic of work makes poverty socially beneficial, and the madhouse, where a metaphysics of reason strips certain men and women of humanity.

Both institutions silence elements of society that contradict the order of things.[22] And in one way or another, both menaced Blake. Poverty dogged him most of his life; only the devoted support of friends like Thomas Butts and John Linnell allowed him to die debt-free. Even so, Blake's penury only substantiated the charge of madness. As Foucault explains it, the relationship between poverty and madness in the Age of Reason grew out of the social ethic of labor that replaced the old religious ethic of faith: "madness was perceived through a condemnation of idleness and in a social immanence guaranteed by the community of labor" (58). This community segregated forms of social uselessness, creating a world apart where the poor and the mad acquired a meaning. Those inhabiting this world bore responsibility for being there, since poverty and madness signified a fall from social grace.[23]

In the Age of Reason, then, the madman, like the poor man, divorced *himself* from the immanent authority of social order. In Foucault's terms, "he crosses the frontiers of bourgeois order of his own accord, and alienates himself outside the sacred limits of its ethic" (58). Once beyond these boundaries, the individual lost the social identity that united him with others. He stepped into that no-man's land Pope describes in the *Dunciad*, a place "where Folly holds her throne," and, "concealed from vulgar eye," there is a cell that holds the quack wordsmith and the enthusiast alike, "The Cave of Poverty and Poetry."[24] Blake knew poverty well enough to understand its political and moral causes:

> Pity would be no more
> If we did not make somebody Poor:
> And Mercy no more could be,
> If all were as happy as we.
>
> (27)

The virtues of pity and mercy are weapons in the arsenal of social order. By attacking this order, Blake alienates himself from it and enters that other world peopled by the economically disinherited: the impoverished and the mad.

Blake's relationship with Hayley illustrates the effect of these virtues upon the social dissenter. Hayley was a popular if inconsequential poet, and his sanctimonious verse helped consolidate taste against the visionary poetry that Blake preferred and practiced. In an indirect way, then, poems like *Triumphs of Temper* made Blake poor, an appropriate candidate for patronage. Hayley's pity of Blake actually reinforced his impoverished condition, since patronage came with the tacit confession of social failure. The insidiousness of such pity appears openly in a letter Hayley wrote to Lady Hesketh concerning Blake:

> I ... shall ever be glad to do Him all the little good in my power, & for extraordinary reasons, (*that may make you smile*) *because* he is *very apt to fail in his art* — a species of failing peculiarly entitled to pity in *Him*, since it arises from nervous Irritation, & a *too vehement desire to excel*, — I have also wished to befriend him from *a motive*, that, I know, our dear angel Cowper *would approve*, because this poor man with an admirable quickness of apprehension & with uncommon powers of mind, has often appeared to me *on the verge of Insanity*.[25]

Hayley explains Blake's poverty as the unfortunate effect of ambition. And, in a single breath, he links social failure and insanity. Blake's poverty—his need for patronage—indicates his proximity to madness: his unruly temperament alone comes between him and a successful career. Hayley's social piety effectively silences vision, reducing a visionary artist to a painter of miniatures.

As Blake's career shows, the visionary in the Age of Reason easily enters the ranks of the socially disinherited. The association of madness with the poet, a notion going back to Plato's *Ion*, for the first time takes on personal urgency as the Enlightenment draws to a close. No era in the history of literature displays so much mental suffering among its poets as the one Northrop Frye calls "the Age of Sensibility."[26] Gray's melancholy and Collins's depression, Smart's monomaniacal enthusiasm and Cowper's obsessive guilt, are all symptoms of chaos at a time when order has not bowed to originality as the standard of value in verse.

Smart and Cowper especially felt the effects of this prejudice, and both ended up in the madhouse.[27] Smart spent seven years there and in that time composed *Jubilate Agno*, the long poem dismissed until recently as the raving of a madman. Cowper spent time in confinement too, and wrote some fine poetry when he was in his own judgment insane. Both poets crossed into that other world beyond the frontiers of social order, victims as much of social exclusion as of their own mental suffering.

For during the Enlightenment, according to Foucault, the madman inherited that world for distinctly metaphysical reasons. The madhouse gave a special kind of visibility to the metaphysics of social power. Leprosy having disappeared from its exclusive position on the margins of Western culture, another affliction—madness—moved in to replace it.

The madhouse became the Enlightenment avatar of the lazar-house because madness, like leprosy, validated the order of things by negating it. Where the leper confirmed the coherence of Christian civilization by being unable to participate in it, the madman proclaimed the authority of reason by embodying its denial. Madness reduced man to beast, placing him, in Foucault's terms, "in immediate relation to his animality" (74). This "fall" involved man as a social being, not as a transcendent spirit, and did not deliver him over to demons, but tore him away from himself and the social order that defined him, until he reached "the zero degree of his own nature" (74). Like the leper, the madman in the Age of Reason made visible the darkness that civilization exists to redeem.

But the difference between what the leper and the madman *signified* was a profound one. A kind of anti-church, the lazar-house signified the same redeeming transcendence—the Almighty God—that medieval culture stood for as a whole. The madhouse in the Age of Reason lacked this transcendental reference. It signified what reason was not; in other words, it signified nothing. In the Enlightenment,

> Madness . . . ceased to be the sign of another world; . . . it became the paradoxical manifestation of non-being. . . . Confinement is the practice which corresponds most exactly to madness experienced as unreason, that is, as the empty negativity of reason; by confinement, madness is acknowledged to be *nothing*. (115–16)

The madhouse became the domain, not of aberration, but of absence, and the madman, the meaningless parody of all that is human.

This is the historical context in which we must situate the "legends" of Blake's madness. To the eye of his age, his poetry and painting appear meaningless because they embody nothing, just that empty negativity that Foucault calls unreason. In such an age poetry must be the oracle of the obvious. To express any but reason's truth is to disturb a universe.

Such, at least, is the implication of certain attacks made upon Blake in his lifetime. The most famous of these, Robert Hunt's review in the *Examiner* of Blake's 1809 exhibition, reduces Blake's visionary art to a madman's maundering. Hunt describes Blake as "an unfortunate lunatic whose personal inoffensiveness secures him from confinement."[28] The attack comes in the name of taste. Blake's art is deranged and even dangerous because it seduces sober minds to mistaken judgments. That the lunatic overvalues his own work is the mark of his lunacy, but when he tempts others to do the same he poses a real threat to the order of things: "That men of taste, in their sober senses, should mistake its unmeaning and distracted conceptions for the flashes of genius, is indeed a phenomenon" (67). To the man of taste, the line that divides meaning from unmeaning is absolute. To cross it is madness, a proud assertion of self, the secular equivalent of impiety. Hunt writes at a time that has begun to witness a rehabilitation of the irrational undertaken by writers like Rousseau, Wordsworth, Coleridge, and others. Even so, he sees in Blake's work only a naive emptiness, and reduces it to silence by labeling it mad. Blake's fate as a visionary artist thus becomes a benign kind of confinement, and it is little wonder that a story eventually circulated of his residence in Bedlam.[29] Blake's solitude and social disenfranchisement mark his work as meaningless, placing him in the curious position of announcing his prophecy in a language that nobody could—or would—understand.

For if, as Foucault argues, reason condemns as mad all that transgresses the frontiers of its order, then Blake's language alone is enough to convict him. Consider the following passage from *The Song of Los*, one which does real violence to the language of reason:

> The Grave shrieks with delight, & shakes
> Her hollow womb, & clasps the solid stem:
> Her bosom swells with wild desire:
> And milk & blood & glandous wine
> In rivers rush & shout & dance,
> On mountain, dale and plain.
> (69–70)

As Blake's poetry goes, this is not a particularly knotty passage. It makes good sense allegorically: in the apocalyptic moment death becomes the source of life, animating the universe with sexual desire. But try to visualize this moment and you run into difficulty. What is that solid stem and how does the grave clasp it? And what does dancing milk and blood *look* like? Blake pushes his language beyond the frontiers of conventional referentiality and into the "meaningless" realm of myth. He makes a sign (the grave) into a metaphor (the grave is a womb), animating the inanimate.[30]

This process of fixing an image and enacting its implications is precisely the way, in Foucault's view, that madness develops: "*Language is the first and last structure of madness*, its constituent form; on language are based all the cycles in which madness articulates its nature" (100). The language of madness is simply the language of reason "enveloped in the prestige of the image," a phrase that accurately describes the method of myth compared to conventional discourse. A sort of poetic speech that has lost its metaphoricity, such "delirious discourse" determines the way the madman acts and talks. To the language of reason, Blake's visionary discourse appears similarly determined by "the prestige of the image." Its sound and fury signify nothing—just the noise of a delirious discourse referring to its own apocalyptic fixations. Blake's visions only confirm what, to the conventional mind, his poetry and painting announce—that he labors in the realm of unreason and chants a tongue men cannot know.

For Blake to accommodate his vision to the language of reason would be to abandon it entirely. In his mocking identification with the madman at the end of his career he confirms his stance outside reason's reach:

> All Pictures thats Panted with Sense & with Thought
> Are Painted by Madmen as sure as a Groat
> . . . .
> When Men will draw outlines begin you to jaw them
> Madmen see outlines & therefore they draw them.
> (510)

Blake opposes the sense and thought of vision to that of his rationalist critics. As the last line insists, Blake believes what he sees, believes *because* he sees. Where reason sees nothing, Blake sees outline, the trace that vision leaves upon the world. The visionary is the man who apprehends this organization, and he shares with the madman the negation of empirical order. As Yeats remarked, "he who half lives in eternity endures a rending of the structures of the mind, a crucifixion of the intellectual body."[31]

The vulgar "legends" of Blake's madness embody the conviction that visionary art stands opposed to empirical order, opposed ultimately to the structure of modern culture. A judgment like Hunt's denies Blake the voice that might have won him a contemporary audience. Without it, he was driven back upon himself, proving his vision on his own pulse rather than on that of his generation. This exclusion from the order of things became his strength *and* his weakness. Yeats has said that "a poet is justified, not by the expression of himself, but by the public he finds or creates; a public made by others ready to hand if he is a mere popular poet, but a new public, a new form of life, if he is a man of genius."[32] Blake created his public posthumously. His artistic solitude gave his work its arresting intensity, but it made difficult the task of marrying vision to the living world of others. He was himself the only representative of "the new form of life" this marriage would bring to birth.

IV

Blake was not unaware that his experience differed from the human norm. He struggled to share it with his contemporaries in terms they could understand and even imitate. His whole mythology is a monument to the effort to legitimize and communicate visionary experience, which clearly deviated from the historical norm but need not therefore become meaningless for us. On the contrary, Blake's visionary art has special relevance to a world shored up by fragments against its ruin. Blake's myth begins in psychological division and ends, at least provisionally, in renewed unity. As Blake struggled to shape visionary experience into artistic expression, he hit upon a uniquely modern conception of madness and its major symptoms.

The visionary lives painfully in the awareness that his experience is not like that of other men and women. While part of him busies itself with worldly affairs, the learning and loving, getting and spending that make daily life possible, part leads another life, equally as real, but insubstantial. No one expresses the dilemma of this existence better than Goethe, whose *Faust* stages one man's quest for a way of uniting this dual nature. Faust puts the dilemma succinctly:

> Alas, two souls within my breast abide,
> And each from the other strives to separate;
> The one in love and healthy lust
> The world with clutching tentacles holds fast;
> The other soars with power above this dust
> Into the domain of our ancestral past.[33]

Two souls, one all-too-human, the other more-than-human: like Faust, Blake faces the problem of fusing them into a living whole.

Blake confronts this problem in personal terms in a curious letter he wrote while at Felpham to his patron Butts (22 November 1802). It contains, in the form of a poem written in loose octosyllabics, one of the most revealing autobiographical passages in Blake's work. Blake describes a visionary encounter he has had with Los, a character of his own mythology whom most critics identify as the Spirit of Time and Prophecy.[34] In this poem, however, Los takes on a more personal—and troubling—appearance. Blake comes as close as he can here to writing a Romantic crisis lyric of the sort developed by Coleridge and Wordsworth. For them such a poem must overcome the burden of a prolific past and the ambiguity of an empty future. But for Blake it must minister to a mind that vision has divided. His poem reflects upon its own genesis in terms that go unnoticed by most Romantic crisis lyrics.

With near Wordsworthian precision, Blake notes the specific time and place at which he wrote these lines: "they were Composed above a twelve-month ago, while walking from Felpham to Lavant to meet my Sister" (*Letters*, 43). The situation here resembles "Tintern Abbey." Blake's sister, like Wordsworth's, anchors the poem in the physical world; she provides a destination for the poet's walk and a context for the visionary encounter he has in the midst of it. This physical frame of reference serves to test the crisis at the heart of the poem.

As it opens, the world appears alive with spirits:

> With happiness stretch'd across the hills
> In a cloud that dewy sweetness distills,
> With a blue sky spread over with wings
> And a mild Sun that mounts & sings,
> With trees and fields of Fairy elves
> And little devils who fight for themselves
> . . . .
> With Angels planted in Hawthorn bowers
> And God himself in the passing hours,
> With Silver Angels across my way
> And Golden Demons that none can stay.
> 			(*Letters*, 43–44)

Blake steps into a world without syntax, inhabited by angels and devils and God Almighty. But he quickly sinks as low in dejection as he was high in joy. The cause of his dismay is the thought of human responsibility. Ghosts of the dead hover around him; his father and two brothers appear to entreat his devotion. Only by ignoring their worldly demands can he walk freely in vision: "Tho' dead, they appear along my path / Notwithstanding my terrible wrath" (*Letters*, 44). Blake releases the energy of family rivalries in vision, and he wrestles with *it* rather than with flesh and blood.

As a result, guilt accompanies visionary experience. Although Blake diffuses oedipal anxieties by turning his attention away from the family, vision does not relieve him of human cares, for it internalizes oedipal and sibling conflicts. Now portions of his being war for primacy and he suffers the guilt of inhabiting a house divided:

> They beg, they intreat, they drop their tears,
> Fill'd full of hopes, fill'd full of fears—
> With a thousand Angels upon the Wind
> Pouring disconsolate from behind
> To drive them off.
> *(Letters,* 44)

Guilt becomes the all-too-human correlative of more-than-human vision.

In contrast to most Romantic crisis lyrics, vision, not lack of it, precipitates Blake's crisis. Blake experiences this crisis as a confrontation between himself and an old man whose existence, like that of Wordsworth's Leech-Gatherer, oscillates between the animate and the inanimate. A thistle acquires human form as the poet quickens the physical world into life:

> What to others a trifle appears
> Fills me full of smiles or tears;
> For double the vision my Eyes do see,
> And a double vision is always with me.
> With my inward Eye 'tis an old Man grey;
> With my outward, a Thistle across my way.
> *(Letters,* 44)

Critics often quote this passage to elucidate Blake's epistemology.[35] When Blake sees an old man in a thistle, his experience of the world turns visionary and sensation ceases to be shareable except through art. The poem itself therefore becomes the medium Blake uses to adapt visionary experience to the human norm. His art, in other words, acquires a therapeutic function.

Blake dramatizes visionary experience, then, to attempt a therapy in personal terms. Like Wordsworth's Leech-Gatherer, Blake's old-man-of-the-thistle reminds the poet of the trials of daily life, the tragic fatality of a life without vision:

> And Los the terrible thus hath sworn,
> Because thou backward dost return,
> Poverty, Envy, old age, & fear
> Shall bring thy Wife upon a bier.
>
> (*Letters,* 44)

This accusing voice announces Blake's anxieties. Los is "terrible" because he remains indifferent to worldly cares. Vision offers little assistance in the business of living; in fact it menaces a man's family with destitution and death.

Blake must reconcile the factious elements within him. The thistle-man voices his human worries, and only by answering them from within can he achieve a victory over his anxiety. This internalizing of the problem of vision explains the peculiar doubling of Blake's self-representation in his poem. Two very different voices speak as Blake here. The first responds to the thistle's accusations in fear:

> 'Must the duties of life each other cross?'
> 'Must every joy be dung & dross?'
> . . . .
> 'The curses of Los the terrible shade'
> 'And his dismal terrors make me afraid.'
>
> (*Letters,* 45)

Vision is the creature's curse because it won't put bread on the table or guarantee joy unmixed with sorrow.

But another self emerges, readier to bear the burden of vision. Blake lashes out at the thistle in wrath, rooting it up, an act that provokes Los's epiphany and gives Blake a new voice. He now speaks as if inspired, out of impulse rather than anxiety:

> 'Thou measurest not the Time to me,'
> 'Nor yet the Space that I do see;'
> 'My Mind is not with thy light array'd.'
> 'Thy terrors shall not make me afraid.'
>
> (*Letters,* 45)

Like Moses, Blake rebukes the vision that burdens him. His defiance liberates a self-sustaining energy from within: "Another Sun feeds our life's streams" (*Letters,* 45). This other sun fires the visionary's activity, giving him a creator's strength to confront his all-too-human anxieties.

With the energy defiance brings, Blake envisions a personal kind of apocalypse:

> Los flam'd in my path, & the Sun was hot
> With the bows of my Mind & the Arrows of Thought—
> My bowstring fierce with Ardour breathes,
> My arrows glow in the golden sheaves;
> My brothers & father march before;
> The heavens drop with human gore.
>
> (*Letters,* 45–46)

Blake answers his crisis of vision, like other Romantic poets, by making poetry out of it, a sublime allegory of mental anguish. Whether the poem solves his dilemma, however, is another question. For ultimately it does not unify the divided experience it depicts. The visionary that Blake becomes masters his human anxieties, but at the expense of the world in which he lives:

> And every soul of men on Earth
> Felt affliction & sorrow & sickness & dearth.
>
> (*Letters,* 45)

There is something compensatory in this fantasy of inspired triumph. Blake does not solve the problem of self-division so much as wish it away.

Blake ends the poem with six lines that are among the most famous he ever wrote:

> Now I a fourfold vision see,
> And a fourfold vision is given to me;
> 'Tis fourfold in my supreme delight
> And threefold in soft Beulah's night
> And twofold Always. May God us keep
> From Single vision & Newton's sleep!
>
> (*Letters,* 46)

The emphasis here upon vision shows how necessary Blake held it for the fullest delight in life. What is surprising, however, is the nonchalance with which he testifies to vision that is "twofold Always." The foregoing poem is a fine example of such, for it dramatizes Blake's dual experience of the world in vision. But as visionary he seeks much more, a fourfold vision of "supreme delight." Therein, presumably, self-division finds healing in a higher synthesis. But Blake explains neither what this synthesis is nor how to achieve it. If his aim as a visionary artist is to awaken men and women to a fourfold vision dormant within them, then he must solve the dilemma of self-division and show how it disappears in that fourfold epiphany. Otherwise a question remains as to the part that compensation plays in his creative labors. To what degree, we must eventually ask, is Blake's great myth compensatory—for the visionary's alienation from the norm of experience, or for the pain, perhaps, of life itself?

Solving the problem of self-division became the aim of Blake's greatest efforts. By placing within what was once beyond, the gods and devils that bless or curse, Blake complicates the issue of human identity. Now men and women must ponder their relation, not to an angry God, but to themselves. Part mortal and part divine, they fall into division when—in vision—the gods awaken. Then the struggle begins, which is as personal as it is poetic, to unite the disparate elements of the self into that tautology of human wholeness signified by the word "identity."

V

The pathos of this undertaking comes with the isolation it inflicts. For as we saw earlier, in certain respects the visionary is, publicly speaking, mad. His "madness" does not simply invert social standards of sanity. It assaults them, leveling them utterly. As Frye remarks regarding oracular poetry in general, "the qualities that make a man an oracular poet are often the qualities that work against, and sometimes destroy, his social personality."[36] Like the hero of old whose greatest strength came through descent to an underworld, the visionary poet must brave these dangers, becoming a greater being by the margin, not of knowledge, but of mental suffering.

For vision disturbs the character of experience, which for the visionary differs from that of most men and women. Life becomes divided between the visionary and the mundane. Blake wrestles throughout his career with this problem, and in this no subsequent thinker resembles him as much as Nietzsche. Like Blake, Nietzsche understands the hazards of visionary experience, as his well-known description in *Ecce Homo* shows:

Has anyone at the end of the nineteenth century a clear idea of what poets of strong ages have called inspiration? If not, I will describe it. — If one had the slightest residue of superstition left in one's system, one could hardly reject altogether the idea that one is merely incarnation, merely mouthpiece, merely a medium of overpowering forces. The concept of revelation—in the sense that suddenly, with indescribable certainty and subtlety, something becomes *visible*, audible, something that shakes one to the last depths and throws one down—that merely describes the facts. One hears, one does not seek; one accepts, one does not ask who gives; like lightning a thought flashes up, with necessity, without hesitation regarding its form—I never had any choice.[37]

Within us there appears to be a power that speaks with the force of a god. In contrast to Blake, however, Nietzsche treats the experience of this power wholly in metaphorical terms. Where Blake takes revelation literally as a supernatural fact, Nietzsche takes it figuratively, *as if* betokening an overpowering force. Because Blake does not interpret visionary experience thus, he betrays, in Nietzsche's terms, an atavistic superstition. But therein lies the greatness of Blake's struggle as a poet. As he labors to marry vision to the living world, he creates an art that transforms the character of visionary experience. Vision turns metaphor in the arena of myth, becoming an aesthetic experience others can share without taking literally. Blake relies upon art to unify the varieties of his experience, displacing much of his ordeal as visionary onto the drama of his myth.

The distinction Nietzsche makes in *The Birth of Tragedy* between the Apollinian and Dionysian elements in art acquires real importance for interpreting work like Blake's. In one sense this duality is aesthetic, opposing the plastic arts to music. But in another, it is psychological, opposing two mental states, dream and intoxication. Apollinian dreams present the mind with a soothing illusion of mere appearance, which compensates for suffering and reinforces individuality. Dionysian intoxication, on the other hand, obliterates this individuality, for it restores all men and women to the primal unity of life, as self-forgetfulness overwhelms them "with the gospel of universal harmony" in which "excess reveals itself as truth."[38] Nietzsche's artistic ideal, which he believes Attic tragedy realizes, unites Apollinian and Dionysian elements in a single form of art that embodies life in all its pain and contradiction.

Both painter and poet, Blake seems to have been capable of expressing either of these states. He sketched designs and he composed songs; the music of poetry found its complement in the hard outline of engraving. He labored to unite these complementary states of mind in the act of creating his "composite art." In the following chapter we shall examine more closely the implications of Nietzsche's inquiry for Blake's myth, which grows out of a lyric impulse and acquires a dramatic form. For now, we need only notice that in Nietzsche's aesthetics a disturbance in the normal experience of the world yields a deeper awareness of life, a knowledge of "the eternal self resting at the basis of things" (50). When given the appropriate form, as in Greek tragedy, this knowledge compensates for the pains of life. Mental suffering, then, can be a means to health if it inspires a therapeutic form of art, one which defends against the disturbance it dramatizes. Blake's myth is such an art.

Harold Bloom, in his study of Blake's poetic argument, suggests that in general myth presents the meeting of a subject with a subject.[39] In Blake's mythology, which dramatizes a psychological dynamic, these encounters occur after the dissociation of the universal human psyche that Blake eventually calls Albion. The fragments that remain emerge as independent voices: not characters that represent individuals, but symbols that represent elements of the mind. The myth dramatizing this psychic *sparagmos* attempts ultimately to overcome it by offering a re-vision of primal unity informed by this vision of its loss.

If dissociation differentiates an originally homogeneous unity, then it relates to that unity as a fall. We usually think of Blake as the great advocate of the individual, crusading for liberty under the banners of "Everything that lives is holy" and "One law for the lion and the ox is oppression." But these phrases celebrate an especially generous individuality, animistic in its force and continuous in its motion. *Life* makes a thing holy. Blake's treatment of the individual apart from this origin paints the horrors of an existence reduced to self-absorption. Urizen, the Ur-ego, falls from eternity when he invents self-consciousness; the individual, in other words, is a solitary bubble defined against an unfathomable abyss. As an illusion of substance, an independent self casts, in Blake's phrase, "a shadow of horror." Once dissociated from an original unity, it lacks an authority for its existence. Its God is not dead yet, just sleeping, but his sleep breeds nightmares. Paradise lost becomes personality lost as the individual splinters away from the primal unity of Albion.[40]

Blake therefore regards individuation, the original violence done to this primal unity, as the true subject of a modern myth of the Fall. In *The Birth of Tragedy*, Nietzsche unravels the strange history of Dionysus, "the god experiencing in himself the agonies of individuation" (73). As a boy, the myth tells us, Dionysus was torn to pieces by the Titans. Nietzsche interprets this event psychologically:

> Thus it is intimated that this dismemberment, the properly Dionysian suffering, is like a transformation into air, water, earth, and fire, that we are therefore to regard the state of individuation as the origin and primal cause of all suffering, as something objectionable in itself. From the smile of this Dionysus sprang man. (73)

The dismemberment of Dionysus resembles the disintegration of Albion. In both cases individuation brings with it suffering as a collective human unity collapses into fragments. Blake presents this process graphically in his emblem series *The Gates of Paradise*, where he psychologizes the four cosmic elements, air, water, earth, and fire (see Erdman's edition, 260–62). In representing them as individuals, he emphasizes their separateness; each wears the look of anxiety that corresponds to the elemental form of his suffering. It is easy to see the Zoas in these images, for the Zoas amount to the mental forms of the four cosmic elements. In their estrangement resides their power; each endures, alone, an abyss.

And yet, as Nietzsche reminds us, Dionysus does not end in his dismemberment. Rather he lives *through* it to be re-membered anew. This pattern of dissociation and renewal—the pattern of the Christian fall—acquires its full significance in what Nietzsche calls the "mystery doctrine of tragedy." The doctrine belongs to art in general insofar as art provides an answer to the pain of individuation. Its main features describes Blake's *credo* with surprising completeness:

> the fundamental knowledge of the oneness of everything existent, the conception of individuation as the primal cause of evil, and of art as the joyous hope that the spell of individuation may be broken in an augury of a restored oneness. (74)

Blake's myth enacts this doctrine, but with this difference: where Nietzsche celebrates a worldly pessimism, Blake, after much struggle, endorses a religious optimism. However different the interpretation each makes, both believe finally that art can reintegrate a splintered unity and redeem the individual. Such art is not static and descriptive but dynamic and prescriptive, moving always in "augury of a restored oneness," a phrase that should remind us of the plenitude implied by Blake's polemic against injustice, "Auguries of Innocence."

In this sense, Nietzsche and Blake both offer their readers a therapeutics of art. Blake writes of his lost painting *The Last Judgment:*

> If the Spectator could Enter into these Images in his Imagination, approaching them on the Fiery Chariot of his Contemplative Thought if he could Enter into Noahs Rainbow or into his bosom or could make a Friend & Companion of one of these Images of wonder which always intreat him to leave mortal things (as he must know), then he would arise from his Grave then would he meet the Lord in the Air & then would he be happy. (560)

Blake believes that visionary art revives in the individual a lost unity that defeats death and redeems life. The therapeutic value of such an art exists in its effect upon the spectator as participant, which Nietzsche describes as "the shattering of the individual and his fusion with primal being" (65). Such a fusion might just help fallen men and women regain their health and happiness.

VI

In its treatment of psychological dissociation and regeneration, Blake's myth is very much about madness. But how relevant is this analysis to our own situation? The empirical method we have been using allows us to compare Blake's myth of mental suffering with the same pattern as it appears in clinical descriptions of mental illness. All the more reason to investigate the possibility that madness, as we understand it today, plays a part in the thematic and structural elaboration of Blake's myth. To Nietzsche's philosophical speculations we can add the fruits of recent clinical investigation. Since for the modern world, schizophrenia is, as Foucault terms it, the "madness par excellence," clinical description of this affliction provides a meaningful context for interpreting Blake's highly psychological mythology.[41] The critic must beware, however, to interpret and not to diagnose, since Blake's experience is historically removed from the claims of twentieth-century clinical research.

Though there are many different descriptions of schizophrenia and the disturbed experience of the world it induces, most agree in this: that the schizophrenic is remarkable for his inability to defend against the pain of life. He feels it intensely and construes the world in his own terms, often retreating into a world of his own devising. Subjectivity proliferates because it is precariously structured. A center of identity will not hold; it splits, like an atom in a smasher, into a legion of competing integers.

What is unique about Blake's visionary art is that it dramatizes this psychological dynamic, the mind's fall into fragments, and its return to health in a restored wholeness. Collectively, this fall accounts for the tendency of human beings to remain isolated from one another, ignoring the call of brotherhood and resisting the appeal of liberty. Understood clinically, however, such a fall is primarily an individual affliction — schizophrenia — whose symptoms seem to recapitulate the psychic history of mankind. The schizophrenic undergoes personally the fragmentation and, if healing occurs, the restoration that Nietzsche identifies as the characteristically Dionysian suffering. To understand Blake's myth deeply, these two views of madness and its method, one clinical and individual, the other philosophical and collective, must be combined. The war within the members of the contemporary schizophrenic closely resembles the collective dissociation that Blake allegorizes in his giant man, Albion. Because the dynamic of this drama is psychological, a myth of the mind's life provides common ground between the Universal Man and individual men and women.

In schizophrenia, as many clinicians understand it, the mind divides against itself. The *Diagnostic and Statistical Manual* of the American Psychiatric Association describes schizophrenia as

> a group of disorders manifested by characteristic disturbances of thinking, mood and behavior. Disturbances in thinking are marked by alteration of concept formation which may lead to misinterpretation of reality and sometimes to delusions and hallucinations, which frequently appear psychologically self-protective. Corollary mood changes include ambivalent, constricted and inappropriate emotional responsiveness and loss of empathy with others. Behavior may be withdrawn, regressive and bizarre.[42]

This clinical description locates in the individual the causes of schizophrenia, which manifests itself in symptomatic relations with others. The etiology of this disorder provokes sharp disagreement. Some investigators claim a chemical origin, a superabundance of neurotransmitters that the normal brain readily diffuses. Others suggest a genetic predisposition that allows strained family relations or other stressful situations to trigger the affliction. A very few still side with Freud, and see in schizophrenia a disordered libido either wrongly fixed upon the self, as in narcissism, or upon a homosexual love-object, as in paranoia. A little reading in the field and the head starts to spin.[43]

These theories agree only in the symptoms they seek to explain. Eugene Bleuler, whose *Dementia Praecox, or the Group of Schizophrenias* remains a masterpiece of clinical observation, named the disease for the sick mind's tendency to split into "different psychic functions."[44] Personality loses its unity and psychic complexes dominate it one at a time, driving out other thoughts and feelings. A patient becomes "depersonalized" as the ego splits up and alien ideas attach themselves to the remaining fragments. He or she loses footing in time and space, and the end can come as a kind of psychic dismemberment, a *sparagmos* of mental unity that is the individual counterpart to the dismemberment at the center of Blake's myth.

For the *sparagmos* of the Ancient Man frees the elements of human identity to war among themselves for power over the whole. As it develops, the drama of Blake's mythology comes more and more to resemble the dynamic of schizophrenia. Both enact the dissociation of a human whole, the proliferation of competing complexes, and the therapeutic effort, perhaps dubious, to achieve a new unity. In this mental strife Blake discovers his great subject: the politics of consciousness, that competition among fragments of the mind for control over the whole.

Blake arrives at this subject, however, by neither accident nor calculation. The politics of consciousness in large part reflect his own struggle to honor vision in a secular society. Blake's visionary experience bears a more than faint resemblance to contemporary symptoms of madness. Critical attempts to distinguish his visual and auditory eccentricities from plain hallucinations are largely unconvincing and tell more about what critics disbelieve in order to serve their cause than what Blake believed in order to serve his. While it is a dangerous thing to speculate about the mental integrity of the deceased, there can be little question that Blake's visionary experience would today hold the interest of clinical investigators. "I am under the direction of Messengers from Heaven, Daily & Nightly," he wrote to Butts (10 January 1803), "but the nature of such things is not, as some suppose, without trouble or care" (*Letters,* 48).

As proof that vision was to him a literal, not merely metaphorical, experience, we have his work and bold claims like the following: "I see Every thing I paint In This World" (9). But there are subtler hints too that visionary experience was quite real—and perhaps pathological. In writing to Hayley (27 January 1804), Blake compares the sound of certain verses to far richer music: "the sound of harps which I hear before the Sun's rising" (80). It is hard to know how to describe such experience without the word "hallucination." Auditory and visual hallucinations, combined with the notion of being assisted by Heavenly ministers, lead to the disquieting conclusion that, in certain respects, Blake's visionary experience falls into a category we today consider at least potentially pathological.[45]

This is not to say that Blake *was* mad, or that his poetry loses any of its value, only to affirm that he was right when he suggested that vision has its liabilities. If the modern world has no place for visionary experience other than the realm of the pathological, then it is a lesser place for it. Even so, we must conclude that Blake's experience of this world deviated in interesting ways from the human norm. Diagnosing and labeling this deviation is a cultural matter that varies historically.

For the critic, the more interesting question than the dubious one of diagnosis is why Blake remained healthy and wrote powerful verse throughout his long career. He alone among the Romantic poets lived *and* wrote great poetry into late adulthood, even though he seems also to have been the one most prone to mental distress. The reason lies in the therapeutic function of his mythological method. We shall see more clearly as our discussion advances that Blake did indeed displace much of his own distress onto the drama of his myth. As the creation of a visionary, that myth functioned literally as a "refuge from unbelief," a psychological defense against both the hazards of visionary experience and the imputations of a secular society.[46] Blake came by his knowledge of mental suffering firsthand. But the therapeutics of his art allowed him to master that suffering and give it a form that all men and women can share in to the extent that they too honor vision. If the visionary suffers for his experience, in art he finds a healing.

T. S. Eliot demonstrates fine insight, then, when he claims that Blake's poetry, like Homer's and Dante's, exhibits for our examination "the essential sickness or strength of the human soul." That Eliot should sense this about Blake's poetry suggests that his own work pursues similar ends. *The Waste Land* also presents a mind besieged by competing authorities, a point made starkly by its original title, "He Do the Police in Different Voices," though for Eliot these voices represent social and historical forces, where for Blake they are primarily psychological. If in a secular age theodicy must proceed not religiously but psychologically, then these poets teach us that paradise is lost and regained by the suffering individual. A divided mind must achieve its own order, a refuge from unbelief.

2

Lyric into Myth

The genius, because of the abnormal ranges of his sensibility, not only accumulates experiences with greater rapidity, but accumulates experiences and qualities of experience accessible only in the extreme ranges of sensibility.
— Wallace Stevens, *"The Figure of the Youth as Virile Poet"*

I

Blake grew up in a world on the brink of a new beginning. An old order of institutionalized repression, buttressed by church and state, was to be leveled and built anew along lines of liberty, equality, and fraternity. The London of Blake's youth was a center of resistance to monarchy. When revolutionary war broke out in the American colonies, sympathies so favored the rebels that their cause became known as "civil war." The spirit of English revolution had returned, but this time in secular guise. Blake himself was swept up in the enthusiasm of the times. In June 1780 rioting erupted to protest government overtures to the Catholic Church made in the hopes of acquiring Catholic troops to help in the fight for the colonies. The rioters sacked papistic churches and businesses, and on the night of June 6th Blake was among them.[1]

Exactly *why* remains unclear, but he participated in the burning of Newgate prison, whose doors were burst and prisoners freed. Nine years before the Bastille fell, Blake witnessed the power of the people when they acted together to defy the institutions of repression. He memorialized this conviction in a sketch, later engraved, that has become familiar to all admirers of his work: *Albion Rose*, once known as *Glad Day*, which depicts a vision of humanity united as one body to rise above enslavement and step into a dawn.[2] Political action, he believed, could work this collective change.

Blake wrote his early lyrics in the service of such hopes. In them he announces a collective vision that challenges the order of both society and the minds that uphold it. In our last chapter we saw how the visionary joins the ranks of the socially disinherited because elements of his experience possess no reasonable meaning. We must inquire further, however, into the pathological potential of vision itself and examine the strategies that Blake evolves to manage it fruitfully. Like the lyrics of his closest poetic contemporaries, the sensibility bards, his early poems begin in vision of vitality that poses a real threat to conventional order, social and psychological. Myth gives a dramatic form to this vision and defends against its menacing intensity.

The poets of the Age of Sensibility, that literary gap between the Augustan and the Romantic periods, share an intensity of vision new to eighteenth-century literature. A reckless animism afflicts their poems, as if the world and the things in it passed through the furnace of the poet's mind on their way to a brighter vitality in verse.[3] But with this profound sympathy for all life comes a heightened sense of separation from it. The sensibility bards intuit an enormous vitality that they sense is beyond them. Their poetry is full of strategies for approaching this life, but rarely engages it directly. To do so would risk dissolution into life's primordial unity and a loss of self so complete as to menace the mind with madness.

It is one of the ironies of literary history that the Age of Reason culminated in an Age of Madness. But it is proof too that rational order comes dearly if it stifles the instinctual life. Augustan poets did all they could to run the passions on reason's track, even if that meant restricting the matter and manner of poetry. Their heroic couplet channeled feeling into manageable measures, displacing the affective elements of poetry onto the more intellectual adventures of balance, symmetry, and period. The favorite form of the sensibility bards, however, was the ode, much better suited than the couplet to the varieties and vagaries of feeling. The ode's irregular line and rhyme patterns make it appropriate for the bards' impassioned meditations. This flexibility marks it as a link between the heroic couplet of eighteenth-century satire and the associational structure of the greater romantic lyric. But the ode remains a form with its own strengths, one of which is to voice the passions that the Age of Reason thought better to repress.

For the ode is an intense medium, the couplet diffuse. Where the latter is especially effective for narration, the former is preeminently lyrical. The stories that get told in sensibility odes usually concern events whose emotional power outstrips their dramatic force, as in Gray's "The Bard," in which the last of an ancient race of bards curses his conqueror, Edward I, and plunges to his death. In such poetry feeling predominates over action to so great an extent that it is difficult to articulate precisely what the poem is *about*. This cognitive indeterminacy is the hallmark of lyrical expression. For the sensibility bards it provides the verbal equivalent of the vitality they see coursing through all things. Gray, however, appears to sense the danger that this vitality poses for the individual. The suicide of his bard, although justified by the scant dramatic situation, exemplifies the sad end of so many sensibility poets, Chatterton especially, but Collins, Cowper, and Smart as well. The life they celebrate is somehow inimical to the integrity of self and mind.

A. E. Housman reaches a similar conclusion in his well-known lecture, "The Name and Nature of Poetry." In his view, a premium upon intellect distinguishes eighteenth-century poetry from that which precedes and follows: "meaning is of the intellect, poetry is not. If it were, the eighteenth century would have been able to write it better." Housman then proceeds to explain what sets real poetry apart:

> As matters actually stand, who are the English poets of that age in whom pre-eminently one can hear and recognize the true poetic accent emerging clearly from the contemporary dialect? These four: Collins, Christopher Smart, Cowper, and Blake. And what other characteristic had these four in common? They were mad.[4]

Madmen, the best of poets? Housman invokes the wisdom of Plato to link inspiration with delirium.[5] Our impulse is to dismiss this belief and the long tradition that supports it as the mystification of unenlightened minds. For what is the value of a literature of frenzy? Precious little, if life reduces to intellect. But if instinct plays a part in who we are, as individuals and societies, then perhaps madmen, creatures of pure instinct, have something to teach us. Of the poets he labels mad, Housman asserts that "elements of their nature were more or less insurgent against the centralized tyranny of the intellect" (38). They waged in poetry a revolution analogous to that underway in politics, a celebration of collective life over and against the claims of a usurping minority class. The sensibility bards engaged in psychological warfare, for the animism they celebrated posed a threat to self-centered identity and the institutions that reinforced it.

Collins, Cowper, Smart, and to a lesser extent Blake, all labor under the conviction that this life flourishes beyond the ego. The first three, though their afflictions were intermittent, were considered mad by the standards of their day. Collins alone avoided an asylum.[6] And although all announce in their poems a vision of vitality, what distinguishes the others from Blake is their inability to interpret that vision by any other standard than religious orthodoxy. Collins and Cowper pine as isolated individuals, fully aware of a vitality they cannot share. Smart soars beyond individuality into vision, but at the cost of all human relations. In both cases a religious transcendence resolves an inner division between an isolated individual and the one life he intuits. Little wonder, then, that Spurzheim, author of the book on madness that attracted Blake's attention, considered religion a "fertile cause of insanity." In a passage Blake noted, Spurzheim claimed that "the primitive feelings of religion may be misled and produce insanity," a situation that, however deplorable, was a real boon to the medical profession, which had "an obligation to Methodism for its supply of many cases" (663).

Collins's "Ode on the Poetical Character" describes the anxiety of the poet as creator in the presence, not only of his precursors, but also of the vitality which merely to intuit is somehow to create. Collins witnesses a cosmic primal scene in which God and his paramour Fancy propagate, thankfully out of our view, both the trappings of the poet's trade and an image of the poet himself in his full glory as creator:

> And Thou, Thou rich-haired youth of Morn
> And all thy subject Life was born![7]

Collins cannot, however, bear the responsibility that attends this sacred rank. The poem ends in a fantasy of destruction that has Heaven overturning the "inspiring Bow'rs" (1. 75) of visionary poetry, as if to repay Collins's satanic offense of having created out of himself the life he intuits. Unable to manage the power that pulses through him, he retreats into himself. The implied orthodoxy of the poem's final stanza places a belittled Collins before a Jealous God who is fully informed on the score of the poet's vision and usurpation of vitality. Collins's mental suffering in part results from this profound self-indictment.

Similarly, and with more fearsome results, Cowper fails to escape the claims of a punishing orthodoxy. His poems reveal a world suffused with life, where oysters speak in allegory to plants and poets, and where the tiniest of creatures possesses transcendent value, even the cricket and the snail. Reverence for life's createdness, however, leads Cowper into the depths of despair. Creation is God's privilege, and the individual is nothing in comparison but a beautifully structured vacuum. In Cowper first appears the sensitivity to the natural world that reaches philosophical dignity in Wordsworth. But Cowper has not Wordsworth's all-assimilating self-confidence and consciousness. To perceive the life in all things is for him to be reminded of his own sinfulness. This heightened self-consciousness turns pathological because Cowper's vision is ahead of his psychology. He has only the orthodox dichotomy of God and man by which to interpret a perception of animistic plenitude, whereas the Romantics have a stronger faith in the mind's ability to create the world it perceives. Like Collins, Cowper retreats into himself and stands condemned as having sinned. Hence his identification with Abiram, the Old Testament sinner whom the earth swallowed whole:

> *Him* the vindictive rod of angry justice
> Sent quick and howling to the center headlong;
> I, fed with judgment, in a fleshly tomb, am
>   Buried above ground.[8]

Abiram at least had the comfort of an earthen tomb. Cowper's is a living death. Like Collins's, his vision hazards him with madness because it unveils a life inimical to the ego and belonging solely to God.

Christopher Smart is the sensibility bard who most resembles Blake. Like Blake, he turns to scripture to find a ground for poetry uncluttered by the debris of an exhausted classical tradition. Not surprisingly, he happens upon themes and techniques that bear striking similarity to Blake's. The unjustly neglected "A Song to David" could be considered a song of innocence worked up to a grand scale. And the bewildering and often beautiful *Jubilate Agno* (modern epic, or madman's scrawl?) anticipates the antiphonal rhetoric and associational method of *Jerusalem*. The tantalizing possibility exists that Blake glimpsed the large folio sheets of Smart's poem, some of which Hayley possessed during Blake's stay at Felpham.[9] Like Smart, Blake makes a Biblical idiom his own, though he works in an independent direction. What these poets share is a devotion to the precious vitality of all living things.

Reading "A Song to David" one might wonder whether, in Smart's view, humanity ever really fell from paradise. Nature lives in the power of David's adoration, from the "quick peculiar quince" (1. 354) to the mermaid's whelp. In David, Smart finds a partial solution to the creative anxieties of Collins and Cowper. David stands halfway between the power of the creator God and the poverty of the creature Smart, interceding, as it were, on behalf of the latter. Smart can displace his own creative ambitions onto David, avoiding the risk of Collins's primal trespass:

> He sung of God—the mighty source
> Of all things—the stupendous force
> On which all strength depends.[10]

Smart's strategy of dramatic displacement anticipates, as we shall see, Blake's use of personae in his lyrics. But in the turn to David, Smart betrays an insecurity about his vocation as a poet. Milton felt able to "sing of God." Not Smart. He sings of David who sings of God, an evasion that forces him into the peculiar situation of being a spectator in his own poem—if, that is, Smart himself can be said to have any existence there at all. The poem's first words, "O Thou," establish a monologue of praise in which the subject of the speaker dissolves into the object of his ovation. Smart fades into David, leaving himself behind.

The effect is a kind of depersonalization, exactly the opposite problem from the one Collins and Cowper face. So complete is Smart's vision of life that it deprives him of individuality and drives him mad. In his poems he lives at the pitch of vision; *Jubilate Agno*, a vast network of correspondences and associations, resolves the human world into a higher one. If the ego dominates in Collins and Cowper to a pathological degree, in Smart it vanishes altogether, revealing the timeless fabric of that eternal world which psychoanalysis calls the unconscious.[11] This disjunction between self and vision is absolute in the sensibility bards. Their Christian orthodoxy forces them to interpret it in terms of a metaphysical dualism. A psychology that locates both identity and divinity within humanity would take a large step toward solving the problems of their poetry and healing the anguish of their minds.

The madness of the sensibility bards is, in cultural terms, a measure of their originality. They represent the first, tragic incarnation of the post-

Miltonic figure that Stevens describes so arrestingly in "The Figure of the Youth as Virile Poet." The muse takes up residence in the mind after Milton, causing a revitalization of the poet and his powers: "a younger figure is emerging, stepping forward in the company of its own muse, still half-beast and more than human, a kind of sister of the Minotaur."[12] This image of youth in the company of a superhuman beast nicely characterizes the situation of the sensibility bards. They and their world are young and vital, but some dark monster shadows their individuality. Their problem is to establish a tenable relation between themselves and the muse within. Stevens senses the great strength that can come of such a relation; the youth "is the spirit out of its own self, not out of some surrounding myth, delineating with accurate speech the complications of which it is composed" (52). The sensibility bards hesitate to claim for their own the vitality which they perceive around them. Remaining thus alienated from their greatest strength, they lapse into madness, lost souls by the standards both of religious orthodoxy and their own originality.

II

Blake's early poetry shows him keenly aware of the dilemma of the sensibility bards. Though his first lyrics have an Elizabethan ring to them, their chief concern is the individual's relation to some apparently superhuman power, whether love or death or divinity. Blake consistently labors to humanize these powers, a strategy best exhibited in the first four poems of his printed volume of juvenilia, *Poetical Sketches*. One would think the seasons beyond humanity, indifferent to its desires. But Blake brings them to life, discovering in them the same vitality perceived by the sensibility bards. His image of summer bears a family resemblance to Collins's figure of the poetical character; it too has "ruddy limbs and flourishing hair" (409). Blake first glimpses here the new figure Stevens describes, that youth as virile poet who sings, self-inspired, a song quickening the world around him. Blake ends his poem in the belief that English bards are capable of the same effect:

> We lack not songs, nor instruments of joy,
> Nor echoes sweet, nor waters clear as heaven,
> Nor laurel wreaths against the sultry heat.
> (409)

That final image suggests that poetry itself provides some comfort against the heat of the inspiring muse.[13]

If Blake perceives the same vitality as the sensibility bards, he knows too their anguished alienation from it. In the startling lyric "Mad Song," he both dramatizes and parodies the pained monomania of a Collins or a Cowper, though probably without having either specifically in mind. The speaker of this poem is in love with darkness and the nightly oblivion of sleep. Therein he seeks to escape the burden of himself, which acquires pathological proportions in the light of day. But Blake uncovers the narcissism at the heart of this anxiety. The speaker inhabits a world animated by his own neurosis, ruled by a sadistic God he has created to punish himself:

> Lo! to the vault
>   Of paved heaven,
> With sorrow fraught
>   My notes are driven:
> They strike the ear of night,
>   Make weep the eyes of day;
> They make mad the roaring winds,
>   And with tempests play.
>
> (415)

Note the irony of the fourth line: the speaker acts in the passive voice. Blake shows a mind utterly dependent upon the very forces that persecute it. The madness of Collins and Cowper, or anyone else so besieged, boils down to a religiously sanctioned self-love, the passion of the sinner for his sins, which give him some distinction, however ignoble, in the face of the Almighty.

But how to avoid the fate of the sensibility bards, balanced precariously on the brink of madness? Blake solves this problem by shaping their metaphysical dualism into a psychological dialectic. It has often been noted that Blake began his career as a poet with a rare lyric gift. Critics once lamented the hardening of that gift into the opaque rhetoric of the later prophecies.[14] Recent scholarship has relieved us of the need to complain where we cannot follow, having thrown much light over Blake's mythology. But we still lack an understanding of why Blake moved beyond the lyric to formulate his vision in myth. His ambition to write an epic like Milton's explains his pursuit of a discursive medium. But the slow emergence of his myth over the course of his whole creative maturity suggests that it originates in an *ongoing* personal struggle to adapt a vision of vitality—intensely lyrical—to the prosaic conditions of existence. Blake's myth, even at its most diffuse, is a dramatic expansion of the lyric.

Any aesthetic approach to the lyric quickly lapses into psychology, for the lyric is like a dream in that it does not exist apart from the mind of the beholder. Shelley makes a similar claim in a famous passage of *A Defence of Poetry*. "Poetry," he writes, "is not like reasoning, a power to be exerted according to the determination of the will. . . . This power arises from within, . . . and the conscious portions of our natures are unprophetic either of its approach or its departure."[15] For Shelley, poetry, especially the lyric, is fundamentally a psychological phenomenon. So it is for Housman, who we saw associates the lyric impulse with madness. His description of his own experience composing poetry emphasizes its morbidity:

> I have seldom written poetry unless I was rather out of health, and the experience, though pleasurable, was generally agitating and exhausting. . . . the production of poetry, in its first stage, is less an active than a passive and involuntary process. (47, 48)

The issue here is the relation of the individual to inspiration, and Housman's comments suggest that the lyric impulse pays no heed to subjectivity as conventionally understood.

It is something of an irony, then, that the lyric is often considered a poem in which the author speaks in his own voice. In our first chapter we noted how Nietzsche argues that Dionysian art, of which his prime example is the lyric, speaks with the authority of "an eternal self resting at the basis of things." Nietzsche implies that the *merely* subjective is beneath the dignity of the lyric. Even so ostensibly subjective a poet as Wordsworth shapes a speaking identity to suit the needs of a particular lyric, as any comparison of his poems with Dorothy's journals will show. In fact the lyric achieves an objectivity of its own, but one that is psychologically rather than physically grounded. "Of art we demand first of all," writes Nietzsche, "the conquest of the subjective, redemption from the 'ego,' and the silencing of the individual will and desire."[16] Even an art that appears subjective must plunge to the heart of things. The disconcerting corollary of this principle implicates the integrity of the "ego": it is nothing, the merest fiction, faced with the power and authority of art.

What, then, is this power, and whence comes its authority? And why does it pose such a threat to the ego? For Nietzsche, we recall, life reveals itself in two psychological and aesthetic categories, the Apollinian and the Dionysian. The power of art derives from the life it manifests, as does its authority. Art returns men to their living origins from which history and society have alienated them. But since life encompasses the contradictions of a primordial pain, this return must only be approximate, or it would demoralize a conscious being to the point of terminal apathy. Art functions to protect humanity from the very life it expresses, either through the delightful illusions of Apollo or the temporary delirium of Dionysus. In either case it seduces human beings into continued existence by imposing a tolerable form upon life's contradictions. The art of Apollo exploits the individuality of men and women to throw a pleasant veil of illusion over the pain of life. The art of Dionysus taps their living unity to give that pain complete expression in communal delirium. In both, art is objective, grounded beyond in the first instance, within in the second. The ego *per se* plays no formative role in either, though its empirical validity (*cogito ergo sum*) is at least compatible with Apollinian art. In Dionysian experience and expression subjectivity has no place: "with the gospel of universal harmony one feels himself not only united, reconciled, and fused with his neighbor, but as one with him ... before the mysterious primordial unity" (37). Through Dionysus, life delights in life, however painful the contradictions it embodies.

The Age of Sensibility witnesses a literary shift from an Apollinian to a Dionysian psychology and aesthetic. The vision of the sensibility bards celebrates the unity of life; individuality becomes a symptom of separation from this vitality. The madness of these poets attests to a psychological upheaval of a sort nicely characterized by Nietzsche's aesthetic duality. For in their pain they confront that primordial rush of life which Nietzsche argues typifies Dionysian experience. Whether by retreating to a fortified ego as do Collins and Cowper, or by absconding from it entirely as does Smart, the bards testify to the presence of this life in the mental agony they endure. They lack a world view that would account for such feelings and an art that would sustain them in their distress.

The project of the Romantic poets generally is to create a poetry of healing, an art that both expresses the one life and protects against its pain. Hence the conservatism of a poet like Wordsworth, who works devotedly to avoid the intensities of the sensibility bards, diffusing their vision of one life over genial landscapes and childhood memories. The Age of Sensibility awakens to a psychology that it lacks the conceptual equipment to sustain. It is for a later generation of poets, with Blake at their forefront, to forge an art equal to the task of life.

Blake's strategy is to introduce into the lyric a dramatic element that diffuses the hazardous strength of feeling. The speaker of "Mad Song," for instance, is not Blake himself, but a persona created to voice certain convictions.[17] A similar dramatic displacement characterizes his nascent myth and allows such feelings to take the form of psychologically objective symbols.[18] As Blake's artistic confidence grows, he elaborates dialectical relations between these symbols (which come to be called Urizen, Los, Urthona, etc.), ultimately organizing them into a comprehensive myth, a myth that dramatizes the dissociation of a unified mind into constituent personae. But in his earliest work he remains content simply to explore the possibilities available to the dramatic lyric. The lyrics in *Poetical Sketches* possess two striking features: an intense musicality and a dramatic persona not necessarily Blake's own. If, as Nietzsche argues, the lyrist works music into symbol, then even in his early poems Blake undertakes to find symbols for the primordial urge of life. For music, in Nietzsche's view (which derives from Schopenhauer), grants life an unmediated expression. In the symbolic efforts of the lyrist, that life acquires psychological objectivity.[19]

Critics have tried and generally failed to find some principle of order among the scattered pieces of *Poetical Sketches*.[20] If a pattern exists, it is the quiet development from the lyrical intensity of the first to the dramatic integrity of the last. Blake may have arranged the poems chronologically, though there is no way of telling. If he did, his literary apprenticeship has him forging a dramatic form for his lyric gift. It is worth noting, incidentally, that the union of music and symbol in the lyric is the verbal equivalent of a marriage between eye and ear. This aberration of the senses facilitates a vision of vitality and is implied by the quiet paradox of Blake's title, *Poetical Sketches*.[21]

The first lyric in Blake's engraved canon, the "Introduction" to *Songs of Innocence*, dramatizes the process of finding a symbol commensurate with a musical intuition of life. Blake is a great writer of songs: literally, if tradition can be trusted.[22] His early lyrics all fall into this category, and even his later works, dense though they be, at least figuratively are set to music. *The Four Zoas* is the "Song of the Ancient Mother" (*FZ*, 3:1) and *Jerusalem* is a "mild song" (*J*, 4:5). The "musical" origins of Blake's verse should alert us to the one life that, according to Nietzsche, all music seeks to express.

The "innocence" of the early *Songs* amounts to the spontaneous human experience of that unity. Those poems embody it in dramatic vignettes, and their "Introduction" details the birth of such a poetry from the spirit of music. Blake opens by dramatizing an encounter between the poet and his wholly human muse.

> Piping down the valleys wild
> Piping songs of pleasant glee
> On a cloud I saw a child.
> And he laughing said to me.
> (7)

This song of innocence begins as songs should, in music. In the first two lines the piper *is* his activity. Playing as he goes, he descends to wild valleys, for a fully human vision of life comes not on the heights but in the depths. And *when* it comes, it seems not a god but a child. Music awakens the piper to the life of innocence; until line three he has no identity, and then only as the recipient of vision.

The poem falls into two parts, the first depicting this musical awakening and the second, the task of symbolizing it. Once again we encounter the disjunction of self and vision characteristic of the sensibility bards. As the poem progresses, the piper's vision becomes steadily mediated. Although he begins in pure music, at the child's bidding he drops his pipe and continues in song. Finally he writes it all out, reducing melody to mere words:

> And I made a rural pen,
> And I stain'd the water clear,
> And I wrote my happy songs
> Every child may joy to hear
> (7)

These lines contain almost as many verbs as the rest of the poem, but with a slight modulation in tone. Where "saw" (l. 3), "pip'd" (ll. 6, 8), and "sing" (l. 11) govern the action of the first three stanzas, "made" (l. 7), "stain'd" (l. 18), and "wrote" (l. 20) govern that of the last. With the passing of his vision of life (embodied in the child), the piper labors alone to communicate it in symbol. He trades a wind instrument, a pipe, for a word instrument, a pen, through which his music cannot immediately sound. As the relentless repetition of the first-person pronoun indicates, he retreats into himself, somehow separated from the joy in his happy songs that only a child can fully feel.

Blake would be in the same position as Collins or Cowper here, cut off from his own vision of vitality, except that he displaces the problem of the sensibility bards onto the persona of his poem. This dramatic displacement of his difficulties as a poet, in this case to communicate the vitality of innocence, allows Blake to evade the anxieties that cripple the minds of his precursors. He neither equates his vision with a God transcendent nor retreats into his own identity. Rather he creates a dramatic persona to symbolize "the eternal self at the basis of things," and through it defends against the one life it manifests. Blake's myth is born in this effort to perceive and symbolize the one life in all its pleasure and its pain.

For Nietzsche, this effort leads naturally to tragedy, where life's primordial unity acquires living symbols in the actors that emerge from the communal chorus.[23] If life is at bottom a contradiction, equal parts good and evil, love and hate, then the manner of Attic tragedy, which unites the Dionysian and Apollinian elements of art and mind, allows its most complete expression. Blake is not generally held to be a tragic visionary, though he once claimed to have written twenty tragedies the length of *Macbeth*.[24] Nevertheless, his early poetry reveals a nascent tragic sensibility. One might take for its slogan a statement that recurs with memorable frequency: "life delights in life." If Blake means life in its pleasure *and* pain, then this statement contains the seeds of tragedy as Nietzsche understands it. Not until Blake places these words in the mouth of the sadistic and willful Enitharmon in *The Four Zoas* does his flirtation with the tragic come to an end. We shall examine more closely in the next chapter Blake's ongoing struggle with tragedy. But it would be unfair to the early poetry not to point out its tragic potential.

Blake's doctrine of contraries, of perennial interest to critics, is potentially more pessimistic than we like to think. The epigram "Without contraries is no progression," provides a better description of Hegel than of Blake, whose poetry makes opposition a value unto itself.[25] When Blake describes innocence and experience as "Two Contrary States of the Human Soul," he resists the inclination of his more Hegelian critics to resolve them into a third and higher state.[26] "Organized innocence" is primarily the product of sentimental reading, though Blake himself eventually turns to a similar solution in Beulah, the earthly paradise of his later myth. Even so, he never uses either the term "organized innocence" or "higher innocence." The closest he comes is a scribble in the margin of page 93 of *The Four Zoas:* "Unorganized innocence: an impossibility!"

The early songs especially stress contradiction and the real pain of inhabiting the natural world. The famous dictum from *The Marriage of Heaven and Hell* all but canonizes contradiction: "Attraction and Repulsion, Reason and Energy, Love and Hate, are necessary to Human Existence" (34). Blake may be writing in the service of energy here, to defy an orthodoxy of repression. But he celebrates a vitality that includes within it the potentially tragic contradictions of natural life. His Proverbs of Hell express a wisdom similarly informed: "A dead body revenges not injuries"; "The weak in courage is strong in cunning"; "Joys impregnate. Sorrows bring forth" (36). The frank naturalism of these statements and others like them allows for at least the possibility of a tragic resolution to their contradictions. *The Book of Thel* ends on a tragic note, as does the beautiful song of innocence, "The Ecchoing Green." Although Blake is by no means a tragic poet, even at his most naturalistic, we should notice the potential for the tragic where it exists in order fully to appreciate the function of his developing mythology.

For that myth has its origin in Blake's relation to his own visionary experience. The contraries of the lyrics grow in dramatic clarity and independence until they acquire, so to speak, a life of their own in Orc, Urizen, and other characters in conflict with each other. The relationships Blake establishes between these "Visionary forms dramatic" initiate a dialectic of deliverance from the fate of the sensibility bards. These forms function just as actors in Greek tragedy, who, according to Nietzsche, symbolize the presence of life's divinity and allow participation in its vitality.[27]

The difference between Greek tragedy and Blake's mythology derives from the status of divinity in an era of enlightenment. The relation of man to the divine has become primarily personal rather than public. The day has passed when a participatory event like Greek tragedy could restore a whole community to primal unity. But individuals, like the sensibility bards, are fully able to intuit that vitality. The displaced drama of this intuition proceeds now in personal terms.[28] For Blake — and here he steps beyond the bards' orthodoxy — divinity is within humanity and lives, as do all things, through humanity: "The Poetic Genius is the True Man... the forms of all things are derived from their Genius" (1). The drama that spins out of participation in this vitality begins in the individual and then works beyond. Blake's myth is, therefore, a monstrous extension of the lyric, for it embodies, in Nietzsche's terms, a Dionysian vision of primordial unity in Apollinian symbols of particularity. Dialectical relations between these symbols constitute the dramatic action of the myth, which moves toward restoring the individual to the divine life within while protecting against its diabolical strength.

III

That is why madness becomes one of the central themes of Blake's mythology. Just as it was madness that put an end to the efforts of the sensibility bards toward an aesthetic animism, so it is madness that is displaced onto so much of the drama of Blake's myth. As a defense against the vision it symbolizes, that myth secures the ego from the pathologies that ruined the sensibility bards. Art of this sort functions as a kind of therapy for the artist devoted to the fullest possible expression of life. Blake himself admits the dangerous potential of the vitality he celebrates in his early poems. On plate 14 of *America* he equates madness and popular revolution:

> Fury! rage! madness! in a wind swept through America
> And the red flames of Orc... folded roaring fierce around
> The angry shores, and the fierce rushing of the inhabitants together.
> (*A*, 14:10–12)

The assimilation of Americans into a revolutionary body politic is madness of a productive sort because it destroys the false integrity of the ego and the oppressive institutions that reinforce it. Notice Blake's use of the wind to symbolize inspiration, an image that becomes a favorite of the Romantic poets. For Blake it expresses the psychological objectivity of the contagious unity that sweeps across America.

Madness, then, takes on thematic importance in Blake's myth for two reasons: first, because it figures metaphorically for the psychological effects of revolution in the name of life; and second because it represents literally the danger that shadows a poet of primordial unity. The ambition to express such a vision requires a readiness to press beyond the norm of human experience, beyond, in other words, the boundary of the ego.[29] Contemporary psychology views the ego as constitutive of the health of the whole personality. Any compromise of its integrity, from either above or below, begins the mechanism of mental dis-ease that reaches completeness in psychosis. Psychoanalytic theory goes so far as to define madness as the total domination of the ego by unconscious instincts and urges.[30] But Nietzsche's discussion of Dionysian experience suggests that dissolution of the ego can, if it becomes an artistic phenomenon, result in psychic renewal. The poet who undertakes this project runs the risk of becoming its victim, as the sensibility bards certainly did. But to succeed would be to discover a new road back to the primal unity of life.

Modern clinical research suggests that certain kinds of mental illness cause something very similar to happen to the mind of the afflicted. The main features of Dionysian art are startlingly similar to symptoms of the affliction that today's clinicians call schizophrenia. Ego-loss gives a patient a glimpse of a world animated by an ubiquitous vitality.[31] Dramatic displacement can reorganize a shattered psyche around emotional complexes that acquire a character and a life of their own.[32] Perhaps the modern schizophrenic has traveled the road to primal unity but failed to find his way back to humanity. His world of symbols signifies nothing, and neither expresses an eternal self nor defends against a primordial pain. In a sense, he is a failed poet, for his vision finds no therapeutic form.[33] Certain existentialist investigators even view schizophrenia as a journey toward the kind of life unavailable to a mind bound by the politics of social experience, a notion as suggestive as it is dubious.[34] The visionary who seeks to express his experience of life fully—in all its pained contradiction—undertakes a similar quest, and may even risk a similar lapse into psychosis. But unlike the schizophrenic, he can return victorious by the margin of his art, which compensates for the dissolution of the ego with a therapeutic drama of restored oneness.

If madness *does* cause the aberration of a socially structured ego, then there is indeed a sense in which it acquires political implications. Michel Foucault and R. D. Laing each in his own way argue that madness is as much a symptom of social as individual illness.[35] It is an easy thing to glamorize the madman, seeing him martyred by a self-centered social order. To do so naively makes light of real sickness. But because treatment of this dis-ease takes place primarily at the social level, in our day either through therapeutic incarceration or the subtler bondage of neuroleptic treatment, the madman does indeed come to inhabit a psychological domain for which no place exists in conventional social order. To pursue the truth of madness, the truth, that is, of ego-loss, is to gamble away a place in society. The sensibility bards who first took this chance, most particularly Christopher Smart, earned confinement either to the madhouse or to the keeping of friends. The trouble we have even today in assessing their achievement may grow out of our uneasiness with its implication that society is so structured as to exclude much of the instinctual life.

Blake was highly sensitive to the political forces that determine the character of madness and the fate of the madman. In his first extended poem, *The French Revolution,* which never saw publication even though partially set in type, he openly associates madness and revolutionary activity. Such activity strips human beings of their social identity and forces them into the psychological no-man's-land of the Bastille, which Blake pictures as having seven towers, each confining a different kind of rebel against social order. The first, named "Order," contains a man "confin'd for a writing prophetic" (*FR*, 1. 29). The last tower holds a being whose benign revolutionary hopes have ended in madness:

> In the seventh tower, named the tower of God, was a man
> Mad, with chains loose, which he dragged up and down:
>   fed with hopes year by year, he pined
> For liberty; vain hopes: his reason decay'd, and the world
>   of attraction in his bosom
> Center'd, and the rushing of chaos overwhelm'd his dark soul.
>   He was confin'd
> For a letter of advice to the king, and his ravings in winds
>   are heard over Versailles.
>   (*FR*, ll. 47–51)

Even here, in one of his most optimistic poems, Blake shows how a strong devotion to liberty ends in madness if the social order resists reformation. The revolutionary lives outside that order, especially when his program pursues a vision inimical to the ego. Blake again uses an image of the wind to represent the spontaneous power of that vision.

This passage betrays a deep suspicion of the prophetic enterprise, as if Blake, at an early stage in his career, feared that his own project were doomed to failure and could even end in madness. In an earlier work, the beguiling prose and verse satire *An Island in the Moon,* he diagnoses in greater detail the social order that condemns the madman. What he discovers is that society, when viewed from an extra-rational perspective, amounts to little more than a collective neurosis. R. D. Laing has called schizophrenia "a successful attempt not to adapt to pseudo-social realities," the most conventional and confining of which is the all-powerful ego.[36] Society nurtures the ego by condemning the instinctual life, until its members prefer aggression to love. Schizophrenia, in Laing's view, is a healthy response to an unhealthy world. We need not accept this disputable position to see that Blake makes a similar if less grandiose diagnosis of his own social milieu in *An Island in the Moon.* The society he depicts there is sick and only a therapeutic art can heal it.

The basic premise of the satire is obvious enough. Viewed from the perspective of the moon, social order in the Age of Reason looks neither reasonable nor healthy. Blake builds his critique around a dialectic of two different kinds of speech: a lunatic discourse that arises as soliloquy, and a lyrical discourse that arises as song. The difference between these forms of speech has primarily to do with their psychological value. The first is individual and exclusive, the second participatory and inclusive.

Lunatic discourse dominates the work and exposes the pseudo-reality of social order, which turns out to be nothing more than a habitual and collective narcissism. Blake's lunar *patois* allows him to record some of the maddest encounters in literature. When Mrs. Gimlet joins a company of islanders, her social demeanor conceals a more profound self-love.

> well she seated & seemed to listen with great care while the Antiquarian seemd to be talking of virtuous cats, but it was not so. she was thinking of the shape of her eyes and mouth & he was thinking of his eternal fame....
> Etruscan Column & Inflammable Gass fixed their eyes on each other, their tongues went in question & answer, but their thoughts were otherwise employed. (449)

Egocentric beings such as these speak a lunatic discourse that circles around themselves. As fictional characters, they are only splinters of a personality, partial beings with no interest in engaging each other as living men and women. A society that reduces its members to self-contemplating shadows is indeed sick, a diagnosis that Blake continues in his great abandoned poem, *The Four Zoas.*

In *An Island in the Moon* the only cure for this social neurosis comes from poetry. When the islanders sing, whether for entertainment or edification, they reach beyond themselves and participate in a larger unity. Blake alternates lunatic and lyric discourse until it becomes clear that the latter is an antidote for the former. When one member sings for the company he or she awakens a collective pleasure that is beyond them, not a product of their meager egos. Some of the lyrics in the satire are the sheerest fluff, while others are more significant. In either case they enter a gathering with power and authority of their own, leveling individual differences and allowing glimpses of a better life. After Obtuse Angle sings a song of particular significance, which Blake later entitles "Holy Thursday," the company for a while forget their mirth: "they all sat silent for a quarter of an hour" (463). By the closing pages of the satire as we have it, Blake is clearly growing impatient with the social lunacy he lampoons, for lyrics come so thick and fast that they drown out the chatter of the self-interested islanders. Blake shows himself ready to pursue the vision of vitality that he only glimpses in the lyrics. His decision to abandon *An Island in the Moon* and the techniques of prose satire, for which he possessed considerable talent, indicates growing devotion to a deeper vision of life and willingness to risk encountering it for the sake of psychic health, both his own and society's.

But that encounter must take dramatic form to secure the mind against the pathological effects of ego-loss. Blake embodies the vision of his lyrics in the drama of his mythology, displacing a menacing intensity onto independent characters and events. His first real effort in this direction comes in *Visions of the Daughters of Albion*, where the relations between the mythological trio Oothoon, Bromion, and Theotormon suggest their filiation in a primal unity. In the story of Oothoon's sexual awakening, rape, and rejection, Blake marries two narratives he found in Ovid, his master in mythmaking. Joining the tales of Persephone and Narcissus, he shows how sexual love becomes so perverted by a self-interested morality that it serves the cause, not of life, but of death. Oothoon plucks the blossom of carnal knowledge, but she discovers that sexuality has been coopted to serve a repressive regime. Blake's poem thus dramatizes a falling away from spontaneous human experience of the one life.

Like Persephone of Greek myth, Oothoon enters sexual experience violently.[37] A rape inaugurates her departure from the vales of Leutha, the sexual equivalent of Enna's fair fields. Blake stresses what the Greek myth suppresses, that the maiden courts sexual love in her flower-gathering and flight:

> Over the waves she went in wing'd exulting swift delight;
> And over Theotormons reign, took her impetuous course.
>
> Bromion rent her with his thunders. on his stormy bed
> Lay the faint maid, and soon her woes appalld his thunders hoarse
> (*VDA*, 1:14–17)

Leaving the land of innocence, Oothoon enters the political arena of Theotormon's reign, where thoughts of God inhibit action and moral codes compete for power. In such a world sex is a means of controlling desire by corrupting it.

Placing Bromion in the position of Dis, Greek god of the underworld, Blake suggests that an accusing morality subjects desire to a kingdom of death. Oothoon enters no heaven of sexual delight but an underworld of sexual repression. Bromion brings her there and rapes her. The word "thunders" describes his phallus and his accusing voice, both of which become instruments of hate instead of love. Not the rape but its significance in Bromion's morality dehumanizes Oothoon. Bromion immediately calls her a harlot and by thus naming her possesses her completely:

> Now thou maist marry Bromions harlot, and protect the child
> Of Bromion's rage, that Oothoon shall put forth in nine moons time
> (*VDA*, 2:1–2)

Accusing language is the weapon that hate uses to pervert the energies of love. The letter of Bromion's morality is scarlet, and it condemns the damnable strength of Oothoon's desire.

At this point Blake modulates expertly from Persephone's story to that of Narcissus. Oothoon's desire becomes an echo of its former strength, in fact an echo of Theotormon's sexual anxiety. Momentarily duped by the morality that accuses her, she howls a defiant plea that identifies her with Theotormon:

> I call with holy voice! kings of the sounding air,
> Rend away this defiled bosom that I may reflect.
> The image of Theotormon on my pure transparent breast.
> (*VDA*, 2:14–16)

Conflating Ovid's details, Blake identifies Echo with the pool in which Narcissus meets his own image. Oothoon is both. She reflects her lover's image verbally and visually. But in doing so she becomes subject to the power-play of his morality. Theotormon's self-denial is a kind of self-enslavement, for it justifies sexual timidity by devaluing the experience of love. His morality masks his narcissism, authorizing what Blake calls, in a fine phrase, "the self-enjoyings of self-denial" (*VDA*, 7:9). Repression becomes pleasurable when it brings power. It gives moral superiority to those whose desire is weak enough to be repressed. Oothoon enters permanently the orbit of Theotormon's anxiety, able to voice the cause of sexual liberty, but unable to pursue it herself. Sexually she has been silenced by the accusing powers that be, and she dwindles into "a solitary shadow on the margin of non-entity" (*VDA*, 7:15), though Blake's final design anticipates the time when Oothoon shall triumph over her oppressors to assert her sexual purity and independence.

The mechanism of sexual enslavement appears with particular clarity in this poem. Morality triumphs over desire by valuing a symbol over life. When a symbol acquires a value greater than the living world, it seduces humanity into a compensatory fantasy, a mechanism that we shall later see resembles the more debilitating one of autistic withdrawal. Religions are built of an idolatry that originates in the frustration of desire:

> The moment of desire! The moment of desire! the virgin
> That pines for man; shall awaken her womb to enormous joys
> In the secret shadow of her chamber; the youth shut up from
> The lustful joy. shall forget to generate. & create an amorous image
> In the shadows of his curtains and in the folds of his silent pillow.
> Are not these the places of religion? the rewards of continence?
> (*VDA*, 7:3–8)

It is a bold stroke on Blake's part to identify religion and masturbation. But his point merits the comparison: in both cases a symbol usurps the place of the living world. Denied physical gratification, the adolescent will seek intercourse with a symbol of his own making, an act of self-love that devalues life and desire. Institutional religion offers a similar idolatry as a substitute for exuberant life. Either way, man walks the path of Narcissus, valuing a symbol of himself over flesh and blood.

Under such conditions sex becomes a perverse acrobatics, a secret sin, a parody of religious possession. Blake pictures it in its full horror on the frontispiece to the poem: a hermaphroditic backward union, eyes staring off in opposite directions. Bromion and Oothoon are chained unhappily together while Theotormon grasps his head in anguish, all beneath the brooding gaze of a single eye in the heavens. In this parody of marriage, in which Oothoon must "bear the wintry rage/Of a harsh terror driv'n to madness" and "drag the chain/Of life, in weary lust!" (*VDA*, 5:24–5, 22–3), Blake offers a lesson in how to read his poem. These figures all inhabit the same cave. They are parts of a single mind roofed over by a human skull. In *Vision of the Daughters of Albion*, Blake approaches for the first time his mature method of rendering in myth the constituent parts of a single fragmented personality. The poem dramatizes a mind's split into incomplete identities, each organized around a particular symbol of life which it takes for the whole. Oothoon's chant of desire could have been a song of innocence, just as the dirges of Theotormon and Bromion could have been songs of experience. Blake links them all together in the dramatic framework of his mythology. His visionary lyricism takes a dramatic form in this symbolism of psychic dissociation. The dialectical relations he creates between these symbols move the drama toward its goal in a restored unity of mind and life.

Freud describes a tension in refined men between tenderness and lust that nicely characterizes the division between Theotormon and Bromion.[38] Where Freud reduces this tension to a disruption in individual men of the proper development of the libido, however, Blake attributes the problem to a dissociation in the human mind in general. Blake's mythological sort of psychoanalysis is both more optimistic and less sexist than Freud's, for it undertakes to resolve divisions—psychological *and* sexual—in a return to primordial unity. In *Visions of the Daughters of Albion*, Blake takes his diagnosis of society a step further than before by dramatizing a mind, not simply narcissistic, but fully dissociated. Self-love (Bromion) has usurped sexual desire (Oothoon), leaving the religious impulse (Theotormon) barren and demoralized. These constituent parts of the mind compete for power over the whole, allowing an early glimpse of the matter and method of *The Four Zoas*. The fall of the mind into the psycho-sexual triad that Blake depicts here haunts his later poetry, as he labors relentlessly to overcome the darker implications of sexual love.

IV

Blake's lyric impulse gives birth to myth, which works to master the potential for madness inherent in vision. Myth aims ultimately at reawakening humanity to a wholeness that society and history have obliterated. The great hope of Blake's early poetry is to achieve this psychological aim within history itself. As if to confirm the vision of the sensibility bards and set life on a collective footing, revolution erupted in America and France. Blake interpreted these social upheavals as historical proof of the validity of his vision of vitality, and at first shaped his mythology around the prospects of a historical renewal of a collective human identity. The drama of the early mythology therefore possesses a specifically political urgency.

The principal characters to emerge define between them the poles of political action: Urizen, the arch-tyrant, and Orc, the implacable rebel. The course of their relations provides an index of Blake's attitude toward politics. In the early poems, their opposition dramatizes a dissociation in the human mind (reminiscent of the sensibility bards) between instinct and intellect, which society has institutionalized by subjecting the masses to a monarch. Blake turns to the *psychology* of this enslavement only after it becomes clear that revolution does not guarantee an end to oppression. In *America* and *Europe,* he simply asserts instinct over intellect, Orc over Urizen, in the hopes of redressing the social imbalance between them and initiating an order that includes both.

The dissociation of instinct and intellect is the cause, in Blake's view, of the collective neurosis that afflicts society. In her anguish, Oothoon gets a glimpse of the mental deity that enslaves both her and her beloved:

> O Urizen! Creator of men! mistaken Demon of heaven:
> Thy joys are tears! Thy labor vain, to form men to thine image.
> How can one joy absorb another? are not different joys
> Holy, eternal, infinite! and each joy is a Love.
>
> (*VDA*, 5:3–6)

Urizen, of course, is a parody of the Old Testament's Jealous God. He embodies the intellect's capacity for reduction from unity to singularity, and by implication from life to death. The premium society places upon this reductive faculty attests to its separation from the instinctual life.

For Blake, this situation is fundamentally psychological, and the figure of Orc, another avatar of Stevens's virile poet, emerges as the dramatic antithesis to the reductive intellect. In *America,* Orc enters life by violating moral sanctions against incest and rape. His encounter with Urizen's representative, the Angel of Albion, is a meeting between contraries, which the latter describes in terms that mix moral, religious, and political imperatives:

> Blasphemous Demon, Antichrist, hater of Dignities;
> Lover of wild rebellion, and transgressor of Gods Law;
> Why dost thou come to Angels eyes in this terrific form?
>
> (*A*, 7:5–7)

Such a question is really an accusation, contrived to maintain the separation of intellect and instinct for the purposes of asserting the power of the status quo. Blake viewed the revolutions in America and France as political harbingers of the psychological transformation that would reunite the mind and allow humanity once again to live as one. His early myth dramatizes a political chiliasm that anticipates the imminent reintegration—in history—of a dissociated collectivity.

But history betrayed him. The American Revolution turned bourgeois and the French Revolution turned bloody. Through no fault of his own except that of too much hope, Blake saw the historical foundations removed from beneath his myth. Agonized lines that he originally included and then suppressed in the preludium of *America* show his disappointment in the failure of politics to restore humanity to one life:

> The stern Bard ceas'd, asham'd of his own song; enrag'd he swung
> His harp aloft sounding, then dash'd its shining frame against
> A ruin'd pillar in glittring fragments; silent he turn'd away,
> And wander'd down the vales of Kent in sick & drear lamentings.
> (*A*, 2:18–21)

The failure of history to fulfill the terms of his vision causes the bard to be ashamed of his own performance. His song has proved untimely, perhaps even untrue. A new element enters Blake's myth at this point. The dissociation of intellect and instinct is no longer the only issue, but, as the example of the sensibility bards suggests, the relation of the poet to this condition as well. The violence that the bard does to his harp suggests a pained discomfort with his vision, as if song itself were the problem as much as its historical applicability. Blake's personal relation to visionary experience and its menacing strength become elements in the drama of psychic dismemberment that is the subject of his later poetry.

Even in *Europe*, the prophecy that follows *America*, Blake steps back from politics, though not completely. Where *America* treats revolution openly, *Europe* places it in the midst of a dream. History has become the nightmare of a devouring female and revolution must awaken both her and the humanity she enslaves. Blake is turning his attention toward the origins in the mind of the dissociation of instinct and intellect. If politics cannot reunite them, perhaps psychology can:

Thought chang'd the infinite to a serpent; that which pitieth:
To a devouring flame; and man fled from its face and hid
In forests of the night; then all the eternal forests were divided
Into earths rolling in circles of space, that like an ocean rush'd
And overwhelmed all except this finite wall of flesh.
(E, 10:16–20)

To prod humanity forward toward a renewed unity, Blake feels he must work backward to examine the origins of the dissociated mind. His politics of revolution becomes a politics of consciousness as his myth pursues the fall from primordial unity into pervasive egotism. He includes himself in this process to the extent that his own activity is conditioned by it. As we shall see, much of his myth betrays a dramatic self-reflexivity that functions to protect Blake from both the temptation to shatter his harp, forsaking song, and the pathological potential of visionary experience. Of the modern poet, Stevens writes that "the consciousness of his function, if he is a serious artist, is a measure of his obligation" (64). Blake fulfills this obligation by displacing his own psychological agon onto his myth. The dialectic of man and myth that develops secures him against the potential madness at the heart of vision.

Like the sensibility bards, Blake faced the problem of assimilating a vision of vitality to the conditions of individual existence. Madness, or at least profound psychological distress, was the reward Collins, Cowper, and Smart won for failing to do so. In the end, these poets became the victims of vision, either separated despairingly from it or possessed maniacally by it. Their suffering suggests a potentially tragic contradiction between the individual and the collective life. Blake labors against this contradiction to escape a similar fate. His early preoccupation and struggle with the tragic, a subject we will turn to next, shows how troubled he was by the possibility that visionary experience cannot be accommodated to the human norm. Blake's myth of madness defends him against the intensity of vision and its antagonism to the world; by making madness an artistic phenomenon, Blake masters it and pursues health. But we must eventually ask whether he is able to do so without recourse to compensation.

3

King, Creator, Madman

Madness in great ones must not unwatch'd go.
—Shakespeare, *Hamlet*

I

From November 1788 to March 1789, George III, King of England, was mad.[1] His physicians attributed the affliction to a long walk on which he thoroughly wet his stockings and failed for hours to change them. A fever set in, and with it an alarming loquacity. The King hurried his words, as if speech were a compulsion, and rambled until his meaning became a jumble. Fanny Burney, then part of the royal household, noted his condition with some concern in her diary:

> The bodily agitation had become extreme and the talking incessant; indeed, it was too evident that His Majesty had no longer the least command over himself. His eyes, the Queen has since told me, she could compare with nothing but black currant jelly, the veins in his face were swelled, the sounds of his voice were dreadful, he often spoke till he was exhausted and the moment he would recover his breath began again, while the foam ran out of his mouth.[2]

At the height of his confusion, King George talked for nineteen hours straight. Sleep came fitfully if at all, and had no renovating effect. He was not without lucid intervals; he often conversed sensibly with his physicians and pages. But his mind would not mend. "Oh my boy," he confessed to the Duke of York, "I wish to God I might die, for I am going to be mad."[3]

The King's deepest fears were realized. His behavior grew so unpredictable and uninhibited that his doctors decided to confine him at Kew palace, where to their surprise his delirium flourished. He mourned the loss of his American colonies when sane enough to remember that he no longer ruled them. Otherwise he imagined they were still his, often believing himself to be George Washington, commander of the American Army. His conduct toward his attendants varied from frivolous to violent. When he became uncontrollable, they resorted to the straitwaistcoat and, on occasion, bound their sovereign to his bed. Even when he was placid, his actions bordered on the bizarre. The faithful equerry Greville noted the King's delirium on Christmas Day 1788:

> Among his extravagances of the Moment He had at this time hid part of the Bed Clothes under his bed, had taken off his Night Cap, & got a Pillow Case round his head, & the Pillow in the bed with Him, which he called Prince Octavius, who He said was to be new born this day.[4]

By identifying his own lost son with Christ, King George put himself in the place of God the Father. His delirium induced a sublime egotism, even as it belittled the dignity of kingship.

The King's domestic affairs during his derangement were unusually open. Declaring all marriages to have been annulled, he spurned the affections of Queen Charlotte and nursed a violent passion for the Lady of her Bedchamber, Elizabeth Pembroke. However contrary to the spirit of his recent Royal Proclamation against Vice and Immorality, the King's passion proved irrepressible. Lady Pembroke was a frequent topic of his conversation, usually erotic, and became the subject of elaborate fantasies. George imagined himself to be King Ahasuerus with Lady Pembroke his Esther. Charlotte was Queen Vashti, who in the Book of Esther was deposed for disobedience to the King.[5] Having thus freed himself from an odious attachment, George descanted his devotion in high adolescent style, scribbling ribald messages to his beloved and singing bawdy ballads in her honor. His delirium removed the inhibitions that, in healthier days, reined in his desire.

The madness of King George could not, however, remain a purely domestic matter. It afflicted the whole body politic, and for a while made chaos of the government. The English monarchy seemed headed for a regency, but, with the King out of his senses, there was no authority to institute one. Greville put the matter succinctly in a letter to the Marquis of Buckingham:

> Parliament cannot proceed to business without the session being opened by the King, or by some Commission authorized by him. No Regent can be appointed or authorized to exercise acts of royal authority but by Act of Parliament; nor can any such Act be valid and binding in law without the King's consent.... It is a heavy calamity that is inflicted upon us in any case except that of his perfect recovery; but in the event which there seems most ground to fear, it may give rise to serious and difficult questions, such as cannot even be discussed without shaking the security and tranquility of the country.[6]

All of England in a sense participated in the King's madness. The populace was informed of His Majesty's condition by daily bulletins from his physicians. To a critical eye like Blake's, however, more was at stake than the king's health. Because the delirium of George III was collective in its effects, the real question was whether England, as a nation, could recover from the madness of its monarch. George regained his reason in March 1789, resuscitating the English monarchy only months before the French doomed theirs by storming the Bastille. Madness returned, however, in 1801 and periodically thereafter, until a later generation viewed George III only as "an old, mad, blind, despised, and dying King."[7]

Such was the political atmosphere in which Blake began to hammer out his mythology. To him the madness of George III was an indictment of monarchy in general, a rare public glimpse of the irrationality of kingship. Blake was not the man to distinguish between the good king and the tyrant. In his view, anyone who asserted himself over his fellows inevitably sacrificed his humanity in the process. George's self-alienation presented Blake with an immediate historical precedent for the psychodrama of his mythology. In *America* he guardedly depicts the deranged monarch's mad reaction to rebellion:

> Albions Guardian writhed in torment on the eastern sky
> Pale quivring toward the brain his glimmering eyes, teeth chattering
> Howling & shuddering his legs quivering; convuls'd each muscle & sinew
> Sick'ning lay Londons Guardian.
>
> (A, 15:6–9)

Open rebellion in the American colonies exposes the madness of the people's guardian. But monarchy as an institution only politicizes a division in the human mind, for in Blake's view the mind that endorses kingship must first have divided against itself, enabling one of its components to lord over the whole. This division and its dynamic constitute the politics of consciousness, the aboriginal psychodrama that becomes the thematic center of Blake's mythology. If the madness of King George awakens Blake to the psychological implications of kingship, it also inspires him to examine and reinterpret the madness of another English monarch, Shakespeare's Lear. As we shall see, Blake shapes his myth in response not only to the self-division inherent in kingship but also to the tragic view of human life that Shakespeare advances in his great play.

II

Blake's failed poem, *Tiriel*, and his minor masterpiece, *The Book of Urizen*, each owe something to both George III's madness and Shakespeare's *King Lear*. Blake's lively struggle against Shakespeare has gone unnoticed by most critics.[8] Those who admit a filiation tend to treat Shakespeare as Blake's forebear in symbolism.[9] While it is true that continuities exist between them, a critical comparison should reveal more than just the similarity of Hotspur and the fiery Orc. Blake wrote no poem entitled *Shakespeare*, so it is easy to underestimate the great tragedian's influence upon his myth.[10] But in a verse-letter to Flaxman, he confides that "Shakespeare in riper years gave me his hand" (*Letters*, 20). If that hand was a helping one, Blake must have taken it as a true friend: that is, in opposition. For in his early myth Blake confronts Shakespeare in a struggle against the dark wisdom of tragedy. Their first encounter comes in *Tiriel*, where allusions to *King Lear* provide a critical commentary upon Shakespeare's play. Blake aims ultimately at revaluing the tragic by creating a myth that endorses a less limiting view of existence.

For the tragic assumes strict limits to human potential. To the ancient

Greeks, who originated tragic drama, the man who aspires beyond his station arouses the jealousy of the gods. His *hubris* provokes *nemesis* to cut him down and reassert human limits. In Aristotle this primitive view of man's subordination to the gods acquires a naturalistic and moral bias. The proud hero offends not so much against the gods as against the natural and moral order which the gods represent and which inheres in all things. Aristotle's endorsement of such an order appears clearest in his remarks upon character in tragedy. Character must be good, he asserts, and that goodness must reveal itself in deeds: "any speech or action that manifests moral purpose of any kind will be expressive of character: the character will be good if the purpose is good."[11] By identifying character and moral purpose, Aristotle suggests that humanity is defined and limited by a moral order larger than itself and embracing nature. The hallmark of the tragic, then, is the belief in this objective moral order and the limits it imposes upon human potential.[12] In Shakespeare this vision acquires even greater naturalistic force. Natural and moral order so interpenetrate that nature itself seems the agent of *nemesis*.

For Blake, as for the other Romantic poets, such a view of life subjects humanity to false limits. He may betray an inchoate sympathy for the tragic in his early, naturalistic poems, but as his myth develops, he turns ultimately away from its pessimism and imperialism. In the late prose tract *On Homers Poetry* (approx. 1820), Blake dismisses both Aristotle's theory of character and the moral order it implies:

> Aristotle says Characters are either Good or Bad: now Goodness or Badness has nothing to do with Character.... a Horse is not more a Lion for being a Bad Horse. that is its Character; its Goodness or Badness is another consideration. (269)

For Blake character is not defined by an objective morality but by its own essence. Tragedy, with its emphasis upon moral order and natural limits, therefore stands in the way of the deepest understanding of human character and the fullest realization of human potential. Blake is not alone in this belief. The Romantic poets share his suspicion of moral imperatives and as a result their poetry is profoundly anti-tragic. Wordsworth's nature, though hard at times, is much more forgiving than Shakespeare's. Byron's dark humor becomes possible only after the passing of an objective moral order. Shelley attacks tragedy directly in his great attempt to subdue its wisdom in *Prometheus Unbound*. All of these poets share with Blake an unwillingness to submit to the conditions of the tragic.

But the effort to forge a less limiting view of human life is not without a struggle. Blake openly confronts tragedy in *Tiriel* and labors against the imposing strength of Shakespeare's vision. The point of contact between *Tiriel* and *King Lear* is a king's madness, the political implications of which became apparent to Blake in the lunacy of George III. In Shakespeare's play, tragedy hinges upon a king's transgression of natural order and the madness that ensues. As king, Lear stands at the pinnacle of human possibility. But he oversteps his authority when he commands the powers of nature to do his bidding. The course of his ordeal becomes an education in what it means to be human; Lear must learn his true place in the order of things. Neither his greatness nor his authority qualify him to usurp nature's powers. When he does, only the deepest suffering and the basest treatment will serve to bring him around to the truth of his own littleness. He confesses as much in the memorable lines,

> When the rain came to wet me once, and the wind to make me chatter, when the thunder would not peace at my bidding, there I found 'em, there I smelt 'em out. Go to, they are not men o' their words: they told me I was everything. 'Tis a lie, I am not ague-proof.[13]

Lear's acceptance of his humanity is a lesson in humility, for he submits to the natural limits whose transgression began his tragedy. For Shakespeare, then, tragedy restores a broken order, returning humanity to a posture of dependence within the scheme of nature.

In this context, Lear's madness is a more metaphysical than psychological phenomenon, involving not merely the mind but the moral imperatives that define the human. Lear's delirium is intellectual evidence of having transgressed against natural order. In trying to become more than man, he becomes less, reduced to the zero degree of his humanity. Hence his passion for the begging Edgar and his crown of weeds and flowers. Lear passes back into nature as madness divides him from mankind. Although in his delirium he sees man at his most vulnerable, debased by life's contradictions, this insight comes at the cost of *all* the civilized conventions that distinguish man from animal. Madness blinds Lear to the value of these conventions for accoutering the animal man. In his moving encounter with the dissembling Edgar, he divests himself of civilization:

> Thou art the thing itself: unaccommodated man is no
> more but such a poor, bare, fork'd animal as thou art.
> Off, off, you lendings! Come, unbutton here.
>
> (III.iv.106-9)

The next time Lear asks to be unbuttoned, he dies only moments later. Shakespeare thus indicates that in his view madness is the psychological equivalent of death. The insight that madness brings Lear, however authentic, comes at the expense of civilized conventions, and cannot be integrated into the natural order he has violated. The dark paradox of Shakespeare's play is that nature has no place for unaccommodated man. Humanity cannot be severed from its civilized lendings, and when it is, death alone reasserts nature's order. Lear's madness, then, is a metaphysical phenomenon that reveals the death of his humanity, but the possibility too of its rebirth in the confession of his offense against the order of nature.

Prior to his madness, however, Lear recapitulates his offense with curses, for by cursing his daughters he turns against the bonds of nature. He oversteps a man's authority when he bids nature to perform the unnatural, claiming as his own a power that is beyond him:

> You nimble lightnings, dart your blinding flames
> Into her scornful eyes! Infect her beauty
> You fen-suck'd fogs, drawn by the powerful sun
> To fall and blister.
>
> (II.iv.165-8)

The patent irony of Lear's cursing is that it remains an empty gesture. Goneril and Regan meet their end, not because of anything Lear says, but because their evil natures drive them to it. Similarly, Cordelia lives to be reunited with her estranged father in spite of his maledictions. Through Lear's curses, Shakespeare marks a limit between man's prerogative and nature's power. Lear's tragedy begins when he oversteps that limit and continues until natural order reasserts itself. By thus limiting human potential, Shakespeare endorses an order that includes humanity, but ultimately extends beyond it. Tragedy is nature's way of putting man in his place.

Blake's ostensible antagonism to the tragic does not mean that he brushes it casually aside. His early efforts to forge a myth show him preoccupied with the possible truth of tragic wisdom. Blake wrote *Tiriel* in 1789, the year that King George recovered his sanity. While most of London feted the King's health, Blake penned this sardonic commentary on the abuses of kingship. It is in its relation to *King Lear*, however, that *Tiriel* reveals most about Blake's nascent myth. The poem is so haunted by the spectre of Shakespeare that it fails to realize a meaning of its own. Blake engages his antagonist directly, but comes away without a victory. Even so, *Tiriel* remains interesting for its attempt to master the tragic. If Blake fails to do so, it is because in *Tiriel* he remains too true to the spirit of tragedy.

One way of viewing *Tiriel* is as a poetic criticism of *King Lear*. Almost every element in Shakespeare's play has its complement in Blake's poem. The most obvious contact occurs where *Tiriel* alludes openly to the great tragedy.[14] Only six lines into the poem, the aged monarch Tiriel curses his offspring. Blake's details differ from Shakespeare's in that Tiriel is blind and his children are male. But the spirit of the scene alludes unmistakably to Shakespeare. Near the end of the opening page, Tiriel delivers a curse worthy of his predecessor, Lear:

> may the heavens rain wrath
> As thick as northern fogs. around your gates. to choke you up
> That you may lie as now your mother lies. like dogs. cast out
> The stink. of your dead carcases. annoying man & beast
> Till your white bones are bleachd with age for a memorial.
> (*T*, 1:42–6)

In its motivation and detail Tiriel's curse differs from those uttered by Lear, but the spirit between them is consistent: both invoke a higher power to disinherit an unfaithful progeny. Allusion becomes an act of criticism when it situates received material in a new context; by alluding so clearly to *King Lear*, Blake's poem becomes a critical reinterpretation of Shakespeare's play.

We should ask, then, *why* Blake alludes to *King Lear* to establish the character of Tiriel. However flawed and fallen, Lear is one of Shakespeare's noblest creations. His curses inspire awe because so great a man hurls them. Blake's Tiriel, on the other hand, could hardly be more unsympathetic. From first to last he acts despicably, subjecting others to the power of his all-consuming self-interest. If allusions to *King Lear* were an effort to ennoble this degenerate being, then Blake would be writing in the service of Shakespeare, receiving his meaning and extending its range. But in fact Blake's allusions are an attempt to overturn the meaning of Shakespeare's tragedy, revealing its inadequacy and revising its conclusions.

Tiriel's curses differ from Lear's in one decisive way: they work. When Tiriel denounces his sons and their society for the last time, the results are devastating. The passage is long, but worth quoting in full:

> And aged Tiriel stood & said where does the thunder sleep
> Where doth he hide his terrible head & his swift & fiery daughters
> Where do they shroud their fiery wings & terrors of their hair
> Earth thus I stamp thy bosom rouse the earthquake from his den
> To raise his dark & burning visage thro the cleaving ground
> To thrust these towers with his shoulders. let his fiery dogs
> Rise from the center belching flames & roarings. dark smoke
> Where art thou Pestilence that bathest in fogs & standing lakes
> Rise up thy sluggish limbs. & let the loathsomest of poisons
> Drop from thy garments as thou walkest. wrapt in yellow clouds
> Here take thy seat. in this wide court. let it be strown with dead
> And sit & smile upon these cursed sons of Tiriel
> Thunder & fire & pestilence. here you not Tiriels curse.
> (T, 5:1–13)

Blake weaves into this long curse the cadences of Lear's oaths. Although he makes no direct quotations, he conjures the memory of Shakespeare's potent phraseology. Behind Tiriel's words we hear Lear's, phrases such as the following: "Nor rain, wind, thunder, fire are my daughters," "oak-cleaving thunderbolt," "Blasts and fogs upon thee," and "Thou art a bile,/A plague-sore, or embossed carbuncle." Shakespeare's language is far more compact and visceral than Blake's, which becomes bogged down in a turgid effort to personify. But Blake clearly wants us to hear Lear's curses in Tiriel's.

Blake courts this comparison to make a point: Shakespeare, in his view, underestimates human potential. No sooner does Tiriel finish than his destructive thought leaps into action:

> at the fathers curse
> The earth trembled fires belched from the yawning clefts
> And when the shaking ceast a fog possest the accursed clime.
> (T, 5:15–17)

These lines come as a bit of a shock, since the preceding allusions lead us to expect such curses to be impotent. But by alluding to *King Lear,* Blake reinterprets Shakespeare's tragedy and implies its incompleteness. The curse no longer marks a limit between human prerogative and natural power. On the contrary, it proves that humanity possesses within a power that Shakespeare places beyond. Humanity is more for Blake than Shakespeare ever allows it to be. Even a despot like Tiriel wields power unknown to the great Lear. In their effect, Tiriel's curses confirm the limitedness of human potential in Shakespeare's play.

One of the results of Blake's reinterpretation is to alter radically the nature of tragedy. If for Shakespeare the order of nature sets strict limits on human potential, for Blake that order exists only as the mind conceives it. Blake psychologizes the tragic, lifting nature into mind and preparing the way for what, in his view, is a less limiting vision of existence. "Where man is not nature is barren": such a claim makes tragedy a mental rather than a metaphysical drama. The paradox of Blake's position, however, appears in his conviction that human nature can overcome natural limits. In Shakespeare's play, this is exactly Lear's error, the impetus for his madness and death. But in Blake's psychological reading of Lear's ordeal, the tragedy lies not in a king's fall, but in a man's failure to perceive his full humanity. This lapse in perception is, to Blake, the only *real* tragedy. Because Tiriel is blind to his own humanity, he condemns himself and his family to death. Blake's psychological reinterpretation of the tragic, then, makes it a phase in a larger mental drama—in fact a late phase, since an ordeal like Lear's becomes possible only after one has lost full humanity and acquiesced to a false natural order. By making nature a function of mind, Blake causes Shakespeare's tragedy to look incomplete, gaining the rhetorical advantage of advancing what seems a more archaic and comprehensive view of humanity.[15]

But does he wholly subdue the possible truth of tragic wisdom? In our last chapter, we noticed a potential for tragedy in Blake's own early poetry. That potential returns in Tiriel's dying lament. Those critics who read the poem as holding out some hope in the form either of a curse-turned-blessing or a "negative prophecy," fail to face up to the unmitigated darkness of its final statement.[16] The poem ends where it begins, in death, but not before Tiriel launches into one last denunciation of life's horrors. This litany of experience runs throughout Blake's later works and should remind us that his myth labors always to confute the debilitating wisdom of tragedy. Tiriel dies unable to explain the tragic contradictions of existence, blind to his own share in the responsibility for their profusion:

> Thy laws O Har & Tiriels wisdom end together in a curse
> Why is one law given to the lion & the patient Ox
> And why men bound beneath the heavens in a reptile form
> A worm of sixty winters creeping on the dusky ground
>
> (8:9-11)

Blake's attempt to answer these questions is the poem itself, for in it he tries for the first time to construct a symbolic structure that would sanction a less limiting view of human potential than the tragic.

Blake extends the implications of his critical allusions by reducing Shakespeare's play to a few major symbols, though in doing so he runs the risk of misreading, since his symbolic method forces him to overlook subtleties of character and motivation. At the center of his poem is the symbol of the mad king, an obvious promotion of King Lear to quasi-allegorical status. Critics have interpreted this symbol variously as a jealous Jehovah, a moralizing body-monarch, the faculty of Reason, the doddering King George.[17] No one would dream of attributing so many identities to Shakespeare's Lear. For Lear is an individual, whereas Tiriel is a type. By ignoring what makes Lear distinctive and his tragedy unique, Blake generalizes his ordeal to include all whose self-love blinds them to their full humanity. The critique that this symbolism provides actually reverses the meaning of *King Lear*. Tragedy becomes for Blake not the just desert of the overreaching individual, but the typical experience of a self-centered being.

Tiriel's madness, unlike Lear's, is just a simple psychological fact. Blake's king is mad, not because he offended against nature, but precisely because he is a king. His madness reveals the mental aberration Blake feels is inherent in kingship rather than the metaphysical implications of violating natural order. Tiriel describes the reasons for his hopeless wanderings with a banality that could never apply to King Lear:

> My Journey is oer rocks & mountains. not in pleasant vales
> I must not sleep or rest because of madness & dismay
>
> (*T*, 3:25-6)

Tiriel seems to take his madness for granted, as if it were the condition and privilege of kingship. Through the banality of this symbolism, Blake attempts to diffuse the pathos of Lear's suffering. The strategy here is to belittle Shakespeare's tragedy with the reductive effects of parody.

So it is that the ageless Har, an enfeebled innocent, parodies the captive Lear, who dreams of flight with Cordelia. Blake echoes Shakespeare when describing Har and Heva in their flower-children's paradise:

> Playing with flowers. & running after birds they spent the day
> And in the night like infants slept delighted with infant dreams
> (*T,* 2:8–9)

These lines call to mind Lear's dream of laughing "at gilded butterflies" and contemplating "the mystery of things." The difference is that for Shakespeare this dream remains an otherworldly fantasy, where for Blake it is as real as anything in his poem. Har's senile innocence is the symbolic complement of Tiriel's despotic madness, and the two must come together in *this* world, according to Blake's critique, if the tragic is to be overcome. Separated, each is unattractive, but if Har's preternatural innocence could unite with Tiriel's embittered experience, then perhaps the tragedy born of their separation would cease. Tiriel's madness and by implication Lear's is in part attributable to a fall away from the primordial innocence represented by Har.

Neither Tiriel nor Har, then, is complete unto himself. Tiriel finds sustenance in Har's innocence. He enters the vales of Har "hungry with travel" (*T,* 2:30), and receives nourishment there for a further journey. When Heva identifies him with Har, she provides a key to understanding the interplay of Blake's symbols:

> Bless thy poor eyes old man. & bless the old father of Tiriel
> Thou art my Tiriels old father, I know thee thro thy wrinkles
> (*T,* 2:37–8)

In a sense, Tiriel *is* Har, for taken together they comprise a single mind. Blake splits Lear's mentality in two, separating the mad king from his psychological double, the senile innocent. The mentality of kingship, in Blake's view, divides man's selfish passions from his native innocence, then institutes this division in the political structure of a monarchy. Such was the real lesson to be learned in the madness of George III. By criticizing this mentality in *Tiriel,* Blake moves toward a political theory that focuses upon the psychological assumptions of social organization.

The conclusion that Blake's symbolic critique of Shakespeare reaches comes to this: the tragedy of King Lear originates in an aberrant mentality, the same supreme egotism that became manifest in the madness of George III. Like Lear and George III, Tiriel is bound upon the wheel of nature, but it is his mind that puts him there, since his selfish passions have divided away from his native innocence. Tiriel gives a private account of this self-division and becomes a psychoanalyst in the process. His personal case history runs like this:

> The child springs from the womb. the father ready stands to form
> The infant head while the mother idle plays with her dog on her couch
> . . . .
> The father forms a whip to rouze the sluggish senses to act
> And scourges off all youthful fancies from the newborn man
> . . . .
>   Such was Tiriel
> Compelld to pray repugnant & to humble the immortal spirit
> Till I am subtil as a serpent in a paradise
> Consuming all both flowers & fruits insects & warbling birds
>   (*T*, 8:12-13, 17-18, 22-25)

Tiriel's analysis of the effects of paternal tyranny and maternal neglect anticipates Freud in its conclusion that childhood relations produce adult mentalities. Tiriel explains his pursuit of power as the result of having had no power as a child. But this explanation becomes a defense when he attributes his mad cunning to the psychosexual determinism of childhood trauma. Blake criticizes a Freudian explanation of behavior even as he anticipates it, showing that psychoanalysis binds our humanity all the more firmly to the wheel of nature by keeping us ignorant of a deeper problem.[18] For Tiriel's madness originates in his dissociation from another self, the innocent Har. By implication, Lear suffers the effects of a similar psychological division, as his selfish plan to remain king in name only suggests. In *Tiriel's* symbolic critique, Blake attempts to defeat tragedy by shifting emphasis away from nature and onto the dissociated mind, thus raising the possibility of overcoming natural limits by healing this aberrant mentality.

    However ambitious this aim, Blake fails to realize it in *Tiriel*. Several forces defeat him. First, in Shakespeare he finds an adversary too powerful to overcome in so slight an undertaking. Blake's allusions and symbolic critique provide a new standard by which to measure *King Lear*, but are inadequate to the task of redefining its values. Blake's strategy is reductive and forces him to misread or just plain ignore subtleties of character and motivation. By identifying madness and kingship, for instance, he vastly oversimplifies Shakespeare's meaning. Lear's greatness as a man qualifies him to be king, and since madness robs him of his humanity, it runs opposite to kingship. After reading *Tiriel,* one comes away with a renewed sense, not of Blake's greatness as a poet and a thinker, but of Shakespeare's. Try as he might to defeat the power of Shakespeare's tragic wisdom, Blake manages only to score a few critical blows.[19] His poetry and his symbols lack both coherence and authority enough to silence the claims of tragedy to be a valid view of life. Like Lear, Tiriel dies in the closing scene, as if in grudging homage to Shakespeare's play, and the overwhelming effect of his ordeal is to substantiate the tragic.

Second, there is evidence that Blake harbors a secret sympathy for the tragic. As we saw in the last chapter, the impassioned naturalism of his early verse forces him into statements fully compatible with tragedy as both Nietzsche and Shakespeare understand it. An assertion like "You never know what is enough until you know what is more than enough" (39) could be the motto of almost any tragedy, and remains unsettling in the company of Blake's more sanguine claims for human potential. Really the only memorable lines in *Tiriel* come in Tiriel's closing lament about the contradictions of existence. For some reason the injustices of natural life fire Blake's imagination, inspiring the best poetry in an otherwise flat and feeble poem. It could be that Blake's secret sympathy for the tragic fuels his endless labor at the forge and anvil, trying feverishly to hammer out a more comprehensive symbolism that would once and for all revalue tragedy. If so, Blake's myth arises in part to deny the truth of tragic wisdom, a truth too pessimistic to tolerate but too strong to dismiss.

Finally, in *Tiriel* Blake still lacks thorough insight into the dynamics of psychic dissociation, which has yet to become, in Nietzsche's phrase, "an artistic phenomenon." The tragic defeats Blake because, as Tiriel's dying lament proves, nature still takes precedence over mind. The presence in the poem of the titanic brotherhood of Tiriel, Ijim, and Zazel shows him moving toward a psychic symbolism whose dynamic can account for tragedy. But it remains undeveloped in *Tiriel* and takes full shape only later, in *The Four Zoas.* Bloom is right when he concludes that "Tiriel's story ends in negation" (30). Blake's first effort to master tragedy fails because his symbols do not go far enough. They do not explain *why* the mind divides or *how* this dissociation can be healed.

III

Blake needs a *myth*, one that puts the madness of psychic dissociation at its center. His first real attempt at one comes in *The Book of Urizen*, where he tries to defeat the tragic by placing it in a cosmological context. If successful, this strategy could explain the origin and anticipate the end of tragedy. Since myth functions etiologically, it does not restrict Blake to the conditions of nature. He can master the tragic with a more comprehensive symbolism that advances a less limiting view of life. As mythmaker, he examines the psychological assumptions of tragedy, incorporating its partial wisdom into a larger myth of psychic dissociation and healing.

Blake therefore becomes a student and an artist of the mind. He mythologizes, not a Miltonic morality of prohibition and reward, but a highly original psychology of self-division and regeneration. It should be admitted, however, that Blake's myth is, perhaps to its disadvantage, demythologized. No one believes in it. And, with the exception of a few credulous graduate students here and there, no one can. This characteristic of the myth has been too little stressed by Blake's critics. Frye gives the impression that, if not itself vital, Blake's myth participates in a universal order of symbols that energizes it. This assumption sanctions a merely peripheral treatment of the text in his landmark study, *Fearful Symmetry*. But the archetypes through which he interprets Blake's myth are the artifacts of exhausted belief systems. In assimilating Blake's symbols to them he risks masking what is unique to a modern attempt at mythmaking.

Georges Bataille comes closer than Frye to the modern reader's experience of Blake's myth. In *Literature and Evil*, Bataille discusses the significance of a mythology that nobody can or does believe in: "the myths which poetry seems to establish only really reveal the void, unless they are objects of faith."[20] There is no evidence that the mythology Blake created was ever an object of faith, not even for himself. His myth cannot be believed in because it lacks the collective assent of a faithful community, a cult of believers. Blake scholars, with their interest in sources and systemization, do not constitute such a community. For them this myth is an object of *study*, not *faith*. Its demythologized character makes it transparently a fiction in a way that does not apply, for example, to the Bible or even to *Paradise Lost*. In mythologizing psychic life Blake renders the mind's dynamic visible, but does not organize its functions into a new belief system. Bataille again puts the point succinctly: "In fact his life was an inner phenomenon and the mythical figures which populated Blake's private world were the negation of external reality, moral laws and all they entailed" (93).

If Blake's myth is not an object of faith, it might be better understood as a hermeneutics of mind, an effort to interpret the experience of psychic dissociation. This mythology narrates a loss of primordial unity with the possibility of recovery. Paul Ricoeur discusses the aim of such mythmaking in suggestive terms:

> It is only in intention that the myth restores some wholeness; it is because he himself has lost some wholeness that man reenacts and imitates it in myth and rite.[21]

These remarks apply equally well to Blake's myth as to primitive man's. Both are evidence of a division within that they seek to explain. The psychic dissociation Blake mythologizes is, as I have suggested, his own as much as it is Albion's. Blake's myth is therefore a defense against the suffering it dramatizes, a hermeneutics of health in the face of madness.

In *The Book of Urizen* Blake tries for the first time to build a comprehensive mythology out of psychic experience. The poem's relation to *Tiriel* is clear enough; the same mad king presides over its action. But the symbol has taken on new, more imposing proportions. Where Tiriel is a despotic king, Urizen is a demonic creator.[22] When Bloom suggests that "Urizen is Tiriel developed on a cosmic scale,"[23] he puts his finger on Blake's strategy: by pursuing a mentality back to its origins Blake, in a sense, becomes its originator.[24] He can expose the limits of tragedy— Shakespeare's or anyone else's—by showing that it constitutes only a part of a much larger view of human life. He may have learned this strategy from the Revelation of St. John, in which, as Leslie Tannenbaum suggests, the tragedy of history is transfigured by the stinging comedy of Divine Judgment.[25] At any rate Blake wants to demonstrate that tragedy mistakes a part of existence for the whole, and that the pessimism it promulgates is the moral counterpart of self-division.

Ultimately he must create an archetypal mythology to make his point convincing. If he can achieve a myth so complete that it both explains and remedies tragedy, then he will be in the position of the artist who, in Kierkegaard's terms, gives birth to his own father.[26] Tragedy will appear to be a phase in a larger system of Blake's own devising, and Shakespeare, his strongest progenitor, will seem his disciple. The issue here is not so much how Blake can be a *poet* in Shakespeare's shadow. Among Romantic poets he betrays disarmingly little anxiety regarding his own powers. But to make room for his larger view of humanity, he must beat Shakespeare at his own game. That does not mean writing more tragedies, though Blake claimed to have written many. It means hammering the symbols of tragedy into a hermeneutic framework that will revalue them, incorporating them into a less limiting view of life.

To achieve this end Blake fashions an archetypal myth that contains all others, a myth of the Universal Man. Such a myth does not fully emerge until *The Four Zoas*, but Blake takes a large step toward it in *The Book of Urizen*. For Urizen achieves a symbolic stature that approaches the archetypal. He is not simply another tragic hero; he embodies them all. When we read the book of his thoughts and acts, what strikes us is not that he resembles Lear, but that *Lear resembles him*. He seems the mythological ancestor upon whom Shakespeare patterns his historical king. By turning king into creator and placing him in a cosmological context, Blake incorporates Shakespeare and sets the stage for his final defeat in the rough comedy of apocalypse.

That defeat can only come about through a kind of symbolic healing, a restoration of tragedy to the larger whole that includes it. For this reason Blake makes a king's madness the central symbol of his mythology. Urizen's tyranny dissociates a primordial psychic unity. After his withdrawal from eternity, Urizen labors to escape its scorching passions "In howlings, pangs, and fierce madness" (*U*, 6:24). By reinterpreting the mad king as a creator, Blake hits upon a fundamentally modern description of madness, one that differs significantly from Shakespeare's. Where Shakespeare treats madness in metaphysical terms, as evidence of nature's moral order, Blake treats it psychologically, as proof that the mind creates all morality. Tragedy now originates in the dissociation of a universal sensibility, a fact that Urizen's fallen acts openly confirm.

This psychodrama, which constitutes the main action of *The Book of Urizen*, recapitulates in mythological terms a mental dynamic typical of the affliction that today's clinicians call schizophrenia. For the universal sensibility Blake imagines as eternity dissociates in two ways: an ego divides from the vitality around it and the capacity of thought separates from feeling.[27] The first of these divisions involves the fabrication of an inner reality that acquires greater value than the outer one, a process dramatized by the autistic withdrawal of Urizen. The second involves the splitting up of idea and emotion, which the "wrenching apart" of Urizen and Los depicts. Although clinically an individual problem, Blake's myth gives madness collective significance. The universal sensibility that dissociates when Urizen retreats into himself includes all men and women as potential victims of a maniacal self-love.

Harold Bloom views *The Book of Urizen* as "primarily an intellectual satire directed at accounts of cosmic and human genesis in the Bible, Plato, and Milton."[28] While it is true that Blake criticizes these cosmogonies, the suggestion that he does not offer one of his own risks underestimating his great contribution to the psychoanalysis of the self. *The Book of Urizen* dramatizes the origin of self-consciousness in the breakdown of an originally collective, undifferentiated mind. Bloom is right to maintain that the poem negates traditional notions of cosmogony. It is important to remember that, in Blake's view, there is no such thing as creation in the traditional sense—no thundering divinities, no rebellious legions, no blissful and ignorant humanity. As it takes shape, Blake's myth is thoroughly demythologized, and in its satirical effect, demythologizing. It simply cannot be literally believed.

But this does not mean it altogether lacks a theory of origins. Blake's cosmogony is wholly psychological, and therefore warrants comparison to modern clinical investigations of mental suffering. One might object that the origins of self-consciousness and psychopathology are two radically different problems. Blake would not agree. Under his prophetic gaze the modern malady of self-consciousness becomes a non-pathological form of a more complete personality breakdown. Blake is not proclaiming, with R. D. Laing, that schizophrenia is a sane response to an insane world. By describing what passes for a normal mentality in pathological terms, he gains the rhetorical advantage of the prophet, who denounces moral degeneracy on a national and collective scale. Overstating his case, Blake awakens us to its urgency: "Enough. or Too much!" (38). The dissociation of psychic unity that he depicts in *The Book of Urizen* accounts for all cosmologies, since in his reading of them they amount to cultural projections of the mind's dynamic. Blake's myth of madness returns cosmogony to its origin in the human mind.

Any discussion of *The Book of Urizen* must begin with its presiding deity. Good analyses of Urizen's function in Blake's myth abound.[29] His name clearly derives from the "Your reason, your reason" of *An Island in the Moon,* and possibly from a more arcane source as well, the Greek word meaning "to limit."[30] Critics agree in interpreting him as Blake's representation of human reason, that portion of the mind that limits, builds, thinks, plans, commands, measures, orders, moralizes, and censures. But how does such a mentality arise?

Urizen comes into being through the division of an originally unified and homogeneous consciousness which Blake describes obliquely in phrases like "forms of energy" and "flames of eternal fury." Tannenbaum argues that Blake noticed the self-divided character of the Biblical creator (whose personality seems split between his Elohim and Yahweh aspects) and transferred this division to his own myth, Elohim becoming Urizen and Yahweh becoming Los.[31] But like most purely intertexual explanations, this one misses Blake's psychological point. If the Bible's creator is self-divided, then man, his real father, must be too, since for Blake all deities reside in the human breast. The act of creation in *The Book of Urizen* represents not so much the *fall* of God as his *birth*, which Blake envisions as a species of madness, the dissociation of a unified psyche. In the original division that separates Urizen from eternity a mentality is born whose individual avatar is self-consciousness and whose collective representation is the jealous god of antiquity.[32] The unsettling implication of this theogony is that such a God comes into being through a pathological dissociation of the mind.

Blake traces this dissociation to its logical conclusion in madness. In its initial phase, consciousness contracts into itself. As the poem opens, the only thing known about Urizen is that he is unknowable; his existence begins in negation:

> Lo, a shadow of horror is risen
> In Eternity! Unknown, unprolific!
> Self-closd, all-repelling: what Demon
> Hath form'd this abominable void
> This soul-shudd'ring vacuum? — Some said
> "It is Urizen", But unknown, abstracted
> Brooding secret, the dark power hid.
>   (*U,* 3:1-7)

As Bloom points out, this passage parodies the creation by contraction of God the Father in *Paradise Lost.*[33] But its psychological implications are of even greater significance. Urizen initiates the withdrawal of consciousness into self, and as a result reason dissociates from the energy that sustains and directs its primordial function.[34] Blake describes the "dark separation" of Urizen as an "abominable void" to suggest that self-consciousness ends logically in solipsism. Unknown to eternity, the self knows only itself, which is why Blake never endorses the traditional wisdom of the temple at Delphi. Urizen invents the modern malady of self-consciousness, then tries to escape it by burying himself in "unseen conflictions" (*U,* 3:14) and "enormous labors" (*U,* 3:22).[35]

But Blake has yet to explain the causes of this condition, and his conception of eternity is an attempt to do so. Eternity is a strenuous place for Blake, full of change and opposition, a Heraclitean fire of energetic flux. Self-consciousness turns pathological when unequal to the task of this existence. Urizen's withdrawal from this reality is an effort to flee its fires and ends ultimately in a kind of autism, the last resort of a mind besieged by life. Valuing its own fantasies over life's pressures and demands, the autistic mind withdraws into itself and creates a surrogate reality where it can be the center of significance. Eventually the outer world comes to figure for the inner world, and all that exists refers somehow to the private workings of the solitary mind. Urizen retreats in this way into a world of his own devising. Life in eternity is too much for him. He has nothing to hold on to, no stability in his existence:

> I have sought for a joy without pain,
> For a solid without fluctuation
> Why will you die O Eternals?
> Why live in unquenchable burnings?
> (*U*, 4:10–13)

The sad irony of this complaint is that Urizen himself is its cause. Self-consciousness separates joy and pain, and allows him to live as if only joy were acceptable and good. So he retreats from the pain of existence into the autistic shell of himself.

Urizen's withdrawal from eternity resembles Thel's fatal withdrawal from life at the end of *The Book of Thel*. In both instances the act defends against existence and ends in the suspended animation of a living death. By applying Thel's defensive maneuver to the hoary Urizen, however, Blake enlarges his critique of consciousness. It is no longer an adolescent fear of sexual experience that precipitates the denial of life, but something in the organization of the mind itself, some principle of self-preservation that paradoxically wills death rather than submit to the contingencies of existence. After building stony defenses against the flames of eternity, Urizen, exhausted, lapses into death:

> But Urizen laid in a stony sleep
> Unorganiz'd, rent from Eternity
>
> The Eternals said: What is this? Death
> Urizen is a clod of clay.
> (*U*, 6:7–10)

Like Lear's proud self-assertion, Urizen's ends tragically in death, but where Lear's error is transgressing natural limits, Urizen's is establishing them.

For a world arises that is the objective correlative of this dissociated sensibility. When Urizen withdraws from eternity, he creates not only himself, but also the natural world of suffering and death—the world of tragedy. As consciousness contracts into the ego, the object-world of barren nature appears. This is the world of Newton and Locke, that Möbius strip of sensory enslavement. It is also the world of the tragic, a "forsaken wilderness" of "dark desarts" inhabited by "fragments of life." The creation of this "dread world" is contemporaneous with Urizen's acquisition of self-consciousness:

> First I fought with the fire; consum'd
> Inwards, into a deep world within:
> A void immense, wild dark & deep,
> Where nothing was: Natures wide womb
>
> (*U*, 4:14–17)

These lines are startling, for they locate Nature's womb *within* the autistic fantasy of Urizen. If all geography is mental, a fragmented mind will create a fragmented world. The most concrete evidence of Urizen's madness is the broken world he inhabits, the brainchild of his autism. By asserting that the natural world of tragedy is the creation of a divided mind, Blake sidesteps its fatality. If he can heal the division that produces such a world, he should be able to triumph over the dark wisdom that binds men to it.

Urizen's madness consists in reducing consciousness to self, asserting part of the mind over the whole. Once his withdrawal is complete, it afflicts all of eternity, for it introduces a principle of division into an originally open consciousness. Symbolically, then, Urizen figures for the paradoxical consciousness of self as *other*. He represents the principle of selfhood that divides the mind through its experience of the natural world. Urizen is alone among the eternals in having a personal history. As Paul Cantor suggests, he literally makes a name for himself,[36] and in the process creates the conditions of a historical existence. Inventing himself, he invents the idea of experience and the authority that arises from the facts of life:

> And self balanc'd stretch'd o'er the void
> I alone, even I! the winds merciless
> Bound; but condensing, in torrents
> They fall & fall; strong I repell'd
> The vast waves, & arose on the waters
> A wide world of solid obstruction
> (*U,* 4:18–23)

Urizen uses his new concept of experience to build a narrative that will subject others to his designs. He codifies his past into a system of law, a song of himself with leaves of brass. Blake demonstrates fine psychological insight here, for none of us can remember a time when we were not. We resort to the authority of experience to advance our interests, just as in Milton Satan's defiance of his creator is based upon memory of his own creation. But Blake shows that Satan could not have indulged in such casuistry had not God first, like Urizen, withdrawn to a position of otherness. Urizen's madness reduces consciousness to self and self to the natural world.

Los advances this dynamic in the second phase of Blake's myth, which dramatizes the dissociation of thought and feeling in the universal mind. Los embodies that part of the mind which both creates and completes the ego through the affections. If Urizen represents this ego, then Los represents a higher identity revealed in time through impassioned activity. The dissociation of Urizen and Los therefore advances the autism begun by the withdrawal of the former from eternity.

> Los wept howling around the dark Demon:
> And cursing his lot; for in anguish,
> Urizen was rent from his side;
> And a fathomless void for his feet;
> And intense fires for his dwelling.
> (*U,* 6:2–6)

Blake's point here is crucial to his myth: divided from thought, feeling becomes subordinate, and identity, which reveals itself by force of the affections, remains paralyzed by self-consciousness. The eternals enjoin Los to contain Urizen's contraction, so Los builds a bodily identity around an empty name. But since all thought belongs to Urizen, Los has no mind of his own, and his whole labor goes into shaping a partial being. The irony of this situation becomes clear when we realize that Los and Urizen, like Har and Tiriel, are broken parts of the same mind. Originally they worked together, every impulse fully known, every idea fully felt, but no longer; their dissociation consolidates Urizen's autistic fantasy.

Under such circumstances, which uncannily resemble the symptoms of schizophrenia, feeling labors strenuously to maintain the image of the self that confronts the real world. Los hammers out a living form for the empty name that inhabits the world of natural history. Many critics have noticed how badly Los's creation turns out, and attribute its failure to Blake's satire.[37] We must look, however, to what motivates this creation to appreciate fully why it fails. Los creates as defensively as Urizen contracts, and under a similar inspiration. Where Urizen fears the activity of life, Los fears the stasis of death:

> Los rouz'd his fires, affrighted
> At the formless unmeasurable death.
> . . . .
> And at the surging sulphureous
> Perturbed Immortal mad raging
> (*U,* 7:8–9, 8:3–4)

Los's fear of finality complements Urizen's fear of futurity, but in laboring against death he ironically substantiates it. The body he builds calcifies Urizen's debilitating changes, giving madness a bodily form. As creator, Los is entirely derivative, and his creation is a pure, petrified *mimesis*.

> He watch'd in shuddring fear
> The dark changes & bound every change
> With rivets of iron & brass;
> (*U,* 8:9–11)

The body of Urizen becomes the organic equivalent of his laws: confining, absolute, and deadly. Los's fear of death inspires a doomed creation that perpetuates the end it would evade.

The striking thing about Urizen's body is its disembodied character. With hallucinatory intensity, Blake numbers the stages of its fossilization, which appear before us with the force of a dream. Cantor reminds us that

Los creates not so much a body as a way of perceiving it.[38] The disembodied quality of his creation attests to the dissociation of thought and feeling in the universal mind. Blake is describing the genesis of the mentality that appears so often in modern literature, pure self-consciousness stripped of feeling and reduced to an automatic bodily response. Urizen prefigures Kafka's K., Camus's Meursault, Sartre's Roquentin, Borges's Funes, and a host of other disembodied moderns. By fabricating Urizen's bodily existence, Los defends himself against the death he fears. Death now belongs to a body that is the unique possession—and perception—of the ego. But this creation is ultimately a botch because it makes final Los's own separation from eternity. Such a defense is an existential fiction, and subordinates man's higher identity to bodily appearance.

Los unwittingly completes the separation of the inner world from the outer that begins in Urizen's withdrawal. R. D. Laing describes a similar situation in *The Divided Self,* his existentialist analysis of schizophrenia. Seeking protection from the dangers of existence, the self withdraws and creates a public fiction that confronts the world in its place.[39] Urizen withdraws to escape the fires of eternity, fabricating a world of death in the process. Then Los forges an image of Urizen to defend against the trials of the natural world. A primordial unity becomes constitutionally divided between thought and feeling, the inner world and the outer. Los reacts in horror to his creation, fading away from eternity into a circumscribed, private existence:

> Los suffer'd his fires to decay
> Then he look'd back with anxious desire
> But the space undivided by existence
> Struck horror into his soul.
> (*U,* 13:44–47)

Los cannot bear the abyss of nature. He too contracts into an autistic existence that remakes the world in the image of his own fantasy.

For pity divides him yet again. In a sobering parody of the classical theory of tragedy, Blake shows how tragic emotion reinforces a divided existence. Having witnessed the tragedy of Urizen's creation, Los stands divided, as Aristotle says he should, between pity and horror.[40] But pity is the stronger, more sinister emotion, and acquires an independent female form. Embodied in Enitharmon, pity becomes a vehicle for self-love as Los seeks to compensate for the tragedy of existence with the perverse pleasure of connubial affection.

> But Los saw the Female & pitied
> He embrac'd her, she wept, she refus'd
> In perverse and cruel delight
> She fled from his arms, yet he followd
> (*U*, 19:10-13)

Blake reveals the pursuit of love to be a compensatory narcissism, a defensive fixation of affection, not upon another, but upon an image of the self:

> Eternity shudder'd when they saw,
> Man begetting his likeness,
> On his own divided image.
> (*U*, 19:14-16)

Los uses Enitharmon just as he does Urizen, to defend himself against reality. Their love perpetuates a division it should heal because it reinforces their selfish passions. Like Urizen, Los finally retreats into private fantasy, ringing his love with the fires of prophecy and wasting his energies in a family romance. Eternity dwindles into the world of time as the universal mind divides against itself.

In its final phase *The Book of Urizen* dramatizes the triumph of nature over the human mind. With the birth of Orc, the positive fruit of Los's union with Enitharmon, Urizen awakens to the autistic world that his withdrawal from eternity has crystallized. It is a grim place, a charnel-house bubbling with lumps of flesh:

> And his world teemd vast enormities
> Frightning; faithless; fawning
> Portions of life; similitudes
> Of a foot, or a hand, or a head
> Or a heart, or an eye, they swam mischevous
> Dread terrors! delighting in blood
> (*U*, 23:2-7)

This fatal geography may seem objective, but Blake has already dramatized the psychic division in which it originates. A solitary wanderer, Urizen finds himself an alien in the landscape of his own autistic fantasy. Even more ironic is the fact that his vitality derives entirely from Orc. As a natural avatar of eternal energy, Orc literally animates a dead world.

> The dead heard the voice of the child
> And began to awake from sleep
> All things. heard the voice of the child
> And began to awake to life.
>
> (*U*, 20:26–29)

Urizen thrives on this energy, but needing to repress its activity in others, he invents religion, a sublimated set of compensatory promises. His net of religion insures, through a kind of contagious *mimesis,* that his fantasy will negate all others, finally reducing eternal life to a self-authorized abyss.

But Blake shows that such a pessimistic view of life arises from mistaking a portion of existence for the whole. When thought lords over feeling, eternity shrinks to appearances and death becomes a way of life:

> No more could they rise at will
> In the infinite void, but bound down
> To earth by their narrowing perceptions
>
> They lived a period of years
> Then left a noisom body
> To the jaws of devouring darkness
>
> (*U,* 25:45–47, 28:1–3)

By the end of *The Book of Urizen* the universal mind stands divided and humanity bows to the order of nature. The world now takes on the limits that make Shakespearean tragedy possible.

Throughout his poem, however, Blake insinuates that, as a view of life, tragedy does not tell the whole story. Rather it blinds humanity to the true origin of its limitations in self-division. This madness, and not nature, forces limits upon human potential. King Lear's anguish, Tiriel's raving, Urizen's insane autonomy, all testify to the delusion that Blake labors to heal by building his highly psychological mythology.

IV

Does *The Book of Urizen* once and for all master the tragic? Ultimately it does not, for several reasons. For one, it is incomplete. Two elements especially, eternity and the Universal Man, remain too vague in *The*

Book of Urizen to be convincing. Eternity is Blake's alternative to natural life. To advance it with conviction he must show how all men and women inhabit it when they live up to their potential. As for the Universal Man, Blake realizes that the success of his archetypal myth depends upon a Being that includes all others, but in this poem he does not draw its lineaments distinctly enough. There are occasional dark hints about "the Immortal," but no clear indication of its relation to Urizen, Los, and the other giant forms in the poem. Eternity and the Universal Man take on a more satisfying appearance in *The Four Zoas,* where Blake enlists apocalypse to complete his myth. But in *The Book of Urizen,* he does not organize his symbols into a comprehensive and redeeming pattern.

In composing the poem, however, Blake discovered that myths proliferate if not thus organized. His giant forms, once separated from primordial unity, all acquire histories of their own. And there is no arbitrating convincingly between them unless apocalypse completes cosmogony. Blake is beginning to understand that myth has its uses and abuses. It becomes a tool in the hands of certain interests to create and to maintain power. In *The Four Zoas* he works to coordinate individual versions of eternal vision with a theory of self-sacrifice that honors individuality even while assimilating it to collective form.

There is finally another reason why Blake cannot revalue the tragic in *The Book of Urizen.* He still secretly endorses it. Bloom points out the subliminal affection Blake must feel for the all-powerful Urizen.[41] As Milton does for Satan, Blake has a deep sympathy for his greatest creation, who embodies the qualities he most suspects. If Urizen's contraction into self-consciousness betrays a preference for the inner world over the outer, in this he resembles Blake. Blake's visions were wholly his own. He fights hard to stay true to them and thus shares Urizen's belief in the primacy of private experience. As a builder of worlds, Urizen bears striking resemblance to that builder of mythologies, William Blake. Urizen constructs a negative image of Blake's myth, as if through him Blake labored strenuously to deny the tyrant within. For by all biographical accounts, not to mention his poems, Blake was an intellectual absolutist. Mental fight meant crossing blades to the finish, as his obsessive revision of other men's ideas suggests.

We must affirm the Urizenic side of Blake along with his more attractive postures. He most betrays it in his private writings, his annotations and oratorical prose. A philosophical antagonist like Reynolds meets there with belligerence, and rival engravers meet with abuse. In the heat of invective, Blake becomes every bit as tyrannical and self-serving as

Urizen: "Such prints as Woolett and Strange produced will do for those who choose to purchase the Lifes labor of Ignorance & Imbecility in preference to the Inspired Moments of Genius & Animation" ("Public Address," 574). About the only people free from this denunciation are Blake himself and those bold enough to hire him. Even his unwillingness to offer his poetry for printing and distribution attests to a dubious integrity; viewed from another angle it appears dangerously close to conceit. To control his imperiousness, Blake displaced onto Urizen this large element of his own character. The myth he forges in later years betrays similar displacements, so much so that it becomes tempting if not particularly rewarding to view it as a systematic fantasy of nearly pathological proportions.[42] As a work of art, however, his myth redeems him. In Urizen Blake wrestles against the very principle of self that sanctions his inner life. Urizen's autistic withdrawal could have been Blake's, had the artist in him not triumphed by making his will to selfhood the protagonist of a universal psychodrama.

Los embodies that artist, the creative power at odds with the authority of the ego. Los's hammer and forge are no mere poetic ornaments; they represent the violence and energy with which Blake must oppose the demands of his own ego. His myth, for all its apocalyptic pretensions, has real trouble actually restoring the Golden Age it envisions. The dissociation that *The Book of Urizen* dramatizes is very much his own. Urizen, Los, Enitharmon, Orc—these deities inhabit the human breast of William Blake, and his myth undertakes to integrate them into a self-redeeming therapy for psychic dissociation.[43] The madness this myth dramatizes might well have been Blake's had not his art provided, first, a stay against confusion, then, a vehicle to new health. Foucault insists that "Madness is the absolute break with the work of art; it forms the constitutive moment of abolition, which dissolves in time the truth of the work of art; it draws the exterior edge, the line of dissolution, the contour against the void."[44] Perhaps that is why Blake placed such a premium upon the wiry "bounding line" in art: it stakes out a defense against the abyss of madness.

Blake's myth stands between the poet and the madness he faces up to. In the winter of 1804 Blake wrote his patron Butts of his harrowing past years: "I have indeed fought thro' a Hell of terrors & horrors (which none could know but myself) in a Divided Existence; now no longer Divided, nor at war with myself I shall travel on in the strength of the Lord God as Poor Pilgrim says" (*Letters*, 104). Here is the inner division Blake mythologizes. His art becomes its best therapy: "I have lost my Confusion of Thought while at work & am as much myself when I take the Pencil or Graver into my hand as I used to be in my Youth" (*Letters*, 104). As we turn to *The Four Zoas* we will observe the agony, both individual and collective, that the mind's dissociation inflicts. If we allow ourselves to participate in Blake's mythology and enter into its hermeneutics, we take upon ourselves, not only his struggle, but also the possibility of his redemption.

4

Schizophrenia
and the Ancient Man

Only a crowd of devils could account for our earthly misfortunes.
— Kafka, *Parables and Paradoxes*

I

Blake's years at Lambeth were among his most productive and perplexing. They began with a burst of creativity, a clear sign that Blake had found the poetic voice he had been searching for in his early verse. In five years (1789–94) he engraved more work than during the rest of his life. But after that, as if to mark the end of something, silence descended for more than ten years. This period of public silence was a time of profound personal struggle during which Blake fought hard to maintain his integrity as an engraver and as an artist. Without his poetry to sustain him, he might have gone the way of the sensibility bards. Indeed, the great work of this period, *The Four Zoas*, is a mythological investigation of madness. For the real subject of that poem is a form of madness that in many ways resembles what we today call schizophrenia, whose fundamental symptoms Blake renders with uncanny fidelity.[1] By making madness an artistic phenomenon, he masters it, securing health and renewed happiness by the margin of his myth.

A business venture first took Blake from poetry in 1795. During most of the following year, he labored on a project that he believed would make his name as a designer and engraver—an illustrated edition of Edward Young's *Night Thoughts*, for which he prepared 543 drawings and 43 engravings.[2] Published in 1797, the first installment failed; others were never printed. Blake's reputation as an artisan fell quickly into eclipse. "I live by Miracle," he wrote in a letter of this period, "for as to Engraving, in which art I cannot reproach myself with any neglect, yet I am laid by in a corner as if I did not Exist, & Since my Young's Night Thoughts have been publish'd, Even Johnson & Fuseli have discarded my Graver" (*Letters*, 11).

With the failure of his commercial venture, Blake was forced to rely upon patronage for a living. Small painting commissions from his faithful friend Thomas Butts kept him afloat. He "published" no more poetry until much later, with the engraving of *Milton* (probably 1808). The years after 1797 were lean ones; the self-confidence displayed in the early work vanished, and in its stead came melancholy. In his self-imposed poetic silence, Blake was wrestling against a crowd of devils. In a letter of 1800, he confides hope of winning the battle: "I begin to Emerge from a Deep pit of Melancholy, Melancholy without any real reason for it, a Disease which God keep you from & all good men" (*Letters*, 17). An offer of patronage from William Hayley looked as though it would provide the security Blake needed to regain his spirits. So in September of 1800 he, his wife, and his sister moved into a cottage near Hayley's estate at Felpham.

Blake was counting on this change to restore his self-confidence as an artist. In a curious letter to the sculptor Flaxman, who recommended him to Hayley, Blake briefly summarized his spiritual history, describing his mental turmoil in guarded terms. The work of the Lambeth years, specifically *America* and *Europe*, was a visionary response to "awful change":

The American War began. All its dark horrors passed before my face
Across the Atlantic to France. Then the French Revolution commenc'd in
    thick clouds
And My Angels have told me that seeing such visions I could not subsist
    on the Earth,
But by my conjunction with Flaxman, who knows to forgive Nervous
    Fear.

(*Letters*, 20)

Without the kind intervention of Flaxman, the visionary Blake could have lost his footing in this world. His visions, Blake confesses, inspire fear because the world is hostile to them. This hostility forced Blake's retreat from public forms of poetry. He remained silent for over a decade, working in private to subdue vision to a presentable form.

The long, unengraved manuscript, *The Four Zoas*, contains a record of this labor. In the course of composing, revising, and finally abandoning the poem, Blake discovered the philosophical and aesthetic assumptions that allowed him to return to publication with *Milton* and *Jerusalem*. But the effort nearly drove him mad.[3] More completely than the earlier poems, and with greater penetration, *The Four Zoas* makes madness the subject of a mythology. Blake enlarges the critique of consciousness begun in *The Book of Urizen* to implicate all humanity in the schizophrenic breakdown of the Ancient Man.[4] But even as he universalizes this critique, he personalizes it, resolving his own psychological crisis through the dynamic of his mythology. Without his myth to rejuvenate him, Blake might have been paralyzed by vision. Thanks to the therapeutics of his art he emerged a tested champion, if not untouched.[5]

The manuscript Blake left unengraved at his death presents the interpreter with a formidable task. The usual approach is to treat the poem as a total vision, surveying its vast geography without attending to local variations.[6] But this approach risks missing details that point to significant changes in Blake's thinking, changes that affect both the shape of his myth and the balance of his mind. As Blake revises he reenvisions.[7] Reading *The Four Zoas* is a little like undertaking an archeological dig: if one does not pay close attention to the stratum in which one is working, concrete history, in this case psychological history, fades into abstraction.[8]

The title page presents a case in point. It is really two title pages: the first recorded in 1797, when Blake made a fair copy of an early draft, and the second penciled in as much as ten years later, when he turned to a Biblical symbolism as the framework for his own.[9] The thematic distance between the titles is huge, belied by the proximity of ink and pencil. When Blake moves from "Vala" to "The Four Zoas," he moves from social to psychological myth. He turns away from the politics of revolution to investigate the politics of consciousness. The whole epistemological status of his poem changes. What had been "A Dream in Nine Nights" now takes place in full view.[10] The nightmares of the sleeping giant that Blake calls the Ancient Man acquire a value equal to waking reality. With three strokes of his pen, Blake assimilates the inner world of the mind to the outer world of humanity, and "the Torments of Love and Jealousy" become the psychological equivalent of "the Death and Judgment of the Ancient Man." Only a profound change in Blake's thinking can account for this transformation.

The aims of the poem's early avatar as *Vala* have become somewhat clearer with H. M. Margoliouth's speculative reconstruction of its text.[11] In the late 1790s, Blake appears to have endorsed a Grecian purity in art derived from the practice of his friends Cumberland, Flaxman, and Fuseli.[12] Although Blake later turned against Greek art in favor of a Hebrew model, in his famous letter to Dr. Trusler, an obtuse would-be patron, he defends his manner of designing thus: "if I were to act otherwise, it would not fulfill the purpose for which alone I live, . . . to renew the lost Art of the Greeks" (*Letters*, 6).

Vala, it appears, was to be Blake's reinterpretation of Homer's *Iliad*, just as *The Book of Urizen* was his reinterpretation of Genesis. As in the earlier poem, his emphasis lay upon the psychology of social injustice. The main question he wanted to answer was this: why does mankind tolerate the oppression of warriors and kings? By asking this question in an epic context, Blake hoped to revolutionize society *and* art, denouncing the martial values that corrupt both. In this view, the Ancient Man becomes Blake's Achilles, whose absence provokes dissension; Urizen becomes his Agamemnon, whose will to power enslaves the nations; and Vala becomes his Helen, the great whore inspiring war. Originally Blake intended to expose the collusion of Urizen and Vala (inverting the values of the *Iliad*) by showing how Vala's solicitations draw off revolutionary energy to fortify Urizen's iron rule:

> The shadow reard her dismal head over the flaming youth
> With sighs & howling & deep sobs that he might lose his rage.[13]

Revolutionary ardor fades into the warrior's devotion to his king's whoring warfare.

But Blake's own king had gone a-whoring in the 1790s, and the publication of an epic denouncing warfare would have been untimely.[14] As Blake worked over his poem he grew to feel more and more the serpent's tooth of his dilemma as a poet of revolution. He possessed a vision of liberty and an epic poem to announce it. But he hid his light under a bushel, revising his poem in private rather than risk publication.[15] Had he too fallen victim to the blandishments of Vala? By the logic of his own myth, Blake stands indicted. The process of revision became a study in evasion, and his swerve away from social action became in part an act of self-betrayal.

II

Blake's annotations to the Bishop of Llandaff's *Apology for the Bible* give some idea of his dilemma. As Schorer remarks, Blake here begins to show traces of "the man who believes that he is persecuted and pursued."[16] Blake ably defends Thomas Paine against the Bishop's glib imputations, but keeps his arguments to himself. His reason: "To defend the Bible in this year 1798 would cost a man his life" (611). He had evidence to support a more judicious formulation of this claim in the incarceration of a fellow dissenter, the Quaker divine Gilbert Wakefield.[17] Even so, Blake insists that a man's first allegiance is to justice: "To him who sees this mortal pilgrimage in the light that I see it, Duty to his country is the first consideration & safety the last" (611). It is a strange duty indeed that thrives when left undone.[18] Blake's final introductory remark vetoes all his fine intentions: "I have been commanded from Hell not to print this as it is what our Enemies wish" (611). What is this demonic censor that lays its scepter across Blake's indignation? In *The Marriage of Heaven and Hell*, hell had been a pit of energy; now it is a place of restraint. As the compulsive quality of this remark suggests, Blake's inner life is acquiring an authority as convenient as it is absolute.

It should come as no surprise, then, to discover that in revising *Vala*, Blake lays steadily more emphasis upon the perilous balance between the inner world and the outer.[19] Like Kafka, he tests the boundary between them and examines incursions from one into the other. And like Kafka as well, he displaces his own trials onto the content of his writing. *Vala* may originally have begun with what is now Night II of the Four Zoas. In revision, Blake heightens the drama of the Ancient Man's retreat from "reality," the very movement that he himself is tracing as he turns from public to private activity. To the poem's economical and precipitous beginning, he adds two decisive lines:

> Rising upon his Couch of Death Albion beheld his Sons
> Turning his Eyes outward to Self. losing the Divine Vision
> (*FZ*, 23:1–2)

Albion's ocular turn outward is the epistemological equivalent of a retreat inward. He no longer sees "reality" sustained by vision, but only himself and his "Sons," his own consciousness, that is, and its factions. With these two lines Blake declares that the inner life and its antagonisms are the true subject of his epic.

Judging from much of the material included in what is now Night I, Blake was using the process of revision to work through the psychological dilemma implicit in his annotations to Bishop Watson's *Apology*. Critics who see this new material as a sophisticated disquisition on the mystification of origins see only part of the issue.[20] Blake begins his epic anew with Tharmas, but not arbitrarily. He labels Tharmas "Parent power" (*FZ*, 4:6) to emphasize the importance of innocence to a fully human existence. Tharmas is a powerful parent in the familiar Romantic sense that the child is father of the man.[21] His sudden awareness of loss is as mystified as, but no more mystified than, everyone's awareness that he or she is no longer a child.

But Blake has darker reasons for beginning his poem with Tharmas. Note the pathos of the following lines:

> Lost! Lost! Lost! are my Emanations   Enion O Enion
> We are become a Victim to the Living We hide in secret
> I have hidden Jerusalem in Silent Contrition   O Pity Me
> I will build thee a Labyrinth also O pity me   O Enion.
> (*FZ*, 4:7–10)

There is a pained self-referentiality about these lines, as if Blake were making the privatizing of his poetry the subject of his epic. They describe a loss of artistic innocence. If Frye is correct in characterizing the emanation as "the total form of all the things a man loves and creates" (73), then Tharmas has lost the production of a lifetime. But mark *how* he had lost it: he has hidden away his emanations, building a labyrinth around Jerusalem and concealing her from the living. The late substitution of "Jerusalem" for "Enion" suggests that Blake is elegizing his own lost vision of liberty, the restitution of which is one of his epic aims. Concealment has been the cause of its passing. The labyrinth that Tharmas builds for his emanation becomes an image of Blake's own poetry, with its allegories and allusions, its unexpected turns and dark passages.

As Blake revises his poem, two things happen: the epic becomes both more personally relevant and more psychologically acute. By the time Blake retitles it *The Four Zoas* (perhaps as late as 1808), he has fought his way through his own crisis of mind to a new confidence in the healing powers of Jesus. The latest strata of revisions are the most explicitly Christian, though by no means orthodox. Blake returns to the fold only after a profound psychological struggle, the drama of which he displaces onto *The Four Zoas*.[22] He adds an epigraph in Greek to characterize the nature of his ordeal:

> For we wrestle not against flesh and blood, but against principalities, against powers, against the rulers of the darkness of this world, against spiritual wickedness in high places.   (Eph. 6:12, KJV)

St. Paul had in mind spiritual enemies like the devil and the false doctrine of the Gnostics. But for Blake the principalities are within; he finds in these words a canonical description of his own psychological ordeal. The epigraph becomes a sort of redemption for the excruciating self-divisions his poem describes.

For *The Four Zoas* mythologizes the dynamic of psychic dissociation, in today's terminology, schizophrenia. It is a crisis poem of epic proportions that counterpoints individual and collective suffering. Blake restates the familiar Christian pattern of fall, redemption, and salvation in psychological terms.[23] Mental health and sickness take the place of good and evil as values for existence. And although Blake displaces his own psychological drama onto that of his poem, he by no means reduces epic to autobiography. A psychologized fall is fully human, one that all men and women participate in by virtue of their humanity. In his *Descriptive Catalogue* (1809) Blake speaks of the division of humanity into the Strong, the Beautiful, and the Ugly:

> They were originally one man, who was fourfold; he was self-divided, and his real humanity slain upon the stems of generation, and the form of the fourth was like the Son of God. How he became divided is a subject of great sublimity and pathos. The Artist has written it under inspiration, and will, if God please, publish it; it is voluminous, and contains the ancient history of Britain, and the world of Satan and Adam. (543)

Apparently God never pleased, for *The Four Zoas* was never published. But the self-division Blake describes, and the existential death that attends it, have their contemporary clinical parallels in the symptomology of schizophrenia, in particular the shattering of the personality and the autistic withdrawal that often ensues. Blake understood, without the terminology or the training, what so few investigators today appreciate: that madness presents an absolute challenge to our humanity, for it strips a mind bare of the garb that makes it human.

In *The Four Zoas,* the Ancient Man undergoes this divestment. He represents the collective identity that, in Blake's view, characterized a preconscious humanity.[24] The name "Albion" is in fact a very late revision for the more felicitous title "the Ancient Man," and reflects the appearance of the historical allegory that Blake develops in his later works. Originally, the Ancient Man included all human reality within his limbs. His *sparagmos* dramatizes an awakening to self, humanity's division into the many and discrete identities that characterize the adult mentality. The fall of the Ancient Man, then, is a fall into self-consciousness, a lapse which turns pathological when independent egos lose the memory of their collective origin. It is a paradox of human development that the collective identity brought by all infants into the world can only be *known* retrospectively. All myths of a lost Golden Age arise to mediate this paradox. When Blake opens his poem with Tharmas's shrill elegy, he locates the origins of consciousness in just such a loss. Innocence, brotherhood, spontaneous love are the price humanity pays for a knowledge purchased with the loss of power. And so the Ancient Man's self-division embodies every man's as well. As Kierkegaard remarks, "man is *individuum* and as such simultaneously himself and the whole race."[25] All individuals share in the dismemberment of the collective identity.

But all are not schizophrenic, only those who lose touch with the human world. Even so, Blake is swift to trace the Ancient Man's division to its logical conclusion in madness. This strategy should make us uncomfortable; to the extent that we are human, it includes us. Valuing the ego above our collective humanity, we create conditions highly conducive to the absolute loss of that humanity in schizophrenia. The dehumanization produced by poverty should similarly awaken a chill: "The Beggars Rags fluttering in Air / Does to Rags the Heavens tear" ("Auguries of Innocence," 491). But of course, it usually does not. Blake mythologizes madness not only to exorcise his own demons, but also to rouse the giant sleeping in all men and women. Through his myth of madness he labors against the pathological potential of the fall into self-consciousness.

In the process he formulates a psychology of the self wholly new to literature and only recently made familiar by clinical investigation. Together, his four Zoas constitute a polyvalent conception of identity. To be sure, this new conception resembles the old psychology of humours, but the proliferating divisions of the Zoas establish a mental rather than a physical dynamic. In his invocation to *The Four Zoas* Blake announces their complex relation to mankind:

> Four Mighty Ones are in every Man;
>   a Perfect Unity
> Cannot Exist. but from the Universal
>   Brotherhood of Eden
> The Universal Man. To Whom be
>   Glory Evermore Amen
>   (*FZ*, 3:4–8)

Albion contains within him four Zoas—but so does every individual—and a psychological unity will only arrive when the Zoas act not for themselves but for their collective humanity, the Universal Brotherhood of Eden. This singular identity has become plural, torn apart by mental fight. On one level, Blake means that our collective identity falls to selfish interests. But on another he means that our individuality can crack under the strain of inner division. The Zoas rage and we are riven both without and within.

The usual way to soften this schizoid psychology is to allegorize the Zoas. Then the Ancient Man's trouble reduces to an imbroglio among instinct, reason, love, and imagination (Tharmas, Urizen, Luvah, and Urthona).[26] This attack provides a place to start investigating *The Four Zoas*, but runs the risk of overlooking Blake's most profound discoveries. For the Zoas are far too human to be adequately characterized by abstract tags. Each is capable of a range of emotions and each fights to assert itself over the others.[27] When discussing the Zoas individually an element of abstraction is inevitable, but it is important to fight against this tendency and remember that all allegorizations are merely heuristic. As our analysis progresses I will resort to such tactics in the interest of clarity, but never to assign an absolute value to any of the Zoas. To take Blake at his word ("Four mighty Ones are in every Man") is to admit that, for him at least, identity consists in the polyvalent interplay of discrete mentalities.[28]

Hence the relevance of schizophrenia to his myth. We saw in the last chapter how *The Book of Urizen* begins to examine the dynamics of psychic dissociation. In *The Four Zoas*, Blake takes his investigations much further, as much out of personal need as poetic interest. A long speech in the apocalyptic last Night of the poem has the Ancient Man describing the dissension within him:

> O weakness & O weariness   O war within my members
> My sons exiled from my breast pass to & fro before me
> My birds are silent on my hills flocks die beneath my branches
> My tents are fallen my trumpets & the sweet sounds of my harp
> Is silent on my clouded hills that belch forth storms & fires.
>   (*FZ*, 119:32–36)

As poetry, these lines are among the finest ever written in an English Biblical idiom. But the psychology they describe is even more startling. The civil "war" Albion suffers resembles the psychic insurrection of schizophrenia, and the "sons" that pass before him appear to be the scattered fragments of a dissociated mind.[29] The self-consciousness that erupts with the fall of the Ancient Man turns pathological when selfish interests turn actively against the unified psyche.

Although the etiology of schizophrenia still escapes its closest observers, its fundamental symptoms have grown quite clear. Eugene Bleuler, who named the affliction, remains its best explainer, even though his observations antedate recent advances in genetic theory and neuroleptic treatment.[30] His great work, *Dementia Praecox, or the Group of Schizophrenias*, deserves to rank with Freud's *Interpretation of Dreams* as an unsurpassed contribution to the psychology of human suffering. Unlike some contemporary investigators, Bleuler pays heed to the existential conditions that contribute to the mind's dissociation: "the overt symptomology certainly represents the expression of a more or less unsuccessful attempt to find a way out of an intolerable situation."[31] To some degree, schizophrenia represents an effort, like the pains of neurosis, to cope with the demands of a menacing reality. But where the neurotic keeps in touch with the world by repressing noxious thoughts and feeling, the schizophrenic withdraws from it by putting another world in its place.

The stakes are much higher in schizophrenia than in neurosis, and its mechanism is wholly different. Rarely does schizophrenia allow a full *restitutio ad integrum*, but this sad fact does not lessen the suffering involved. Precisely because this form of madness can reduce man to the zero degree of his humanity, it provides Blake with a metaphor for an absolutely fallen existence. An earlier age had its crucifixion, an even earlier its Dionysian rites. Both are metaphors for human suffering that work to transcend the pain they glorify. So too Blake's myth of madness. Albion's split into warring factions is the psychological equivalent of a crucifixion that befalls the collective identity of mankind.

Bleuler describes the mechanism of schizophrenia as a splitting of psychic functions in which certain complexes dominate the personality while others remain impotent:

> single emotionally charged ideas or drives attain a certain degree of autonomy so that the personality falls to pieces. These fragments can then exist side by side and alternately dominate the main part of the personality. (143)

A better description of *The Four Zoas* could hardly be given. The poem dramatizes the dissociation of the eternal mind into bellicose factions and investigates the politics of consciousness that characterizes this fallen state.

The Ancient Man himself gives the best evidence that such madness is what menaces him. Blake articulates this affliction beautifully:

> In this dark world a narrow house I wander up & down
> I hear Mystery howling in these flames of Consummation
> When shall the Man of future times become as in days of old
> O weary life why sit I here & give up all my powers
> To indolence to the night of death when indolence & mourning
> Sit hovring over my dark threshold. tho I arise look out
> And scorn the war within my members yet my heart is weak
> And my head faint Yet will I look again into the morning
> Whence is this sound of rage of Men drinking each others blood
> Drunk with the smoking gore & red but not with nourishing wine.
> (*FZ*, 120:3–12)

Fallen, the Ancient Man inhabits a world of existential paradox. Though in a narrow house, he wanders homeless; though a creature of time, he lacks a meaningful present. He suffers the depersonalization of Bleuler's typical schizophrenic, who "loses his boundaries in time and space" (143).

According to Bleuler, four main symptoms characterize the schizophrenic mind, and all appear to varying degrees in the harrowing passage above. They are the famous "Four A's": association disturbance, ambivalence, affective disturbance, and autism. In association disturbance, the associations that impel thought lose their continuity and thinking becomes bizarre. Ambivalence appears when opposed feelings or ideas are held with equal conviction. In affective disturbance emotional experience deteriorates until indifference becomes the rule. Finally, autism occurs as a withdrawal from reality into an inner world of fantasy.

In the lines above, the predominance of the inner war over eternal reality illustrates the same debilitating mechanism of autism that we saw at work in *The Book of Urizen*. Though Albion scorns this inner warfare, it preoccupies him completely, becoming more real than the eternity around him. An attenuated affect appears in his weak heart; the inner life has drunk up all his passion, leaving him emotionally indifferent to all but his private fantasies. Hence his ambivalence; indolence weighs him down, for it is easier to endure his disorder than to cure it. Disturbance in association, which Bleuler places foremost among his symptoms, is harder to identify here. But Albion's solipsistic preoccupation with his problems betrays a mind revolving in ever-tightening circles around the same ideas. Blake sees the Ancient Man bound by the competing demands of a few privileged complexes. Thinking grinds to a halt, and the process of association that guides it spirals inward.[32]

The Four Zoas dramatizes, then, the effects of a madness in the universal mind. But it would be wrong to suggest that this subject infects the integrity of its form. Poetry itself cannot be mad, however unstable its content or creator. In this case poetry provides a therapy for the sort of suffering it depicts. Though Blake did not succumb to the madness so often imputed to him, *The Four Zoas* gives ample evidence that he had an intimate acquaintance with its fundamental symptoms. Poetry steps between Blake and such suffering, allowing him to turn away from its abysses and toward a healthy mind. Albion's words could just as easily be those of a prophet unheeded in his time, unheard amidst the wrack of war. No wonder Blake in later years celebrates the therapeutic powers of art ("Art is the tree of Life," *Laocoön*, 274). Through it he brought himself from the brink of darkness back into light.

But if Albion in some sense stands for Blake, so do all the Zoas. Few critics have grasped the significance of this psychic affiliation. E. D. Hirsch argues that "Blake's own tumultuous spiritual history is the central theme of *The Four Zoas*."[33] Hirsch is on the right track, though he hobbles his insights with a historical absolutism. Blake may indeed have undergone, as Hirsch suggests, a conversion away from his youthful naturalism. But the world never ceased to delight him, even if in his later years he found it ultimately unfulfilling. Together the Zoas constitute a psychology of the self that assimilates revolutions in consciousness without absolute denials. Their shifting alliances stand for modulations in the internal dynamic of the polyvalent identity.[34]

For the Zoas are the primary symbols of this identity, and Blake labors to organize and interpret them in his myth.[35] They are to Albion as complexes are, in clinical terms, to the personality. They split away from the whole mind of the Ancient Man as it falls into the psychological ambivalence that Blake calls "the sleep of Death" (*FZ*, 23:6). Blake finds that he can never retreat with assurance to the cause of this fatal lapse. Having fallen away from primal unity, each Zoa constructs a personal myth of origins to assert his authority against all comers.[36] But the overall mechanism of their dissociation is autistic, the pathological usurpation of reality by an inner world built to stave off an onerous existence.

In *The Book of Urizen*, Urizen retreats inward to create a world of his own *ex nihilo*. Blake softens his role in *The Four Zoas*, realizing that the fall into consciousness must have satisfied human needs, or it never would have occurred. Urizen becomes "the great Work master" (*FZ*, 24:5) and marshals his minions with the command, "Build we a Bower for heavens darling in the grizly deep" (*FZ*, 27:7). But Albion is sleeping, and this bower is quite literally a fantasy. Blake's irony here is worthy of Kafka — and every bit as pathetic — for Albion gives a nightmare the value of reality. He falls into that limbo that Bleuler knows so well:

> The reality of the autistic world may ... seem more valid than that of reality itself; the patients hold their fantasy world for the real, reality for an illusion.... When autism gets the upper hand, it creates a complete isolation around the sick psyche. (66, 94)

Urizen rules over this state of confusion as the other Zoas pursue their own political designs. Consciousness has become a chaos of competing interests.

In a significant advance over the cosmology of *The Book of Urizen*, Blake attributes this chaos to the flight of love from the heart of the Ancient Man, in clinical terms the loss of affect from the once unified psyche. The earlier poem charts the dissociation of thought and feeling characteristic of schizophrenic breakdown. *The Four Zoas* follows this course further in the struggle between Urizen and Luvah, the Zoa most critics identify with love. Blake lays special stress upon the disappearance of love from the geography of the universal mind. The east, Luvah's quarter in eternity, becomes a void as the Ancient Man falls into sleep — a brilliant figure for the loss of body-consciousness that characterizes the state of dreams. Disembodied, the Ancient Man diverts the energy of love into the internal works and wars of fantasy. Luvah wastes away in iron furnaces that channel his energy into psychic defenses:

> Luvah was cast into the Furnaces of affliction & sealed
> And Vala fed in cruel delight, the furnaces with fire
> Stern Urizen beheld urg'd by necessity to keep
> The evil day afar, & if perchance with iron power
> He might avert his own despair;
>
> (*FZ*, 25:40–44)

Confining Luvah away from bodily existence in the perverse intellectual gratifications of "cruel delight," Urizen creates an abyss to avoid an abyss. As in dreams, the energy of the caged Luvah fuels the confusion of the war within.

Cut off from bodily intercourse, Luvah succumbs to the delusion that Blake calls "reasoning from the loins" (*FZ*, 28:2), fabricating an elaborate system of explanation based upon a false premise. This compensatory fantasy, a paradigm of all the Zoas' personal myths of origins, resembles in its form and function the delusions of persecution that characterize the paranoid schizophrenic.[37] Both attribute a false importance to the afflicted individual and reinforce that belief with elaborate fantasies of power and privilege. Luvah considers himself "Valas King" (*FZ*, 26:5), and chronicles the creation of the natural world through the word of his command: "When I calld forth the Earth-worm from the cold & dark obscure / I nurturd her I fed her with my rains & dews, she grew / A scaled Serpent" (*FZ*, 26:7–9). Luvah is playing Christ here, though the nature he creates turns out to be a venomous Leviathan.

Bleuler notes that delusions of persecution usually arise when a wish meets with obstacles to fulfillment. Precisely because Luvah cannot possess Vala, he imagines himself her creator and king. And he has an explanation ready for her disappearance:

> I loved her I gave her all my soul & my delight
> I hid her in soft gardens & in secret bowers of Summer
> Weaving mazes of delight along the sunny Paradise
> Inextricable labyrinths, She bore me sons & daughters
> And they have taken her away & hid her from my sight
> They have surrounded me with walls of iron & brass,
>
> (*FZ*, 27:4–9)

The Pynchonesque use of "they" to suggest an organized persecution helps explain why Bloom calls Luvah's claim "simply a madness"

(*Commentary*, 952). Luvah builds a system to justify the aching unfulfillment of desire, and uses it to assert himself over a unified humanity:

> The hand of Urizen is upon me because I blotted out
> The Human delusion to deliver all the sons of God
> From bondage of the Human form,
> (*FZ*, 27:16–18)

Here is the false premise upon which Luvah builds his compensatory system. Blake discovers that myths conceal as well as reveal, organizing falsehood as easily as truth. To the extent that Luvah's delusion of persecution is also Albion's, consciousness itself becomes the arena of a power struggle between the autonomous components of the dissociated mind.[38]

For when Albion lapses into the autistic sleep of death, consciousness becomes a function of the needs that condition it. The mind of the Ancient Man breaks up with the lassitude of withdrawal, but by no means arbitrarily. *The Four Zoas* and their proliferating kin divide it between them, reducing its unity to the component parts, to speak abstractly, of reason, love, hope, and imagination. This division becomes pathological when it extinguishes the memory of humanity's collective identity. As in the madness of schizophrenia, a once unified consciousness "becomes the plaything of the complexes" (361), which Blake embodies in his Zoas. It is important to understand that he does not, in the traditional sense, personify these powers. For in schizophrenia, to quote Bleuler again, "the patient appears to be split into as many different persons or personalities as they [sic] have complexes" (361). Consciousness comes under the sway first of one, then of another autonomous personality, not abstract personification. In Blake's poem, the Zoas, as individuals, vie for control of the whole mind. The politics of their struggle receives Blake's particular attention because all individual personalities are fragments of the Ancient Man's collective identity. Blake aims to reunite them.

III

But what is the logic of their dissociation? In a sense, Blake's myth is an epic attempt to answer this question. It offers three basic versions of the fall, upon which the Zoas play their variations: as usurpation of Urizen by Luvah, as seduction of Albion by Vala, and as relaxation of Albion's will to live.[39] This last conforms closely to schizophrenia's dynamic. But we need to consider the mechanism that drives the Ancient Man into autism and splits his mind into factions.

Ahania presents the clearest picture of what happens in her personal myth of origins. Trying to placate the melancholy Urizen, she describes the Ancient Man's deluded self-devotion:

> Above him rose a Shadow from his wearied intellect
> Of living gold, pure, perfect, holy; in white linen pure he hover'd
> A sweet entrancing self delusion, a watry vision of Man
> Soft exulting in existence all the Man absorbing
>
> (*FZ*, 40:3–6)

Fatigued by thought, the Ancient Man invents God, and in that moment devalues his own existence utterly.

> Man fell upon his face prostrate before the watry shadow
> Saying O Lord whence is this change thou knowest I am nothing
>
> (*FZ*, 40:7–8)

The thought that human life is meaningless is the condition for Albion's dissociation, for it allows the idea of God to acquire a pathological predominance over what is real. But the idea of one God breeds many gods, and the Zoas split away from the universal mind along the lines of its most basic needs, the needs to love, think, hope, and imagine (Luvah, Urizen, Tharmas, and Urthona). Sublimated into a vision of holiness, Albion's self-love annihilates his humanity, and the Zoas appear to serve the many needs of the mind by isolating one and excluding the others.

The *sparagmos* of the Ancient Man does not, however, stop with the four Zoas. The Zoas have feminine portions, which Blake calls emanations, and sons and daughters too. Blake's psychological insight is quite acute here, as others have shown, for the division between Zoa and emanation symbolizes the separation of the hard and the soft passions in the minds of most men and women.[40] But it would be oversimplifying Blake's myth to maintain that Zoa and emanation sum up between them its sexual psychology. Their division is symptomatic of the larger one that afflicts the Ancient Man and exemplifies the same polyvalence in the psychology of love that characterizes the psychology of the self in general.

For Blake, love too often exaggerates divisions in the mind. As early as *Visions of the Daughters of Albion*, he locates within a single psyche the conflicting interests of the love relationship. In *The Four Zoas* he continues this method, expanding it to include the wide range of nuance represented by the Zoas and their emanations. All men and women are at least capable of this whole range; Albion's "Torments of Love and Jealousy" unite them in one vast mind.

The basic psychological split that love inflicts is usually tripartite: the agonizing cycle of surveillance that Blake depicts in the notebook lyric "My Spectre around me night and day." This little poem remains beguiling until it dawns upon the reader that the three players in its lovedrama inhabit the same mind. The poem's voyeuristic quality derives from the calm deliberation of a self contemplating its own ambivalent emotions. Sexual hunger and moral prohibition divide and dissipate its energy until only one fatal course of action remains:

> Till I turn from Female love
> And root up the Infernal Grove
> I shall never worthy be
> To Step into Eternity.
>
> (476)

The smug Christian piety of these lines is the libidinal equivalent of autism. The dilemma here bears directly upon *The Four Zoas*, because in writing his long poem Blake discovers that there is something fatal about the psychology of sexual love. Sex exacerbates the internal dissension of the divided mind, becoming a barrier to healing, not a balm. Little wonder, then, that his rough sketches in *The Four Zoas* manuscript are among his most erotic creations, and often painfully so.[41] Sexual love cannot in itself provide a therapy for the dissociated mind.

In revising his poem, Blake places increasing emphasis upon the sexual character of psychic dismemberment. His apparently original beginning has the Ancient Man calling upon Urizen to stabilize his "sickning Spheres" (*FZ*, 23:3). But working backwards, Blake adds a whole new Night that places this dissension in a sexual context. As we have noted, he now begins the poem with Tharmas, focusing upon this Zoa's separation from Enion, his emanation. Their division into separate identities consolidates the autistic lapse of the Ancient Man. Becoming opaque to one another, they divide reality between them into a sexual fantasy of pious restraint and libidinous pursuit.

This division in the Ancient Man prods him toward a dissociation of schizophrenic proportions, for it dissipates his humanity in a cycle of sexual pursuit. Frye describes Tharmas as man's original "power to bring what he creates into complete existence" (274). He is the mind's organ of hope, and Enion is its agency of actualization. When they divide into sexual counterparts, hope becomes acquisitive and its agency accusatory. Blake senses that madness is the sure end of this dissociation, for when faced with systematic and absolute suspicion, the mind's power of innocent conviction will seek a suicidal comfort. Tharmas confronts his once androgynous ally (now his sexual adversary) with the full implications of their separation:

> Why wilt thou Examine every little fibre of my soul
> Spreading them out before the Sun like Stalks of flax to dry
> The infant joy is beautiful but its anatomy
> Horrible Ghast & Deadly nought shalt thou find in it
> But Death Despair & Everlasting brooding Melancholy
> (*FZ*, 4:29–33)

Enion murders hope to dissect its motive. When every innocent wish is tested against the moral fibre of a negating piety, the power of hope ceases to sustain the Ancient Man.

And when wishes meet consistently with negation, fantasy worlds arise to compensate, as Bleuler knows well: "If anyone attempts to actualize such unfulfilled wishes in real life, he experiences disappointments which may bring him to the brink of disease" (374). Blake dramatizes this dynamic in sexual terms to underscore the damaging effects of a legislated sexuality. As sexual morality grows obsessive, it turns hope against itself, for sexual fulfillment is the body's glimpse of the most that men and women can hope for.

> Thou wilt go mad with horror if thou dost Examine thus
> Every moment of my secret hours Yea I know
> That I have sinnd & that my Emanations are become harlots
> I am already distracted at their deeds & if I look
> Upon them more Despair will bring self murder on my soul
> O Enion thou art thyself a root grown in hell
> Tho thus heavenly beautiful to draw me to destruction
> (*FZ*, 4:34–40)

Tharmas shares in the madness with which he menaces Enion, for it is his secrecy that gives her the privilege of piety. The separation of hope from its agency of actualization means that Tharmas spins fantasies in secret while Enion substantiates them by negating them. It is tempting to see in this drama Blake's battle with his own creative conscience, accusing him of betraying his revolutionary hopes by hiding them from plain view. At any rate, with hope working at cross purposes, the Ancient Man lapses into an existential coma.

In one of Blake's bitterest ironies, Enion's preoccupation with the venery of Tharmas incites him to sin. Blake remarks in another context that "All Penal Laws court Transgression & therefore are cruelty & Murder" (*Annotations to Watson*, 618). Enion's sexual morality courts transgression, buttressing a fallen status quo. Her power resides in the ability to weave a moral body for innocence, but she finds to her horror that hope turns despotic when reduced to a rigid standard. Tharmas is woven into her moral fabric,

> In gnawing pain drawn out by her lovd fingers every nerve
> She counted. every vein & lacteal threading them among
> Her woof of terror.
> . . . .
> Wondring she saw her woof begin to animate. & not
> As Garments woven subservient to her hands but having a will
> Of its own perverse & wayward Enion lovd & wept
> (*FZ*, 5:16–18, 20–22)

The acquisition of independent wills finally splits Tharmas and Enion into deluded individualities.[42] "Exalted in terrific Pride" (*FZ*, 6:8), Tharmas wills his independence at Enion's expense, accusing her of the sin he sought to evade:

> If thou hast sinnd & art polluted know that I am pure
> And unpolluted & will bring to rigid strict account
> All thy past deeds
> (*FZ*, 6:10–12)

With a will of his own Tharmas plays God, trying others by the morality that animates him. Hope has been perverted into righteous judgment.

The cycle of accusation that erupts between Enion and Tharmas illustrates the burden of the mind under the moral law. Each represents to the other an unfulfillable standard, so each stands accused of sin without hope of reprieve. When we recall that their recriminations occur inside the Ancient Man, we can see that the mind has become its own tribunal, and the guilty verdict it returns is tearing it apart. More extremely even than St. Paul, Blake senses the despair this self-accusation must breed. The will to righteousness becomes a will to death when it shuts man off from existence. Psychologically, this living death is madness, a willful retreat into compensatory fantasy. Kierkegaard calls this condition despair, and he defines it as "a disrelationship in a relationship which relates itself to itself," an accurate if somewhat cumbersome characterization of the psychic dismemberment of the Ancient Man.[43] The war within his members creates a fatal self-alienation: Kierkegaard's "sickness unto death," a despair so complete that even death offers no comfort.[44]

In Tharmas hope turns lethal. Night III of *The Four Zoas* ends with some of the maddest and uncannily moving lines in English literature:

> Tharmas reard up his hands & stood on the affrighted Ocean
> The dead reard up his Voice & stood on the resounding shore
>
> Crying. Fury in my limbs. destruction in my bones & marrow
> My skull is riven into filaments. my eyes into sea jellies
> Floating upon the tide wander bubbling & bubbling
> Uttering my lamentations & begetting little monsters
> Who sit mocking upon the little pebbles of the tide
> In all my rivers & on dried shells that the fish
> Have quite forsaken.
>
> (*FZ*, 44:21–45:1)

Tharmas's despair fills his world with a chorus of accusation. But to his further torment, he discovers that he cannot will his own death. Kierkegaard's diagnosis of the sick self for whom even the hope of death is not available is illustrated chillingly in lines that open Night IV:

> Deathless for ever now I wander seeking oblivion
> In torments of despair in vain. for if I plunge beneath
> Stifling I live. If dashd in pieces from a rocky height
> I reunite in endless torment.
>
> (*FZ*, 47:12–15)

On one level this passage illustrates the persistence of life against all odds. On another it announces a conception of the self at once terrifying and attractive. For even at its most alienated, identity cannot die. The burden of existence is to find a way to will life instead of death, the only real therapy for Tharmas's madness. Blake devotes the labor of his whole poem to the discovery of such a therapy.

He seems to admit, however, that the odds are against him. Separated from Tharmas, Enion becomes a voice crying in the void. From the handmaiden of innocence she has turned into the sphinx of experience, and her dark wisdom sounds through the poem's early nights like a canticle of despair. She voices the inequities of nature, society, and finally herself until she dwindles into nothing.[45] Shut away from existence, she represents the existential alternative to Tharmas's lust for oblivion. At last she begs Tharmas for relief:

> Driven by thy rage I wander like a cloud into the deep
> Where never yet Existence came, there losing all my life
> I back return weaker & weaker, consume me not away
> In thy great wrath. tho I have sinned. tho I have rebelld
> (*FZ* 45:21–24)

Enion plunges into silence as Tharmas rages in his chaos. Their sexual and moral antagonism forces the Ancient Man into a simultaneous consciousness of inevitable death and ineradicable life. Only when these visions can again unite into a whole will Albion overcome his debilitating ambivalence and arise from his grave of nightmares.

Similar splits occur between the other Zoas and their emanations with similar results, all reinforcing the dismemberment of the Ancient Man. Blake ties these agonies to time in the all-too-human antipathies of Los and Enitharmon.[46] They are the children of Tharmas and Enion, and are heirs to their parents' psychic division. In the earliest strata of the poem, Los seems to have been accounted a full-fledged Zoa, a position similar to the one he holds in *The Book of Urizen*. But Blake demotes him in revision, making him the temporal avatar of the eternal imagination, Urthona. Los enters the fallen world through Enion's loins, a child with Enitharmon of the disillusioned intercourse of hope and piety. As such, these fragments of the Ancient Man share his inner division, warring against each other rather than seeking the peace of a healing union.

Through them Blake examines the forces that keep the Ancient Man a thrall to the madness that dehumanizes him. Foremost among these is a selfish will to power that can only arise, in Blake's view, in the vacuum left by shattering the collective human identity. Los and Enitharmon knowingly pursue their own advancement at the expense of Albion's health. Their earliest conversation concerns a strategy for maintaining the fallen status quo in which they exist independently. When Los remarks upon the sad and secretive manner of their parent powers, Enitharmon replies,

> To make us happy let them weary their immortal powers
> While we draw in their sweet delights while we return them scorn
> On scorn to feed our discontent; for if we grateful prove
> They will withhold sweet love, whose food is thorns & bitter roots.
> (*FZ*, 10:3-6)

It is a fallen world indeed in which love feeds upon contempt. These lines show Blake fully aware of the potential for selfishness in the heart of a child. Their tone dates back to the hard wisdom of "Infant Sorrow": Enitharmon plots to please herself without regard to the sorrow she inflicts.

Such self-advancement is only possible, Blake suggests, when some pathology menaces our humanity. In a startling compromise of the conventions of myth, he reminds us that even Los and Enitharmon are only mental constructs whose partial life obscures the human whole. Los, who as Urthona's residue is the spirit of Prophecy, offers his consort a momentary glimpse of this higher life:

> Sickning lies the Fallen Man his head sick his heart faint
> . . . .
> Tho in the Brain of Man we live, & in his circling Nerves.
> Tho' this bright world of all our joy is in the Human Brain.
> (*FZ*, 11:10, 15-16)

Even Los and Enitharmon are fragments of a suffering personality. Their individuality is a neurological fiction. When they assert themselves over their parent powers, they reduce the "Brain of Man" to only one of its components. Such is the seduction of self-consciousness according to Blake: to value the ego at all costs is to shackle the mind to a fixed idea.

Enitharmon cannot bear the implications of Los's prophecy. In a long passage that Blake added quite late and that shows him moving steadily away from a purely sexual solution to human suffering, Enitharmon leagues with Urizen to maintain her place in the fallen world. Doing so, she shows herself her mother's daughter, displacing sexual energy onto religious devotion. Rather than seeking a union with her beloved and brother Los, she pursues independence with Urizen in the ranks of death:

> Descend O Urizen descend with horse & chariots
> Threaten not me O visionary thine the punishment
> The Human Nature shall no more remain nor Human acts
> Form the rebellious Spirits of Heaven. but War & Princedom & Victory & Blood
>
> (*FZ*, 11:21-24)

What is unnerving about these lines is the awareness they attribute to Enitharmon. She willingly slaughters humanity to maintain her own reality. Blake is moving toward the theory of psycho-sexual enslavement that dogs his later work like an obsession. The point to note here is that Enitharmon cannot be sure of her own existence without the collusion of an angry God.

In sexual terms this means preferring the church bench to the marriage bed. When Los approaches with the look of love, she retreats into a holy trance. Evading his embrace, she initiates a cycle of recriminations that sap the visionary of sexual and imaginative energy:

> Demon of fury If God enrapturd me infolds
> In clouds of sweet obscurity my beauteous form dissolving
> Howl thou over the body of death tis thine
>
> (*FZ*, 34:24-26)

Enitharmon's religious rapture disembodies her, leaving Los to fondle a corpse. The split within her between body and mind has grown into a pathology that participates in Albion's. She enjoys an intercourse with his delusions through a delirious sexuality quite characteristic of the schizophrenic.[47] Blake exposes the compensations that derive from an otherworldly religion, and suggest that they are the fruit of a disordered mind, a point that Bleuler makes as well when he compares Catholic symbolism to autistic delusion: "Homo Dei as the image of mortals could just as well have been the brainchild of a modern schizophrenic" (438n).

Los also participates in Albion's autism, but retains a conviction that it must end. In him, Blake dramatizes his own dilemma as an artist in the Age of Reason.[48] Urizen's intercourse with Los's beloved suggests that the artist's prostitution of his talents comes through no fault of his own. But the solution to this abuse exacts a high price, ultimately requiring a revolution in Blake's own understanding of his duties as an artist. Suffering Enitharmon's lascivious taunts, rendered in one of the truly corrupt courtly lyrics in the language (34:58–93), Los seeks comfort in the sadistic vengeance of alienating Urizen from his own beloved, Ahania. Los adds his jealousy to Enitharmon's, conspiring with her to bring Enion's unanswerable dirge to Ahania's notice:

> And Los & Enitharmon were drawn down by their desires
> Descending sweet upon the wind among soft harps & voices
> To plant divisions in the Soul of Urizen & Ahania
> To conduct the Voice of Enion to Ahanias midnight pillow
> (*FZ*, 34:1–4)

This conspiracy of Los against Urizen makes a significant change in the pattern of *The Book of Urizen*. It implicates the artist (Los) in both the end of one deluded system and the beginning of another. Urizen, the "great Work master," has built a world of admirable complexity and design, even if draconian. Los helps put an end to it, for less than laudable reasons. Blake is beginning to admit his own share in the sickness of the fallen self, however liberating or therapeutic his works may be.[49] Los may represent the artist in the Age of Reason, but his creativity begins in a personal grudge.

Unlike the Los of *The Book of Urizen*, who creates by eternal command, Los in *The Four Zoas* confronts a world whose ruin is in part his own doing. Blake means to suggest that destruction must precede creation, but without a naive Yeatsian revel in the terrible beauty of rebirth. Urizen is the victim of secret cunning, a conspiracy motivated by jealous hate. Los must rebuild Urizen's world anew, guided not by an eternal command, but by the mad ambitions of his raving father Tharmas, the fallen Zoa of hope. Blake seems to be confessing the unreasoning origins of his own creative enterprise; he too must work against the inclination of all fallen production toward death. Tharmas inspires Los's labors with a compensatory fantasy of nature's deadly cycle.

> But thou My Son Glorious in brightness comforter of Tharmas
> Go forth Rebuild this Universe beneath my indignant power
> A Universe of Death & Decay.
> . . . .
>   renew thou I will destroy
> Perhaps Enion may resume some little semblance
> To ease my pangs of heart & to restore some peace to Tharmas
> (*FZ*, 48:3–5, 8–10)

The creator begins in a foul rag-and-bone shop, hoping to achieve some semblance of the heart's desire. The danger exists that his creation will become pure compensation, that a fantasy of death will usurp the reality of life.

This danger besets Los and through him even Blake, as the events that follow prove. Los at first defies his father's orders, preferring solipsism to service: "Los remains God over all" (*FZ*, 48:18). But Tharmas subdues him by stripping him away from his apathetic paramour, Enitharmon:

> O how Los howld at the rending asunder all the fibres rent
> Where Enitharmon joind to his left side in griding pain
> He falling on the rocks bellowd his Dolor. till the blood
> Stanch'd, then in ululation waild his woes upon the wind
>
> (*FZ*, 49:7–10)

This event marks a turning point in Los's creative life, for it motivates his rehabilitation of his old rival Urizen, which he undertakes in order to resuscitate Enitharmon. It also locates the origins of creative labor in pain, specifically the pain of thwarted love. The artist must create to achieve healing, both for himself and for humanity.

Los begins his labors as his father's son, "Frightend with cold infectious madness" (*FZ*, 52:28). He might have succumbed to this despair were it not for another event that attends his alliance with Tharmas. Though holding Enitharmon hostage, Tharmas enlists as her guard the Spectre of Urthona, a shadowy figure, but like Los a remnant of eternal imagination in the fallen world. The Spectre builds a bower for Enitharmon and participates through his labors in the creative agonies of Los. His presence eventually proves their resolution, but for the moment he works the furnaces, helping Los to hammer out the body of Urizen. With the fortuitous collusion of Los, the Spectre, and Enitharmon, Blake has set the stage for healing the psychic dismemberment of the Ancient Man, for their relationship provides a way of reviving the memory of their collective human identity.

The central irony of Nights IV–VII, however, is severe: though all the ingredients for a cure are present, madness persists. Even as he labors to rebuild the universe, Los touches the nadir of mental suffering:

> Infected Mad he dancd on his mountains high & dark as heaven
> Now fixd into one stedfast bulk his features stonify
> From his mouth curses & from his eyes sparks of blighting
> Beside the anvil cold he dancd with the hammer of Urthona.
>
> (*FZ*, 57:1–4)

The madness of the Ancient Man afflicts even the eternal prophet. Nowhere is the danger of a final retreat into autism more real than now, when Los takes on the stony features of Urizen, for Urizen, as in the book that bears his name, has withdrawn into the shell of himself: "Urizen slept in a stoned stupor in the nether Abyss" (*FZ*, 52:20).

There can be little doubt that Blake is describing his deepest fears in the image of the mad Los. He had ample precedent for such feelings in the mental anguish of the sensibility bards. Los stands metaphysically between Urizen and Urthona, embattled between reason and imagination. His madness is a function of his position beyond the stony face of reason, open to the ordeal of a thundering inspiration. A hint of this creative unreason lingers in Frederick Tatham's account of Blake's fits of composition, whose furor could only be moderated by the patient attendance of his wife Catherine.

> She would get up in the night, when he was under his very fierce inspirations, which were as if they would tear him asunder, while he was yielding himself to the Muse, or whatever else it could be calld, sketching and writing. And so terrible a task did this seem to be, that she had to sit motionless and silent; only to stay him mentally, without moving hand or foot: this for hours, and night after night. Judge of the obedient, unassuming devotion of her dear soul to him.[50]

Los's madness in part begins in his consort's disobedience and lack of devotion. Faced with similar betrayal, we can surmise, Blake would have been subject to similar suffering, for this description of inspiration resembles nothing so much as the psychic dissociation characteristic of some forms of madness. Without Catherine to anchor him in *this* world, he ran the risk of a pathological lapse into that other. Blake relied similarly upon his art, displacing a profound psychological struggle onto the drama of his myth. Through the image of Los's madness he maintains a healthy distance from his own creative distress.

Likewise the Spectre of Urthona: he comes to represent Blake's tendency in the other direction, toward abstraction, away from art and into abstruse meditation or petty anxiety.[51] In a letter written to Butts while laboring at Felpham, Blake confesses his attraction to the abstract:

> I labor incessantly & accomplish not one half of what I intend, because my Abstract folly hurries me often away while I am at work, carrying me over Mountains & Valleys, which are not Real, in a Land of Abstraction where Spectres of the Dead wander. (*Letters*, 34)

Blake gives an unforgettably concrete description of this abstract world at the end of Night VI of *The Four Zoas,* where the Spectre, who "rejoicd along the vale," wields a mighty "Club whose knots like mountains frownd / Desart among the stars them withering with its ridges cold" (*FZ,* 76:12, 14–15). Blake senses the menace of his spectral musings as heavily as the burden of his visionary inspirations. The division between Los and the Spectre signifies his own inner division between these faculties of mind. He must integrate them or dis-integrate, a victim of their competing interests.

That is why the drama of *The Four Zoas* becomes progressively more personal and less veiled in allegory. As Tatham's account of those nocturnal visions suggests, Blake needed to ballast his creative life with something solid. Hence the desperate pursuit throughout the poem of Enitharmon by the afflicted Los. Their conflicts represent the apparent incompatibility of artistic integrity and domestic love, the tension within Blake between the creative urges of art and sex. In a deeply moving confessional passage, Los approaches Enitharmon to explain the contradiction he feels within him between these interests:

> Why can I not Enjoy thy beauty   lovely Enitharmon
> When I return from clouds of Grief in the wandering Elements
> Where thou in thrilling joy in beaming summer loveliness
> Delectable reposest ruddy in my absence flaming with beauty
> Cold pale in sorrow at my approach trembling at my terrific
> Forehead & eyes thy lips decay like roses in the spring
> (*FZ,* 81:23–28)

Visionary interests rob Los of Enitharmon's physical love. He can only love an idealized image of her, which her physical presence withers into a disappointing reality. Bleuler underscores the perilousness of this attitude when he discusses masturbation, for to the practitioner thereof "the imaginary mistress is more real than a real one" (343). As Blake shows in *Visions of the Daughters of Albion,* such abstraction of the beloved contributes to the elaboration of an autistic fantasy. Enitharmon, in turn, finds Los's loving looks fearsome, for they partake of the same intensity that calls him away to vision. Neither can love the other bodily, and their sexual life becomes a vacuum.

Blake's confession of a pained marriage could hardly be more frank and flatly contradicts Tatham's sanguine description of Catherine's absolute devotion. In fact, the subtitle of *The Four Zoas* could easily be "The Heaven and Hell of Marriage." Whose are the terrific forehead and eyes in the passage above but Blake's own? The sexual anguish of the following lamentation belongs to him as well:

> All things beside the woful Los enjoy the delights of beauty
> Once how I sang & calld the beasts & birds to their delights
> Nor knew that I alone exempted from the joys of love
> Must war with secret monsters of the animating worlds
> O that I had not seen the day then should I be at rest
> Nor felt the stingings of desire nor longings after life.
>
> (*FZ*, 82:4–9)

Note the opposition Blake establishes between "the joys of love" and "secret monsters of the animating worlds." It defines two phases of his poetic career, the exuberant naturalist and the retiring metapsychologist. He returns to the delicate language of *The Book of Thel,* and by applying it to himself discovers the naiveté of his earlier sexual vision. Unlike Thel, Blake remains inside the Northern Gates, and finds love ill-equipped to tame the monsters that war within. He must seek a darker therapy or, like Tharmas, succumb to the vain, mad hope of death.

Art itself becomes that therapy, as through it Blake finds the comfort he needs. He must, however, enlist his wife's aid, so that artistic creation can effect a mutual satisfaction comparable to sexual love. And he must achieve within his own mind a productive harmony among the conflicting interests that divide it. Blake's latest revisions show him in the grips of a personal crisis so profound that it ends, if we can trust the evidence, in religious conversion—of both man and myth. The key player in this drama becomes the Spectre of Urthona, who acquires a double function as both a barrier to and an agent of reintegration in the dismembered mind. In a late addition to Night I, the Daughters of Beulah, Blake's pastoral guardians of lower paradise, openly condemn the Spectre: "The Spectre is in every man insane & most deformd" (*FZ*, 5:38). He is the mind's organ of pride, which prizes material gain over visionary glory. And yet the great lesson of *The Four Zoas* is the importance of the Spectre to mental health and wholeness, for in this poem, the Spectre is a potentially positive figure, not merely the withering accuser of Blake's later myth. It is the Spectre who possesses Enitharmon with a pride that Los cannot muster.

> Loveliest delight of Men. Enitharmon shady hiding
> In secret places where no eye can trace thy watry way
> Have I found thee have I found thee tremblest thou in fear.
> (*FZ*, 82:28–30)

Though insane if left to his own designs, the Spectre can initiate the miracle of regeneration when allowed to combine his desires with another. Through him Blake arrives at the conviction that self-love, and all the worldly ambitions that go along with it, can be a vehicle for reviving the whole Man.[52] The Ancient Man's mind shattered in part because he bowed down and worshipped his own image. If that image can be put into action as a means of mutual love, then it might, by asserting itself, transcend itself, opening a way to a healing of humanity. As the Spectre unites with the Shadow of Enitharmon, an unexpected thing happens: for the first time in the poem discrete individualities exchange visions of a common psychic ancestry. Both are fallen fragments of Urthona, and through each other perceive their affiliation.

This human interaction and the relationship it inaugurates keeps the schizophrenic dissociation of the Ancient Man from remaining a deadly pathology. Through the sacrifice of self to the collective humanity of all, Albion's inner division finds restitution in a new psychic unity. Blake's art becomes the arena for this therapeutic reintegration of the Ancient Man. But this activity must begin at home. Blake's own life functions more and more as a paradigm of Albion's rather than vice versa. Los must recognize and assimilate the separate existence of the Spectre, just as he must approach Enitharmon with an accommodated passion. In biographical terms, Blake is affirming the importance of duty and restraint in order to achieve the fullest life. In lines marking the moment of his rejuvenation—and through him the Ancient Man's—Los confronts the Spectre and as never before sees himself from a perspective different from his own:

> Los embracd the Spectre first as a brother
> Then as another Self; astonishd humanizing & in tears
> In Self abasement Giving up his Domineering lust
> Thou never canst embrace sweet Enitharmon terrible Demon. Till
> Thou art united with thy Spectre Consummating by pains & labours
> That mortal body & by Self annihilation back returning
> Tho thus divided from thee & the Slave of Every passion
> To Life Eternal be assurd I am thy real Self
> Of thy fierce Soul Unbar the Gates of Memory look upon me
> Not as another but as thy real Self I am thy Spectre.
> (*FZ*, 85:29–38)

In this crucial passage, added quite late, Los faces both a remedy for his suffering and a temptation to renew it. The Spectre stands before him, his material double. He holds out the remedy of assimilation: if Los affirms that he is, in part, this spectre, then he will have taken a step toward reintegrating the Ancient Man, humanizing *all* the elements of the collective identity, however repugnant. But there is a substantial difference between seeing in the Spectre "another Self" and "thy real Self." For Los to succumb to the Spectre's temptation and reduce mental to material life would be to complete the madness of the Ancient Man. Los avoids this danger and embraces the Spectre as simply "another self," taking it into his bosom. The Spectre remains an independent portion of a new composite identity. The polyvalent identity that comes into being when the Ancient Man dissociates must be reconstituted *within* the individual. Only then will the collective identity of humanity revive.

United with the Spectre, Los can integrate art and love. He anticipates a quieter life:

> My lovely Enitharmon. I will quell my fury & teach
> Peace to the soul of dark revenge & repentance to Cruelty
> . . . .
> Lovely delight of Men Enitharmon shady refuge from furious war
> Thy bosom translucent is a soft repose
> (*FZ*, 86:11–12, 90:5–6)

Not surprisingly, Los woos Enitharmon with the rhetoric of the Spectre. He now knows how to manage his pride in a way that awakens her desire. Together they "fabricate embodied semblances" (*FZ*, 90:9), forms of artistic pleasure conceived as a refuge from a wearying existence. Art intervenes to couch humanity when it falls away from the task of living. But it could not do so without the active participation of the Spectre in the regenerated self, for the Spectre, more than any other element, connects a fantasy of comfort with the real world. Through him Blake guards against the possibility, so real to a man of profound visionary gifts, of substituting an autistic world for the real one, and retreating into the shell of a partial self.

IV

But we must not exaggerate Blake's victory. It comes at a high price. Promising as the reunion of Los, the Spectre, and Enitharmon may be, it arises only as the correlative of a deeper transformation of vision. Los and Enitharmon function together because, through each other, they get a glimpse of something greater than themselves.

> Then Los said I behold the Divine Vision thro the broken Gates
> Of thy poor broken heart astonishd melted into Compassion & Love
> And Enitharmon said I see the Lamb of God upon Mount Zion
> Wandering with love & Awe they felt the divine hand upon them
> (*FZ*, 99:15–18)

In the absence of this mutual vision of the Lamb of God, the Ancient Man would lapse forever into Ulro, that autistic world of living death. The logic of Blake's myth seems to demand this final descent, for as we have seen, Los's creative activity, Spectre or no Spectre, is infected by Albion's madness. Perhaps Blake senses what investigators have since confirmed, that once turned chronic, a madness like schizophrenia rarely allows a spontaneous recovery. Bleuler holds out hope for recovery, but admits that "essential improvements of chronic states are rare and cannot be counted on" (328). The myth Blake creates to contain the symptoms of such a condition provides a therapy for psychological distress, but not of itself a remedy. That comes in the turn to the Divine Vision as a complete and compensatory restitution, for conversion provides Blake's visionary experience with a lasting defense against its pathological potential.

Even a cursory reading of *The Four Zoas* betrays the profound change in symbolism that characterizes Night VIII. Suddenly a new set of villains takes over—Satan, Rahab, and the like—while a new hero arrives on the scene—Jesus, the Lamb of God. When Bloom maintains that this revision indicates a crisis in Blake's poetry that is "only a structural rather than a spiritual one" (244), he falsifies the complexity of Blake's poem and the pain that inspires it. We must not confine the idea of crisis to the poet in a man. Blake's latest revisions are the fruits of some sort of conversion and suggest a turn away from wholly human answers to psychic suffering and toward a religious healing.[53] We will examine the motives for this transformation in greater detail in the next chapter, but we misconstrue *The Four Zoas*, which I believe to be Blake's greatest poem, if we do not admit openly the effect of this change upon it. Blake revises his text obsessively, neither wholly canceling his earlier version nor smoothly integrating his later, until a kind of double-think afflicts the whole. He imposes upon the original myth the machinery of a later, more explicitly religious solution, whose integrity derives from Biblical parallel. He thrusts Jesus into Luvah's void, providing an orthodox comfort for an unorthodox condition. And as a last attempt to redeem his poem, he adds pages 22–24 and 55, the scenes concerning the Council of God, which introduce a saving transcendence where none can rightly be imagined if the Ancient Man, as originally conceived, contains within him all reality.[54]

Blake makes these changes in order to work a kind of conversion upon his own poetry, healing the psychic dissociation it dramatizes with a vision descending from above.[55] His letters richly verify that he benefited personally from such a conversion. He describes his experience to Hayley in terms drawn from his own myth:

> he is become my servant who domineered over me, he is even as a brother who was my enemy. Dear Sir, excuse my enthusiasm or rather madness, for I really am drunk with intellectual vision whenever I take a pencil or graver into my hand, even as I used to be in my youth, and as I have not been for twenty dark, but very profitable years. I thank God that I courageously pursued my course through darkness. (*Letters*, 101–3)

Blake has found a meaningful context for his mental suffering. That "madness" becomes a mark of health indicates that, in the context of a visionary Christianity, the psychic dissociation that he displaces onto the events of *The Four Zoas* has become intelligible and therefore redeemable.

Blake revises his poem accordingly, and in one surprising passage even confesses his new aims:

> First Rintrah & then Palamabron drawn from out the ranks of war
> In infant innocence reposd on Enitharmons bosom
> Orc was comforted in the deeps his soul revivd in them
> As the Eldest brother is the fathers image So Orc became
> As Los a father to his brethren
>
> (*FZ*, 90:44–48)

These lines narrate the conversion of Blake's mythology from an oracle of psychological revolution to one of spiritual prophecy. Until now, Orc has been the bound embodiment of natural energy. Blake draws him from his poem's ranks in new forms: Rintrah, prophet of wrath, and Palamabron, prophet of pity. These figures become central to the later myth, signifying the spiritual conversion that underwrites it.

Describing the psychology of such an upheaval, William James remarks that "to say that a man is 'converted' means that religious ideas, previously peripheral in his consciousness, now take a central place, and that religious aims form the habitual center of his energy."[56] If we are to read Blake's late works aright, we must take into account the new, or at least renewed, centrality in them of religious ideas.[57] Jesus descends from above to put an end to the maddening politics of consciousness and to provide a center around which Blake can organize the scattered fragments of the Ancient Man.[58]

The price paid for this new order is the censorship of his greatest work. The method of his later poems is only apparently more personal than *The Four Zoas*. Blake deals with his own experience as visionary, but wraps it in the mists of an explicitly religious symbolism. The open vistas of *The Four Zoas* narrow as he encloses vision in a system. He retreats from an unabashed confidence in his own experience, looking to verify it in the humanity of Jesus. Even on the first page of *The Four Zoas*, Blake tampers with the autonomy of his vision. The nature of his Zoas, which it had been the aim of his poem to describe, is rendered inscrutable, the privileged knowledge of the kind of Nobodaddy Blake usually loathes:

> [*What*] are the Natures of those Living Creatures the Heavenly Father
>   only
> [*Knoweth*] no Individual [*Knoweth nor*] Can know in all Eternity
>
> (*FZ*, 3:7–8)

The spirit of an invocation allows for no irony here. Blake pencils in these lines, a very late addition squeezed between lines of earlier verse that alters their meaning significantly. Blake has not become a mystery-religionist—far from it. But he affirms the new religious context in which visionary experience must thrive to be intelligible and psychologically tolerable.

Without this context, the Zoas' war can only end in sorrow, not the reintegration of the Ancient Man. Such at least is the implication of a passage in *Jerusalem* that seems a recantation of *The Four Zoas:*

> The Four Zoa's in terrible combustion clouded rage
> Drinking the shuddering fears & loves of Albions Families
> Destroying by selfish affections the things that they most admire
> Drinking & eating, & pitying & weeping, as at a trajic scene.
> The soul drinks murder & revenge, & applauds its own holiness
> (*J*, 37:26-30)

Blake senses the self-indulgence of a poetry that places his own psychic struggle at its center, shoving aside the concerns of his beloved wife and country. He senses too the danger of such an enterprise: it can become a self-consuming infatuation, as pessimistic and imperial as the tragic wisdom he struggled with and rejected. So *The Four Zoas* goes unengraved, and its apocalypse, the finest we possess, remains a revelation unrevealed. Like *The Prelude*, whose surface differences hide deep spiritual affinities, *The Four Zoas* stays hidden until after the poet's death, too personal for publication.

The Four Zoas is so great a poem because in it Blake wrestles against the principalities and powers that war within. But the madness he mythologizes pertains ultimately to all. The *sparagmos* of the Ancient Man dramatizes not only the fall of humanity into self-consciousness but more importantly the pathological potential inherent in this divided condition. Blake labors to revive in all men and women the memory of their collective human identity, the loss of which creates conditions sadly conducive to mental breakdown. After much struggle and much anguish Blake at last embraces a religious optimism, offering the divine humanity of Jesus as the one authentic proof of a collective identity. If this solution lacks credibility in the purely psychological terms of Blake's original myth, it nonetheless satisfies profound needs of his own and becomes the foundation of his later work.

The burden of vision drove Blake to Felpham in 1800, then back to London in 1803. By the time he announced that vision publicly in *Milton* and *Jerusalem*, however, it had acquired a new evasiveness. For Blake would pass through an ordeal confirming his profound fear that to publish would mean to perish. On January 11, 1804, he stood trial for sedition. Before this difficult event he could write to Butts of redoubled devotion to his private schemes:

> Now I may say to you, what perhaps I should not dare to say to any one else: That I can alone carry on my visionary studies in London unannoy'd, & that I may converse with my friends in Eternity, See Visions, Dream Dreams & prophecy & speak Parables unobserv'd & at liberty from the Doubts of other Mortals. (*Letters*, 55)

Blake's resolve to value the inner world if need be in defiance of the outer is a plan rife with dangers. His trial only strengthens this resolve, but exacerbates as well a growing sense of persecution. As a result, a compensatory element enters his late myth and sanctifies a newfound political quietism. The politics of consciousness rages still, but in the arena now of a religious order.

5

Trial and Defense

O my Lord, by the vision my sorrows are turned upon me, and I have retained no strength.
— Daniel 10:16

I

On the afternoon of August 12, 1803, a soldier entered the garden of Blake's cottage at Felpham. Private John Schofield of His Majesty's First Regiment of Dragoons had been invited in by the gardener to lend a helping hand. Blake found him lounging, and sensed immediately an archetypal danger: a hireling had crept into his garden, undoubtedly with wicked intent. After an exchange of words, the nature of which remains a mystery, Blake asked the dragoon to leave. When he refused, Blake forcibly expelled him, grabbing him by the elbows and pushing him down the road to the inn where he was quartered.[1]

To avenge his rough treatment, Schofield charged Blake with sedition, and the case was tried publicly the following January in Chichester. Schofield's charge hinged upon Blake's allegedly seditious utterance in both the garden and the road. Only Schofield's crony Cox could substantiate the evidence, but his corroboration was enough to force the prosecution of, in Blake's phrase, "a very unwarrantable warrant" (*Letters*, 63). This encounter left its mark upon Blake and his poetry, inspiring in both a defensive posture that secures vision from its natural adversaries. As a result, Blake's personal relation to his myth and the madness it allegorizes comes to dominate the content of his late, long poems.

The utterance Schofield attributed to Blake is a farrago of matter mixed with impertinence.² Some parts are obvious fabrications. But in certain moods Blake was unquestionably capable of the brash declaration Schofield attests to hearing: "if Bonaparte should come, he would be the Master of Europe in an Hour's Time"! Other statements possess the curious blend of republicanism and suspicion that colors Blake's late works. Schofield's complaint states "that he damned the King of England— his Country, & his Subjects, that his Soldie[r]s were all bound for Slaves, and all of the Poor People in general" (*Letters*, 62). The reciprocal enslavement of oppressor and oppressed is an idea compatible with Blake's prophecies. The whole statement reads like a gloss on *America*. If Blake did not speak these words he must have felt them, as another passage of Schofield's complaint suggests:

> Blake, then addressing himself to this Informant, said, tho' you are one of the King's subjects, I have told what I have said before greater People than you, and that this Informant was sent by his Captain or Esquire Hayley to hear what he had to say, & to go and tell them. (*Letters*, 62)

This much at least Blake spoke in his anger: it is a statement that implies so much more, implies in fact both a spiritual endorsement of sedition and a natural fear of its repercussions.³ In such a statement we can hear the defensive tones of an aging republican who feels persecuted for convictions he dare not openly express.

We do a disservice to Blake's poetry when we ignore the enormous psychological tension required for him to maintain a private allegiance to his vision while denying it in public. Blake writes to his patron Butts that "as to Sedition, not one Word relating to the King or Government was spoken by him or me" (*Letters*, 63). But isn't he splitting hairs? He speaks such words in the privacy of his own margins, annotating his copy of Bacon's *Essays* with statements like "Every Body hates a King" (623) and "When the Reverence for Government is lost it is better than when it is found" (624). Unable to stand up for these convictions, Blake ran the risk of quietism. His trial put his revolutionary principles to the test, forcing him ultimately to interpret his political dilemma in psychological terms. The public division between man and prophet becomes a private dualism between self and vision, while the psychic warfare of *The Four Zoas* takes a surprisingly conventional shape in this context.[4] The politics of consciousness finds its resolution in a psychological dualism that secures Blake's health and happiness, but at the high price of abdicating social action.

To read the defense presented by Samuel Rose, Blake's lawyer, is to sense some of the tension that Blake carried with him through his trial and into his late poetry. Rose begins by admitting "the atrocity & malignity of the charge" laid before the jury and pledges his own presence as evidence of Blake's integrity. Then comes the declaration of innocence, which should make any lover of Blake's poetry happy that Rose never bothered to read it:

> I am instructed to say, that Mr Blake is as loyal a subject as any man in this court: — that he feels as much indignation at the idea of exposing to contempt or injury the sacred person of his sovereign as any man: — that his indignation is equal to that, which I doubt not every one of you felt, when the charge was first stated to you. (*Letters*, 75)

Rose skillfully deflects the issue away from Blake, who listened in silence to a testimonial of his obsequiousness. Blake resists confronting openly the very powers he denounces in prophecy, as if the judges and the jury, the lawyers and the witnesses, were somehow less real than the giant forms that represent them in his poems.[5] What better arena than *Rex v. Blake* for a prophet to arise and denounce the oppressors of Jerusalem and the agents of her captivity? But Blake remains silent, guarding his health and welfare while promoting a false appearance in the public eye.

Rose's remarks about Blake's occupation only widen the gulf between public and private. As an engraver, according to Rose, Blake benefits from the soothing influence of his craft,

> an art, which has a tendency, like all the other fine arts, to soften every asperity of feeling & of character, & to secure the bosom from the influence of those tumultuous & discordant passions, which destroy the happiness of mankind. If any men are likely to be exempted from angry passions it is such a one as Mr Blake. (*Letters*, 76)

The slightest acquaintance with Blake's poetry proves the disingenuousness of this description; cantankerousness and unruly passion had much to do with his lackluster success as an engraver. Blake shows himself willing to submit to the duplicitous terms of Rose's defense, if only to win his freedom to return to the streets of a fallen metropolis. Rose carried the day, though before he could finish he broke down with a cold that eventually killed him. Blake stood exonerated of the public charge of sedition, to the general satisfaction of his friends and neighbors, but he had done nothing to advance the cause of his prophetic calling. Instead, he copped a plea and prepared the way psychologically for the disintegration of man and prophet that afflicts his last poems.[6]

Blake gives a glimpse of this psychological dualism in a letter to Hayley dated Oct. 7, 1803, some months before his trial. Playfully maintaining his innocence, he describes his current situation in terms of inner division:

> When this Soldier-like danger is over I will do double the work I do now, for it will hang heavy on my Devil who terribly resents it; but I soothe him to peace, & indeed he is a good natur'd Devil after all & certainly does not lead me into scrapes—he is not the least to be blamed for the present scrape, as he was out of the way all the time on other employment seeking amusement in making Verses, to which he constantly leads me very much to my hurt & sometimes to the annoyance of my friends. (*Letters*, 69–70)

Note Blake's readiness to admit the antagonism between poetry and daily living.[7] Using the language of *The Marriage of Heaven and Hell*, he distinguishes between creative identity and mundane ego, valuing the former above the latter even though it distracts him from the facts of life.[8] This psychological dualism provides the foundation for his last opaque efforts at myth. Upon such a dualism he builds *Milton* and *Jerusalem* to defend the integrity of vision against the encroachments of a fallen world.

The happy outcome of his trial did little to lessen Blake's sense of persecution. The growing emphasis in those poems upon the accuser "Who is God of this World," not to mention the private barbs cast in his notebook, show him convinced that the world has betrayed him. As an engraver he was passed over and as a painter ignored. He made several attempts to awaken the public to his merits, designing illustrations for Blair's *Grave* in 1808 and holding an exhibition of his own paintings in

1809, but neither event succeeded in advancing his reputation. The hesitation of the public to embrace his works confirmed his calling as one "crying in the wilderness" (1), and drove him in upon himself, an aging stranger in a strange land.[9]

In an extended piece of private invective that has dubiously come to be called the "Public Address," Blake defends his abilities against his persecutors with almost paranoid conviction. He writes as one "Now surrounded by Calumny & Envy" (571), and promises to mete out a poetic sort of justice:

> the manner in which I have routed out the nest of villains will be seen in a Poem conern[in]g my Three years Herculean Labors at Felpham which I will soon publish. Secret Calumny & open Profession of Friendship are common enough all the world over but never have been so good an occasion of Poetic Imagery. (572)

Blake's deep feelings of persecution come through clearly here. What is startling, however, is his explicit confession of the use to which he puts his poetry. Blake both routs his persecutors and celebrates his own heroism through the medium of epic verse.

The relation of this strategy to similar Romantic efforts is clear enough: the private doings of the individual become the arena for heroism rather than the social exploits of the Great Man. But we must not deny the compensatory function of Blake's new epic strategy.[10] Feeling powerless, he creates in poetry the conditions of a heightened personal power. The sense of persecution, after all, originates in the frustration of wishes and the confirmation of fears.[11] Blake himself says much the same thing when he writes, "if any could desire what he is incapable of possessing, despair must be his eternal lot" (2). When consistently frustrated, aspiration turns against itself, ending finally in delusions of persecution.

It should come as no surprise, then, that an element of paranoia creeps into Blake's later works. According to contemporary research, paranoia, a species of schizophrenia, represents an effort to compensate for frustrations by exaggerating personal importance.[12] The paranoid schizophrenic typically imagines that he is special, destined for great things, and that the world keeps him under surveillance in order to frustrate his designs. Events that occur around him, however accidental, come to refer directly to himself and his thwarted aspirations. If he receives an insult on the job, it indicates a plot against promotion. If he gets a visit from a stranger, it must be with bad intent. Such "delusions of reference" provide compensation for frustrated desires and often arise in the company of pathological jealousy or exaggerated religiosity. It is therefore not unusual for the paranoid schizophrenic to feel singled out by God. With enough frequency, these delusions acquire a systematic character, until an individual spends more time and energy elaborating a system than experiencing life. It was this characteristic that led Freud to postulate the therapeutic value of such systems: "the delusional formation, which we take to be a pathological product, is in reality an attempt at recovery, a process of reconstruction."[13] The elaborate delusions of the paranoid schizophrenic work to restore his relation to the world. In a sense paranoia is a pathology against pathology, a mental illness that contains within it the seeds of its own healing.

I raise the issue of paranoia not to diagnose Blake's mentality, but to suggest that certain elements of his late poetry become meaningful in light of clinical research. Granted such meaning is wholly our own, significant for us in ways unknowable to an earlier age, but Blake's poetry is the richer for it, acquiring a new psychological urgency. We have seen that *The Four Zoas* performs a therapeutic function; this function gains importance in Blake's later poems. Blake's ambition to inherit Milton's vision is the real subject of the poem—*Milton*—that routs the villains who would deprive him of his laurels. And though Blake, in my estimation, realizes that ambition in his poetry, his failure to do so in the prosaic world forces him further into a psychological dualism that separates his private identity as prophet from his public one as artisan and Englishman. While it would be crude to label Blake paranoid, his feelings of persecution account at least in part for both the privatizing and the systematic elaboration of his late myth. In *Milton* and *Jerusalem* myth functions as much as a defense against a hostile world as an indictment of its fallenness. Blake encloses himself snugly within the walls of Golgonooza, his imagined city of art, creating a system to avoid enslavement by another, protecting his mind against the madness it fears.[14]

This retreat into systematic thought—not at all characteristic of Blake's earlier work[15]—has its correlative in a withdrawal from social action. The usual way to explain this late aversion to politics is to maintain that Blake turned his attention to the psychological revolution that must precede political reform, a change of emphasis derived from the failure of the French Revolution.[16] And undoubtedly he was right to do so. The aftermath of the French Revolution proved that a people must be ready, in mind and spirit, for reform or it will lapse into that cultural compulsion to repeat the fall diagnosed in the Orc Cycle.

But the boundary between psychological speculation and political quietism is as fine as it is absolute. Blake's late disgust with politics, clearly inspired by his trial, relieves him from the burden of providing a program for reform of the sort he labored so hard to articulate in his early prophecies and even *The Four Zoas*. In the "Public Address" he expresses his chagrin at the political preoccupations of Englishmen:

> I am really sorry to see my Countrymen trouble themselves about Politics. If Men were Wise the Most arbitrary Princes could not hurt them If they are not Wise the Freest Government is compelled to be a Tyranny Princes appear to me to be Fools Houses of Commons & Houses of Lords appear to me to be fools they seem to me to be something Else besides Human Life. (580)

Here is republicanism at its most banal and quietistic—and its most bigoted as well, for if Princes and politicians, however misinformed, are not representatives of human life, what are they?

Blake appears to be wrestling with the same contradiction between wisdom and politics that Shakespeare examines in *King Lear*. But where Shakespeare places between them a tragic abyss, Blake dismisses their antinomy outright; the wise man transcends the need for politics. In essence, Blake answers Shakespeare with a religious solution of the sort only implied by *King Lear*. "Are not Religion and Politics the same thing?" he asks in *Jerusalem*. "Brotherhood is Religion" (*J*, 57:10).[17]

The problem Blake faces, then, is the advancement of Brotherhood, and it is here that his vision fails him. Men become wise, according to *A Vision of the Last Judgment*, "whenever any Individual Rejects Error & Embraces Truth [and] a Last Judgment passes upon that Individual" (562). By thus casting out error, all men and women labor in the service of true Art and Science, "the Foundation of Society which is Humanity itself" (562). When Blake defines Humanity by its intellectual activities, however, he impoverishes his own earlier claims. Although he devoted ten years of his life to diagnosing humanity's debilitating "Torments of Love and Jealousy," he now confidently dismisses passion as a function of the intellect: "The Treasures of Heaven are not Negations of Passion but Realities of Intellect from which all the Passions Emanate Uncurbed in their Eternal Glory" (564). This unity between intellect and passion is a profound ideal, well worth pursuing. But the whole thrust of Blake's production until now has been to explain their dissociation, especially in *The Marriage of Heaven and Hell* and *The Four Zoas*. Blake fails to provide a program for their reintegration, and his myth becomes mired in the double ruts of so much idealist thought. Damrosch argues quite convincingly that Blake's recourse in his late poems to a doctrine of Error ends inevitably in a Platonic sort of dualism, for if Humanity equals truth, then the error that individuals fall into is of a lesser order.[18] The "apocalyptic humanism" that Bloom celebrates so avidly is a sublimated ideal, on the edge of otherworldliness.[19]

II

A measure of Blake's greatness, however, is his unwillingness to rest comfortably in the implications of his own idealism. Above all a psychologist, Blake creates a context that dramatizes, in myth, the inner division he suffers. Between *The Four Zoas* and the brief epic *Milton*, he retreats from an innovative polyvalent psychology to a more conventional dualism. But psychic dissociation is no less his subject. The politics of consciousness now plays itself out between the poles of a visionary identity and a mundane ego. By abandoning the sophisticated and highly satisfying mental allegory of *The Four Zoas* and collapsing it into the psychological dualism of the late poems, Blake wins a victory over the mind's dissociation, positioning visionary experience in the cultural context of a long-standing religious tradition.

The central dramatic episode of both *Milton* and *Jerusalem* involves the confrontation of an eternal Human identity with its fallen spectral selfhood. In *Milton*, the great Puritan poet returns to earth from the confines of his own heaven "to wash off the Not Human . . . in Self annihilation and the grandeur of Inspiration" (*M*, 41:1–2). In *Jerusalem*, Blake's visionary alter-ego Los compels his Spectre to build the halls of Golgonooza. Both poems locate the origin of individual suffering in that inner division we met with in our first chapter between visionary and worldly experience. Both, in other words, allegorize psychic dissociation, but of a milder sort than appears in *The Four Zoas*. This new psychological dualism concerns the individual; the collective implications of *The Four Zoas* take shape only in a general call to awakening. Blake circumscribes his vision in his late poetry, no longer identifying the individual and the race.

Damrosch has pointed out the similarity between Blake's psychological dualism and the "schizoid" personality that R. D. Laing describes in *The Divided Self*. Though a promising observation, Damrosch applies it to *The Four Zoas*, a poem much more sophisticated than this concept.[20]

The drama of *Milton* and *Jerusalem*, however, fits nicely into Laing's psychology of the schizoid, for these poems focus upon individual rather than collective identity. Laing argues that the psychological dualism of the schizoid personality derives from a profound conviction of the world's hostility: "The person I am describing feels persecuted by reality itself."[21] Such a person responds to his feelings by dissociating his authentic identity from the ego that confronts a hostile world. A psychological dualism evolves, rife with dangers for the unity of the personality:

> If the whole of the individual's being cannot be defended, the individual retracts his line of defense until he withdraws within a central citadel. . . . But the tragic paradox is that the more the self is defended in this way, the more it is destroyed. (77)

From within his own central citadel, Golgonooza, Blake senses the danger of this tragic paradox. His city of art defends against this danger, but also provides a therapy, through creative labor, for healing the mind's dissociation. Blake's solution to this division is just the opposite of Laing's. Rather than assimilate the ego, he subordinates it to the higher claims of visionary experience. Hence the tension in his later poetry between the competing interests of vision and the world.

This psychological dualism is the reason Blake is often taken to be a mystic.[22] With the mystic he shares that inner cleavage between power and poverty, Los and the Spectre. Blake does not arrive at this position by chance. In the tradition of religious mysticism, among whose most important members for him were Boehme and Swedenborg, he discovers a cultural context in which he can situate his psychological dilemma.[23] His turn away from the highly original psychology of *The Four Zoas* is a turn toward the much more traditional psychology of mystical experience. By assimilating his own experience to this time-honored tradition, Blake finds a context which can validate his visions. Mysticism could well provide a stable structure of meaning for certain mild neuroses or even psychoses, domesticating them and integrating them into a manner of living conducive to health and happiness. The explicit religious strain in Blake's late verse indicates that he takes some comfort in such a structure, as well he should, for it has always been the function of religion to reconcile humanity to the demons that divide it.[24] Blake ends up in a position reminiscent of the sensibility bards, except that their dualisms are religiously absolute, whereas his is psychologically serviceable.

Even so, *Milton* and *Jerusalem* both ameliorate the madness of psychic dissociation by treating it in an explicitly religious context. The primary concerns of each are the character of visionary experience and its relation to the natural world. The poems relate as species to genus, *Milton* being a private application of *Jerusalem's* public statement. In the former Blake looks *up* to vision from the vantage of his worldly ego; in the latter he looks *down* upon the natural world from a visionary perspective. Together, *Milton* and *Jerusalem* constitute one long poem that defends the visionary and his experience against an inhospitable, fallen world.[25]

Blake confesses the religious character of this defense in a passage from *Milton* that glosses the aesthetic principles of his late works. Notice the relationship of Architecture, Poetry, and Religion in the following lines:

> But in Eternity the Four Arts: Poetry, Painting, Music,
> And Architecture which is Science: are the Four Faces of Man.
> Not so in Time and Space: there Three are shut out, and only
> Science remains thro Mercy: & by means of Science, the Three
> Become apparent in Time & Space in the Three Professions
>
> Poetry in Religion: Music, Law: Painting, in Physic & Surgery:
> That Man may live upon Earth till the time of his awaking,
> (*M*, 27:55–61)

Blake describes all kinds of science, *scientia*, as fallen forms of architecture because for him humanity's intellectual achievements are stays against confusion. By identifying Poetry and Religion, he emphasizes their common visionary heritage, for religion organizes the eternal art of poetry in the lineaments of time. Blake's late poems are just such an organization, a religious defense of visionary experience against the threats of time and space. As a species of architecture, they shelter a comatose humanity until the hour of its awakening. In *Milton* and *Jerusalem*, then, Blake builds a defense of poetry—for the sake of his own mental health as much as humanity's. If the elaborate architectonics of these poems bear some resemblance to the "wondrous golden Building" (*FZ*, 32:10) of Urizen's Mundane Shell, it is because Blake himself now builds defenses to protect visionary experience against the world's rebukes.

Much more explicitly than his earlier work, the late poems concern the burden of vision. In poems like *Europe* and *The Book of Urizen*, Blake dismisses this issue in a short preludium or invocation. But in *Milton* it becomes the substance of the whole poem, the center around which a highly psychological drama revolves, for Blake labors to build his own structure in which to validate his visionary experience. Mystical tradition provides a cultural context for this undertaking, but he remains too loyal to the details of his own experience to tolerate an orthodox emasculation of it.

For his vision includes something more harrowing than the infinite love encountered by the Christian mystic. On plate 23 of *Milton* Blake describes visionary experience in terms that arouse a shudder:

> Like the black storm, coming out of Chaos, beyond the stars:
> It issues thro the dark & intricate caves of the Mundane Shell
> Passing the planetary visions, & the well adorned Firmament
> The Sun rolls into Chaos & the stars into the Desarts;
> And then the storms become visible, audible & terrible,
> Covering the light of day, & rolling down upon the mountains,
> Deluge all the country round. Such is a vision of Los;
> (*M*, 23:21–27)

How comforting it would be to dismiss such a passage as a mere trope, a synecdoche that signifies the self turning against itself in an awareness of its partiality.[26] But at question is the nature not of poetic origins but of pathological experience, for what Blake describes here is the sort of hallucination that he took for inspired revelation. Blake situates the details of this experience in the aesthetic arena of his mythology in order to interpret them and direct them toward productive rather than debilitating ends. A vision of Los descends menacingly from beyond the borders of rational order and takes possession of the "vegetable" senses.[27] Whether they originate in God or in his imagination, the "visible, audible & terrible" storms that engulf Blake are hallucinatory experiences and pose a direct threat to his peace of mind. Blake represents their disturbing effect in lines that come after the climactic vision of judgment that closes *Milton:*

> Terror struck in the Vale I stood at that immortal sound
> My bones trembled. I fell outstretched upon the path
> A moment, & my Soul returnd into its mortal state
> (*M*, 42:24–26)

Such visions have their dangers, which Blake avoids by returning to this mortal world.

But rather than turn against his visions, he works to integrate them into a system of psychic defense that liberates their significance and mitigates their dangers. If, as Foucault argues, "where there is a work of art, there is no madness," then Blake's aesthetic strategy becomes intelligible.[28] With its rhetorical thunder, Blake's later poetry transforms pathology into prophecy. Visions that could otherwise qualify Blake for confinement in Bedlam become, through the artful mediation of myth, an indictment of the world's fallenness. To quote Foucault once again,

> through madness, a work that seems to drown in the world, to reveal there its non-sense, and to transfigure itself with the features of pathology alone, actually engages within itself the world's time, masters it, and leads it; ... it is now arranged by the work of art, obliged to order itself by its language. (288)

The beguiling opacity of Blake's late poetry performs just this function: it judges the world by the standards of vision and compels either agreement or confused silence. In either case we stand convicted of our world's poverty *vis-à-vis* the greater power of vision.

It would be wrong, however, to suggest that Blake places faith in art alone to achieve this end. The visions he records in *Milton* ultimately find a religious resolution. In a description that is astonishing for anyone familiar with his poetry, Blake empties himself before the divine influence that informs his vision:

> O how can I with my gross tongue that cleaveth to the dust,
> Tell of the Four-fold Man, in starry numbers fitly ordered
> Or how can I with my cold hand of clay! But thou O Lord
> Do with me as thou wilt! for I am nothing, and vanity.
> (*M*, 20:15–18)

Echoing Albion's solipsistic devotion to his own image in *The Four Zoas* (*FZ*, 40:12–18), Blake returns in *Milton* to a conception of God he had explicitly rejected. The whole passage seems a confession of his inability, or worse, his unworthiness, to tell the story of the fall and resurrection of the Ancient Man. What Blake is admitting here is the poverty he feels in the absence of visionary power. The only alternative to visionary experience, it appears, is nothingness and a compensatory deity. The problem he therefore faces in *Milton* is to integrate vision and the world in such a way that the intensity of the former does not drain the latter of human meaning.

This is why he elaborates his myth so exhaustively: to mediate the visionary experience it defends. For all its murkiness, as others have noticed, *Milton* boils down to two moments of illumination.²⁹ The first comes when Milton enters Blake's left foot, bringing with him a conviction of prophetic election:

> Then first I saw him in the Zenith as a falling star,
> Descending perpendicular, swift as the swallow or swift;
> And on my left foot falling on the tarsus, enterd there;
> But from my left foot a black cloud redounding spread over Europe.
> (*M*, 15:47–50)

Blake encourages the conclusion that he experienced this moment just as he describes it, for he pictures it in a full-page illustration preceding plate 30. The second visionary moment comes when Ololon descends into his garden, an event he illustrates on plate 36:

> There is a Moment in each Day that Satan cannot find
> Nor can his Watch Fiends find it, but the Industrious find
> This Moment & it multiply. & when it once is found
> It renovates every Moment of the Day if rightly placed[.]
> In this Moment Ololon descended to Los & Enitharmon.
> (*M*, 35:42–47)

The quality of a whole day depends upon the use made of its visionary moments. The latter passage illustrates Blake's relation to his vision especially well. He must guard it closely, for worldly powers seek to find and to exploit it. And yet he must multiply it to renew the fallen time in which he lives. His late myth answers this double need as it defends, through its symbolic opacity, against intruders, and mediates, through its systematic continuity, the renovating moments of vision. Myth functions in *Milton* as memory does throughout Wordsworth's poetry, mediating past experience of vision to effect a renovated present.

But myth itself does not overcome the psychological dualism that divides the mind. Only Jesus can do that. Blake retells the tale of this division in the Bard's song of *Milton*, which runs from the end of plate 2 to the beginning of plate 14.³⁰ His mythic strategy should be familiar by now. He parcels out the portions of a whole mind among the interests that divide it. Satan, Palamabron, and Rintrah, as well as their emanations, all belong to a larger whole, divided by the competing interests of poetry and daily life. What differs here from the great myth of *The Four Zoas* is

Blake's severely narrowed scope. So confined to the dilemma of the poet is the Bard's complaint that it has become the custom to interpret it as an allegory of Blake's mental war with Hayley. Blake's method transcends this limitation to be sure. But even so, he resorts in the Bard's song to the kind of poetry of compensation that he works hard to avoid in his earlier work. The judgment of the Eternal Counsel and the ensuing descent of Milton is an almost painfully obvious vindication of Blake's behavior at his own trial and a belated declaration of his prophetic right.

In *Milton*, then, Blake solves the problem of psychic dissociation with a myth that compensates for his neglect as an artist and advocates a dualistic separation of man from Satan rather than a wholly human reunion of man with man. Such a dualism is a defensive strategy that remakes a psychological division into a religious one, allowing it to be assimilated to an authoritative cultural tradition. The whole tenor of the following chant sung by Los seems to reject human mire and blood and to celebrate a quietism uncharacteristic of Blake's earlier poetry:

> Crave not for the mortal & perishing delights, but leave them
> To the weak, and pity the weak as your infant care; Break not
> Forth in your wrath lest you are vegetated by Tirzah
> Wait till the Judgement is past, till the Creation is consumed
> And then rush forward with me into the glorious spiritual
> Vegetation; the Supper of the Lamb & his Bride; and the
> Awakening of Albion our friend and ancient companion.
> (*M*, 25:56–62)

Albion will awaken, it appears, not when his scattered portions reunite, but when judgment consumes creation. In *Milton*, as ultimately in *The Four Zoas*, it is Jesus who heals the mind's maddening dissociation and lifts life to the level of vision:

> with one accord the Starry Eight became
> One Man Jesus the Saviour, wonderful! round his limbs
> The Clouds of Ololon folded as a Garment dipped in Blood
> Written within & without in woven letters: & the Writing
> Is the Divine Revelation in the Litteral expression:
> (*M*, 42:10–14)

After witnessing this theophany, which unites the disparate moments of vision recorded in *Milton*, Blake can but return to his "mortal state"

(*M*, 42:26) to await the day of apocalypse when all divided selves shall become one in Jesus.[31]

III

Until that day, however, the mind remains divided. Blake devotes much of his last, great poem, *Jerusalem*, to the ordeal of living in the midst of this division. Recent criticism has come to see in the mental fight of Los with his Spectre the thematic center of the poem, for it is here that Blake dramatizes his personal struggle to live up to the terms of his own prophecy. There has been a tendency, however, to whitewash the disturbing character of this struggle and to disregard its darkest implications. So persuasive is Blake's rhetoric, not to mention that of his strongest critics, that our sympathies turn unreservedly to Los, and away from his grotesque parody, the Spectre. But the fact that Los himself cannot dismiss so lightly the Spectre's obsessed complaint should alert us to its urgency, and to Blake's deep attraction to it.

In the continuing dissension between these psychic fragments, Blake dramatizes once again the inner division that afflicts him. The battle between Los and the Spectre in *Jerusalem* allegorizes what we might call a schizoid experience of the world, a chronic dissociation in the mind that yet does not lapse into psychosis. This condition allows Blake to serve simultaneously the interests of vision and the world and to vent his profound feelings of persecution without becoming their slave. In its relentless systemization, *Jerusalem* resembles the systematic delusions of the paranoid, with this difference: as a work of art, its therapeutic value does not apply to Blake alone. In no other poem does he explore so deeply the tribulations of the visionary artist, divided by the power of vision and the poverty of mere self.

Critics have taken a growing interest in the Spectre since Frye first clarified its status in the pantheon of Blake's late mythology. Frye somewhat overzealously identifies the Spectre with the will, that portion of man's being which is "the instrumentality of the mind" (293). I say overzealously because all of Blake's giant forms possess a will of their own, Los as much as the Spectre. Their dis-integrated willfulness is the legacy of the Fall. Frye comes closer to the mark when he equates the Spectre with the "man" in the poet, his all-too-human being that must toil to make a living amidst the fever and the fret.[32] Bloom advances this notion in two important ways. First, he emphasizes the baser elements that necessarily participate in the poet's lofty ambitions, his pride as an artist, but his anxiety too that when the body dies all is finished.[33] Second, he interprets the insanity of the sensibility bards as a human precedent for the Spectre's complaints. In the Spectre, Blake satirizes their despair in order to overcome it and take up the trumpet of prophecy.[34] Damrosch argues somewhat to the contrary that prophecy itself arouses this anxiety. The Spectre embodies a false self behind which Blake can conduct his prophetic activity with some security.[35] Finally, Paley suggests that Blake creates the Spectre out of the darkness of his own soul, drawing upon deep feelings opposing conscious beliefs and personality traits inspiring disgust.[36] Paley steps back from the implications of his own analysis, however, when he disinfects it with a caveat: "The construction of Blake's myth tends toward integration, not schizoid bifurcation" (252). This may be true of *the Four Zoas,* but it no longer holds for *Jerusalem,* where Blake never dramatizes the *reintegration* of Los and the Spectre.

What all of these important readings fail to notice is the madness inherent in this division—mastered through the therapeutics of Blake's art, but menacing nonetheless. The Spectre confronts Los and through him Blake with a highly appealing antithetical vision, a temptation to despair that hounds the visionary like a demon.

The Spectre does not, however, spring *ex nihilo* onto the cluttered stage of Blake's late myth. His ghostly presence appears throughout Blake's poetry, as if biding its time, like Milton's Satan, until the moment is ripe for temptation. He is the spirit of the early lyric "Mad Song," who crowds after darkness and fills the waking world with his anxiety. He shadows *Songs of Experience* with his moral imperatives. And he puts in an especially brash appearance in *The Marriage of Heaven and Hell.* On plate 5, which contains the famous vindication of Milton's Satan, Blake recounts a visionary journey to hell from which he returns with a load of proverbs. The journey requires a psychic dissociation that apparently poses no threat to the mind's integrity. Blake slips with ease back into the sensory world, but not before he gets a disembodied glimpse of his own body:

> When I came home; on the abyss of the five senses, where a flat sided steep frowns over the present world. I saw a mighty Devil folded in black clouds, hovering on the sides of the rock, with corroding fires he wrote the following sentence. (35)

Anyone familiar with Blake's late myth will recognize the Spectre in this Devil plying the corrosives of the etcher's trade. His appearance does not, however, confirm the consistency of Blake's canon. On the contrary, it refutes this claim. Here the Spectre is a Devil, participating in the bliss of creation, whereas in the late myth he is a Covering Cherub inhibiting the return to paradise.

This evolution charts the descent of Blake's psychology from an ideal pluralism to a functional dualism. The Spectre is no mere trope. Blake's illustrations of it confirm its psychological reality.[37] It takes the form of a vaginal bat on plate 6 of *Jerusalem*, closing itself to the visionary utterance of Los. And in its most grotesque appearance it parodies the visionary moment of Milton's union with Blake (a moment illustrated with a full plate in *Milton*). Famous and strange, *The Ghost of a Flea* shows the Spectre in a position just the opposite of Blake's, with a star falling toward its right foot to indicate a hostile disregard for vision. These representations of the Spectre, running from early poems to late paintings, document the history of a psychological double that takes its most menacing avatar in *Jerusalem*.[38]

For in *Jerusalem* the Spectre embodies an explicit challenge to Blake's vision, a challenge that originated in Blake's trial and that has the potential for turning pathological. Los exhorts Albion to awaken from his spiritual stupor and answer this challenge:

> I feel my Spectre rising upon me! Albion! arouze thyself!
> Why dost thou thunder with frozen Spectrous wrath against us?
> The Spectre is, in Giant Man; insane, and most deform'd.
>
> (*J*, 33:2-4)

Los and Albion suffer the same anxiety here, but not, as in *The Four Zoas*, simultaneously. Los's battle with his Spectre cannot in itself achieve the awakening of the Ancient Man. This distinction significantly limits the aims of Blake's late myth. Mental fight is now primarily a private matter, and a victory guarantees no collective response. Blake centers his final efforts at awakening in the individual and labors to secure, first and foremost, his own mental health.

Why then does Los, Blake's visionary alter-ego, characterize his own Spectre as "insane & most deform'd"? Blake describes here his conviction that the very impulses most hostile to his sanity arise from within. He does not use the word "insane" lightly. His whole treatment of the

Spectre and its relation to Los bears resemblance to the mental process that Bleuler calls "automatism," in which a complex splits off from the personality to be experienced as an alien power.[39] In Blake's case what splits off is not a wish, as is usual, but the subtler awareness of the obstacles to its fulfillment. These take the form of a psychological double, the Spectre, whose presence is a constant reminder, not only of the limitations that hinder vision, but also of the bad faith involved in denying them.

For Los, the Spectre is an alien power originating in his own deep suspicion of his prophetic vocation. Its projection outward is functional, a necessary risk the prophet must run if he is to serve his vision truly. But the separation of the Spectre from the whole mind is potentially pathological because it sets up a psychological dualism that tempts the prophet to despair, a fearsome temptation since it originates within. Blake describes the division of Los in the following terms:

> His spectre driv'n by the Starry Wheels of Albions sons, black and
> Opake divided from his back; he labours and he mourns!
> . . . .
>   and the Spectre stood over Los
> Howling in pain: a blackning Shadow, blackning dark & opake
> Cursing the terrible Los: bitterly cursing him for his friendship
> To Albion, suggesting murderous thoughts against Albion.
>
> (*J*, 6:1–2, 4–7)

Not only must Los and through him Blake endure the agony of the mind's dissociation, but both must bear the added burden of guilt for harboring alienated impulses known only to the Spectre. In the embattled relations between Los and his Spectre, Blake dramatizes a schizoid experience that threatens to lapse into psychosis. Split away from Los, the Spectre is insane, and menaces the prophet's whole personality with madness.

In biographical terms, the Spectre, described in *Milton* as "the Idiot questioner" (*M*, 41:12), is the voice of the conspirators who accused Blake of seditious utterance against the King. In Los's defiance of his Spectre's charges, Blake reenacts his trial, a purpose he develops in *Jerusalem* by giving cameo appearances to his adversaries, including Schofield and his crony Cox. A profound feeling of persecution clearly inspires Blake's labors, but it is a feeling that originates as much in himself as in others. For in *Jerusalem* Blake focuses primarily upon the trial of the visionary, tempted to betray his vocation by the arguments of reason. Having done just that during his trial for sedition, Blake elaborates a system that is part compensation, a retrial, so to speak, that gives him a second chance to take a stand. The voice of an accuser haunts him continually. *Jerusalem* is in part a defense against those accusations, an epic attempt to cope with the frustration of self-betrayal.

For as others have suggested, the Spectre presents Los and through him Blake with a constant temptation to despair.[40] It articulates that sickness unto death voiced so fearsomely by Tharmas in *The Four Zoas*, but the Spectre speaks in accusatory tones rather than tearful lamentations. And it substantiates Los's deepest fears with rational demonstration:

> This is the Spectre of Man: the Holy Reasoning Power
> And in its Holiness is enclosed the Abomination of Desolation
> (*J*, 10:15-16)

Blake is at his canniest when he equates reason with insanity. But any intellectual activity that reinforces the mind's dissociation participates therein. The Spectre threatens to reduce a schizoid experience to a despairing psychosis by substituting his own holiness for the indemonstrable convictions of vision:

> Where is that Friend of Sinners! that Rebel against my Laws!
> Who teaches Belief to the Nations, & an unknown Eternal Life
> Come hither into the Desart & turn these stones to bread.
> Vain Foolish Man! wilt thou believe without Experiment?
> And build a World of Phantasy upon my Great Abyss!
> A World of Shapes in craving lust & devouring appetite [?]
> (*J*, 54:19-24)

The Spectre shows himself an acute psychologist, accusing the sinner's friend of building a sublimated world of fantasy. But the Spectre is playing God as well. To capitulate to his higher criticism would be to succumb to that "madness of the will" which Nietzsche describes as a "*will* to erect an ideal—that of the 'holy God'—and in the face of it feel the palpable certainty of ... absolute unworthiness."[41] Such is the insanity that the Spectre counsels—the sacrifice of the self to itself in a deluded worship of the abyss.

Even so the Spectre's temptation has great appeal for Los, and for Blake, too, to the extent that he follows vision. It could be that Blake is a poet of the Spectre's party without knowing it—at least without wanting to. For he puts into the Spectre's mouth accusations that qualify the integrity of his own prophetic vocation. It is to Blake's credit that he voices these objections through his accuser. But he doesn't really overcome them except in the dazzling moment of vision that ends *Jerusalem*. Only by keeping his suspicions at a distance can he advance the prophet's task and remain true to visionary experience.

In the above passage, for instance, he confesses the possible compensatory elements in his own imaginative production. His idealism, he suspects, might be autism, tricked out in literary style. Depending as he does so entirely upon the imagination to sustain him, Blake cannot afford to question its integrity directly. The Spectre performs this function for him, at a safe psychological distance from the prophetic personality. Other of the giant forms in *Jerusalem* reinforce the Spectre's suspicions, as when Albion, on the opening plate of the poem proper, dismisses the Divine Vision as a "Phantom of the over heated brain! shadow of immortality!" (*J*, 4:24). Los must master the Spectre's imputations to convince Blake himself of his visionary purpose and to secure his mental health.

Far more cutting and closer to home, however, is the Spectre's charge of willful isolation and exploitable hypocrisy. He accuses Los of self-destructive impulses that masquerade as large-hearted brotherhood:

> And thus the Spectre spoke: Wilt thou still go on to destruction?
> Till thy life is all taken away by this deceitful Friendship?
> He drinks thee up like water! like wine he pours thee
> Into his tuns: thy daughters are trodden in his vintage
> He makes thy Sons the trampling of his bulls, they are plow'd
> And harrowd for his profit, lo! thy stolen Emanation
> Is his garden of pleasure! all the Spectres of his Sons mock thee
> Look how they scorn thy once admired palaces! now in ruins
> Because of Albion! because of deceit and friendship!
>
> (*J*, 7:9–17)

The Spectre voices Blake's dark suspicion that his mythic method is deceitful and his vision of brotherhood therefore clandestine. For his myth confronts its public with a surface so opaque that it wins no following. Blake's isolation, the Spectre hints, is at least in part willed. As a result he bears responsibility for the commercial exploitation of his talents. A prophet who will not stand up and shout his prophecy can only sit by and see it coopted by profiteers and talent-mongers. Cromek's treatment probably confirmed these fears, for Blake saw his designs to Blair's *Grave* executed by another, but not before Blake himself dedicated them to, of all people, the Queen.[42] The tensions involved in playing the prophet at home and the artisan in the street find their way into Blake's poetry through the Spectre, who claims that, for all Los's talk of brotherhood, isolation is his native element.

The dissociation of Los and the Spectre therefore dramatizes the schizoid experience that allows Blake to play the prophet *in absentia.* Blake admits the necessity of this inner division, both for his poetry and his occupation, when he has Erin, his personification of the spirit of Irish liberty, describe the reduction of vision to time:

> The Visions of Eternity, by reason of narrowed perceptions,
> Are become weak Visions of Time & Space, fix'd into furrows of death;
> Till deep dissimulation is the only defence an honest man has left.
> (*J*, 49:21–23)

Blake concentrates all of his frustration as a visionary into these lines, especially the last. Deep dissimulation is a defense that the honest man, Blake's definition of the prophet, must take up to evade death. No wonder, then, that the Spectre's accusations of deceitful friendship tempt Los to despair. They are true.[43] Los cannot wholly overcome them, and neither can Blake. Both must turn them to productive uses, like Freud's paranoid, who elaborates his delusions to reconcile himself with the world. Los enlists his Spectre in the ranks of vision without denying the validity of his accusations:

> I know that Albion hath divided me, and that thou, O my Spectre,
> Hast just cause to be irritated: but look stedfastly upon me:
> Comfort thyself in my strength the time will arrive,
> When all Albions injuries shall cease, and when we shall
> Embrace him tenfold bright, rising from his tomb in immortality.
> (*J*, 7:52–56)

In a dramatic change from *The Four Zoas,* where Los embraces the Spectre of Urthona as a brother and a friend, Los defers reuniting with his Spectre until the day of awakening. Until then they must endure their dissociation without allowing it to lapse into psychosis.

IV

In *Jerusalem*, then, Blake renders a familiar Romantic dilemma, the inner division between creative power and existential poverty, in terms of a pathology. His own problem is to achieve a balance, through his poetry, between the competing claims of Los and his Spectre. He dramatizes in their continuing fight the psychological opposition in the Romantic between creature and creator.[44] Blake interprets this opposition in pathological terms because he senses the danger it poses to a unified humanity. The Spectre condenses all of our creaturely aspects into a critical mass of existential complaint:

> But my griefs advance also, for ever & ever without end
> O that I could cease to be! Despair! I am Despair
> Created to be the great example of horror & agony: also my
> Prayer is vain I called for compassion: compassion mockd
> Mercy & pity threw the grave stone over me & with lead
> And iron, bound it over me forever: Life lives on my
> Consuming: & the Almighty hath made me his Contrary
> To be all evil, all reversed & for ever dead: knowing
> And seeing life, yet living not; how can I then behold
> And not tremble; how can I be beheld & not abhorrd
>
> (*J*, 10:50–59)

It is hard to read these lines without hearing the complaint of the monster in Mary Shelley's *Frankenstein*. Like Mary Shelley, Blake reduces the human sense of our own createdness to one grotesque image of alienated ugliness. The Spectre reproaches Los as the monster does Frankenstein, with selfish disregard for the living death he creates. Where Mary Shelley propounds the tragic nightmare of an uncompromising idealism, however, Blake maintains a resolute faith in its power, so long as his own creative labor can answer the Spectre's accusations.

For as Blake's representation of the creator in man, Los depends heavily upon the Spectre for assistance in building Golgonooza, the city of art that shelters humanity. Imagine Victor Frankenstein sitting down with his monster to compose a poem—or build a mate! But for Blake, the creator in man must work through the creature if vision is to become anything other than fantasy or pathological delusion. By driving the Spectre to the furnaces, Los answers anxiety with activity:

> Los. compelld the invisible Spectre
> To labours mighty, with vast strength, with his mighty chains,
> In pulsations of time, & extensions of space
> (*J*, 10:65-11:2)

Only the productive complicity of creature and creator can overcome the tragic outcome of Mary Shelley's novel. Blake makes a significant concession to the fallen world when he allows that it should bring him metaphors for poetry. On the 91st plate of *Jerusalem*, Los transforms the Spectre's "stupendous Works" (*J*, 91:32) into the stuff of vision:

> Los beheld undaunted furious
> His heavd Hammer; he swung it round & at one blow,
> In unpitying ruin driving down the pyramids of pride
> . . . .
> Then he sent forth the Spectre all his pyramids were grains
> Of sand & his pillars: dust on the flys wing: & his starry
> Heavens; a moth of gold & silver mocking his anxious grasp
> (*J*, 91:41-43, 47-49)

The mind's division ends in an act of violence that subordinates creature to creator. The schizoid experience that makes their relations productive inspires a climactic vision of Albion's awakening on the closing plates of the poem.

But we must ask whether Blake ever really answers the Spectre's creaturely complaint. For either Blake or Los to have succumbed to it would have meant a lapse into psychosis, the psychological equivalent of Frankenstein's tragic end. But Los's whole treatment of the Spectre resembles nothing more than the mechanism of repression, especially when compared with the brotherly assimilation dramatized in Night VII of *The Four Zoas*. Vision triumphs by force in *Jerusalem*, answering dissociation, after a long struggle, with denial.

Bloom makes an important observation when he suggests that Blake satirizes the sensibility bards in his portrayal of the Spectre. He points to the profound personal ordeal that Blake displaces onto the Spectre's battle with Los.[45] Bloom errs only in seeking external correlatives, like Cowper and Ezekiel, for a fundamentally internal drama: the confrontation between the new Blake and the old. The sensibility bard Blake fears most is the poet of the early prophecies—Blake himself in the flush of revolutionary fever, willing to risk his security for the sake of principle.

An indication of this anxiety appears in Blake's revision of his myth. In *Jerusalem* he takes the three main characters of his earlier mythology, Urizen, Los, and Orc, and reduces them to two, Los and the Spectre. What becomes of Urizen and Orc? As most critics agree, Urizen slips into the Spectre, though there is something in Los's belligerence that harks back to the primeval priest. The fate of the fiery Orc is a bit more startling. In *The Four Zoas* he becomes entangled in the web of Urizen's morality. In *Jerusalem* he lives an attenuated existence in the rebellious Spectre's defiance of Los. The Spectre describes himself, in terms reminiscent of Orc, as "all evil," a being created by the "Almighty" to be His "Contrary" (*J*, 10:57, 56). Los senses this hostility and promises to put the Spectre in its place:

I know thy deceit & thy revenges, and unless thou desist
I will certainly create an eternal Hell for thee. Listen!
Be attentive! be obedient! Lo the Furnaces are ready to receive thee.
(*J*, 8:7-9)

On plate 3 of *The Marriage of Heaven and Hell*, Blake *celebrates* the revival of "Eternal Hell." But here Orc's element has become a punishment. By collapsing three characters into two, Blake revises the values of his earlier myth. Both Los and the Spectre possess Urizenic qualities and both at times resemble Orc, Los in his wrath and the Spectre in his rebellion. Blake's new myth may be more faithful to the subtlety of human psychology. But in his effort to absorb Orc, his former hero, Blake betrays an anxiety about the overwhelming strength of his own earlier works—and the younger poet who composed them.[46] In *Milton* Blake goes so far as to link the once-heroic Orc with the antichrist: "And Satan is the Spectre of Orc" (29:34). By thus discrediting rebellion, Blake attempts to repress the revolutionary fervor of his own youth.

When scraps of his earlier myth appear in *Jerusalem*, it is often the Spectre who recites them. In his very first speech he recounts the ordeal of Luvah in the Furnaces of Affliction, pirated from the twenty-fifth page of *The Four Zoas*. As the poet of an unpublished mythology, the Spectre attests to Blake's discomfort with that self-censored work. But what is most striking about the earlier material included in *Jerusalem* is the extent to which Blake parodies it. Enion's pathetic lament over her lover's sin becomes a cunning seduction when it issues from Vala's lips (*J*, 22:10-15). And when Blake returns to the Zoas, he simplifies their dealings radically:

> But when Luvah assumed the World of Urizen Southward
> And Albion was slain upon his Mountains & in his Tent.
> And fell towards the Center, sinking downwards in dire ruin,
> In the South remains a burning Fire: in the East. a Void
> In the West, a World of raging Waters: in the North; solid Darkness
> Unfathomable without end: but in the midst of these
> Is Built eternally the sublime Universe of Los & Enitharmon.
> (J, 59:15-21)

While a good thumb-nail sketch of a complex poem, this summary amounts to a misreading, for it completely belies the subtlety of the psychology Blake advances in *The Four Zoas*.[47] To clear literary ground for the more conservative message of his later myth, Blake must misread his earlier work, reducing it to caricature. When the Spectre offers himself as its author and apes the behavior of the rebel Orc, he betrays Blake's anxiety of *his own* influence, the fear that he cannot overcome the demonic power of his youthful prophecy. The psychological dualism of *Jerusalem* works against that prophecy, pushing it aside to make room for Jesus, the evangel who stills the demon Orc. But the price Blake pays for this security is a decline in the power of the prophet in him after *The Four Zoas*.

The psychic division between Los and his Spectre, then, separates the young Blake from the old. Blake must repress his former glory in the interest of present peace of mind, which is just what he does when he withholds *The Marriage of Heaven and Hell* from sale to prospective patrons.[48] But the division within him remains, sustained perhaps by the lingering guilt of the one-time rebel:

> O that I could abstain from wrath! O that the Lamb
> Of God would look upon me and pity me in my fury.
> In anguish of regeneration! in terrors of self annihilation:
> Pity must join together those whom wrath has torn in sunder,
> And the Religion of Generation which was meant for the destruction
> Of Jerusalem, become her covering, till the time of the End.
> (J, 7:59-64)

These lines rationalize Blake's return to the religion of Jesus, a provisional security until apocalypse. When the Lamb descends, and not before, the old Blake will unite with the young. Until that hour, the two Blakes wrestle for priority, neither gaining a victory without the annihilation of the other.

Blake gives some idea of this ordeal when he describes the way he composes his poetry to Henry Crabb Robinson. Admittedly a credulous observer, Robinson recorded Blake's curious comments in his diary:

> I write he says when commanded by the spirits and the moment I have written I see the words fly abo[u]t the room in all directions—It is then published and the Spirits can read—My MSS [are] of no further use—I have been tempted to burn my MSS but my wife wont let me She is right said I [Robinson]—You have written these, not from yourself but by a higher order The MSS. are theirs not your property—You cannot tell to what purpose they may answer; unforseen to you—He liked this And said he wo[ul]d not destroy them.[49]

There can be no stranger account than this of the experience of inspiration. The important thing to note is that Blake makes a clear distinction between the visionary command of Los and the mundane temptations of the Spectre, who would see those manuscripts burned (and who possibly did, if Robinson's report of 100 volumes of now-missing manuscript is credible). Blake's failure to find an audience for his late work only reinforces the cleavage within him between Los and the Spectre.

This dissociation proves quite functional, however, as plate 17 of *Jerusalem* shows. Blake solves the problem of sexuality that so disturbs him in *The Four Zoas* by separating the sexual act from its more sublime origins. Mark the peculiar relationship in the following passage between Los and the Spectre, who pimps on behalf of his purer alter ego:

But Los himself against Albions Sons his fury bends, for he
Dare not approach the Daughters openly lest he be consumed
In the fires of their beauty & perfection & be Vegetated beneath
Their Looms, in a Generation of death & resurrection to forgetfulness
They wooe Los continually to subdue his strength: he continually
Shews them his Spectre: sending him abroad over the four points of heaven
In the fierce desires of beauty & in the tortures of repulse! He is
The Spectre of the Living pursuing the Emanations of the Dead
Shuddring they flee: they hide in the Druid Temples in cold chastity
Subdued by the Spectre of the Living & terrified by undisguisd desire.
(*J*, 17:6–15)

Damrosch points to this passage as evidence of Blake's schizoid personality.[50] The dissociation of Los and the Spectre separates desire from its dangerous sexual expression—dangerous because sex places the Divine Humanity into the possessive grasp of mother nature. The Spectre pursues the Daughters of Albion so as not to involve the visionary in too permanent a contact with fallen love.

For love leads directly to entanglement in *Jerusalem* as pretensions to chastity coopt desire.[51] Blake no longer celebrates unreservedly the physical facts of sexuality, as he did in *The Marriage of Heaven and Hell*, where he boldly proclaimed "the genitals[:] Beauty" (37). In *Jerusalem* he qualifies his enthusiasm, pointing out the proximity of the genitals to organs of pure bodily function. When the Spectre makes the following remark, it voices Blake's deep suspicion that, for all its joys, sexual love too often forces men and women into the tragedy of natural existence:

> The Man who respects Woman shall be despised by Woman
> And deadly cunning & mean abjectness only, shall enjoy them
> For I will make their places of joy & love, excrementitious[.]
>
> (*J*, 88:37-39)

Blake is not endorsing the tragic wisdom of Yeats's Crazy Jane here. He confesses through the Spectre the facts of natural life in the visionary effort to overcome them, "Circumcising," in his own phrase, "the excrementitious Husk & Covering" (*J*, 98:18-19). In spite of his aims, however, Blake is in *Jerusalem* spiritually at his closest to Freud. The enormous stress he lays on a primary narcissism as the origin of moral systems allies him with that other great psychologist in the conviction that, at bottom, sickness begets sexual love, which the demands of culture then repress. Psychological dualism is hence a defense also against the tragic facts of fallen sexuality.

In chapter 3 of *Jerusalem*, Blake devotes long, disturbing passages to the horrors of natural existence. A social order based upon the natural man commits, in his view, a grisly human sacrifice. Los's vision of such rituals, conducted by the pious Rahab and the bloodthirsty Tirzah, are a denunciation of thinkers who follow Rousseau in attempting to build a society on nature's foundations. Like Sade, Blake exposes the fallacy of expecting natural man to give up his baser pleasures for the sake of social order. Nature is an epiphany of nothingness in the face of which cruelty brings the relief of an intoxication:

> Look: the beautiful Daughter of Albion sits naked upon the Stone
> Her panting Victim beside her: her heart is drunk with blood
> Tho her brain is not drunk with wine: she goes forth from Albion
> In pride of beauty:
> . . . .
>   to cut the flesh from the Victim
> To roast the flesh in fire: to examine the Infants limbs
> In cruelties of holiness: to refuse the joys of love:
>
> (J, 68:11-14, 57-59)

There is an obsessive quality in Blake's enumeration of nature's cruelties that suggests his own proximity to the Spectre's insanity. Madness would indeed be an appropriate response to the inhuman atrocities of natural man. Sade composing furiously in the confines of the Bastille presents a circumstance curiously parallel to Blake's solitary prophecy. It is not surprising, then, that the tone of Blake's denunciation lapses into the sadistic. Both writers assert the nothingness of nature and suggest the madness that this conviction can inspire. Foucault argues that in Sade's work "Nature enters madness," and finally destroys itself: "The nothingness of unreason, in which the language of Nature had died forever, has become a violence of Nature against Nature, to the point of the savage abolition of itself."[52] Something similar takes place in Blake's descriptions of humanity consuming itself on the altars of sacrifice. Blake's own solution is the psychological dualism he displaces onto the drama of Los and the Spectre. The Spectre provides a defense for the vision that Los opposes to nature's nothingness.

V

The alternative to this schizoid experience, as Blake sees it, is the florid schizophrenia of the Ancient Man. The Albion of *Jerusalem* differs significantly from the Ancient Man of *The Four Zoas*. Blake is now less interested in the genealogy of Albion's affliction than in elaborating its symptoms and effects. Los is still the temporal avatar of the eternal prophet Urthona, but his relations with Albion are less those of son to father than those of brother to brother. Albion must master his own Spectre just as Los masters his. Because he does not, his mind splits up, proliferating personalities wildly. Blake greatly increases his cast of characters between *The Four Zoas* and *Jerusalem*, and their interactions are always divisive, elaborating Blake's systematic defense against feelings of persecution. A stunning visual representation of this schizophrenic collapse appears on plate 50. It shows a giant sprouting heads as fragments of his mind split off into independent personalities. This dissociation is the condition of the poem's action, for Blake begins by having Albion insist upon its necessity:

> But the perturbed Man away turns down the valleys dark;
> [*Saying. We are not One: we are Many, thou most simulative*]
> Phantom of the over heated brain! shadow of immortality!
> Seeking to keep my soul a victim to thy Love! which binds
> Man the enemy of man into deceitful friendships:
> Jerusalem is not! her daughters are indefinite:
> By demonstration, man alone can live, and not by faith.
> (*J*, 4:22–28)

Unlike the Ancient Man of *The Four Zoas*, whose psychic dissociation is dynamic and moves toward a therapeutic resolution, the Albion of *Jerusalem* consciously resists any attempt at healing.[53] Los must fight against this recalcitrance, first by subduing his own Spectre, then by exhorting Albion to do likewise.

Having achieved the former, however, is no guarantee of the latter. Albion's madness requires the explicitly religious therapy that Blake resorts to in *The Four Zoas*. Blake's last poems confess the inadequacy and even danger of visionary experience not centered in the religion of Jesus, the religion he rejected in *The Marriage of Heaven and Hell*. Albion's many sons and daughters are not reconciled to him, but cast away as he offers himself for another in the mutual sacrifice of religious brotherhood. Albion admits as much to Jesus:

> Albion replyd. Cannot Man exist without Mysterious
> Offering of Self for Another, is this Friendship & Brotherhood
> I see thee in the likeness & similitude of Los my Friend
> (*J*, 96:20–22)

Only when an individual sees another in Jesus does the division that afflicts humanity disappear in a vision of brotherhood.

Blake's Jesus is distinct for his humanity and Blake's God for his intellectual abundance. The history Blake offers of Christ's birth on plate 61 of *Jerusalem* shows just how little use he has even in his latest thought for a wholly other, transcendent Jesus. God too belongs in the last analysis to Man, as Blake makes clear on the poem's great ninety-first plate. Los commands his Spectre to play evangel of the Divine Humanity:

> Go, tell them that the Worship of God, is honoring his gifts
> In other men: & loving the greatest men best, each according
> To his Genius: which is the Holy Ghost in Man; there is no other
> God, than the God who is the intellectual fountain of Humanity;
>
> (J, 91:7-10)

Bloom uses these lines to affirm the consistency of Blake's thinking over the course of his career.[54] But it is one thing for a young, ambitious poet to maintain that Genius merits the most love, and quite another for an aging, neglected prophet to make the same claim. Meeting with these lines in *Jerusalem* is a bit like reading a newly written *Don Quixote* — the words take on another meaning in their new psychosocial context. Blake asserts his right to homage at least in part to compensate for neglect.

Moreover, identifying God with "the intellectual fountain of Humanity" is not precisely the same thing as identifying God with Man, as Blake does on plate 23 of *The Marriage of Heaven and Hell* and in the second *No Natural Religion* tract. In his late poems Blake interprets a psychological dualism as a religious one. The individual must identify himself with the God in him, casting off the fallen selfhood "In Forgiveness of Sins which is Self Annihilation. it is the Covenant of Jehovah" (J, 98:23). Only through this internalized covenant can man live fully in vision. The schizoid experience dramatized by Los and the Spectre disappears in the last magnificent plates of the poem, absorbed into a religious vision that concentrates the whole epic into its final word: "Jerusalem."

Before we have done with it, however, we must investigate the psychological prestige with which Blake endows this vision. The new premium that he places upon forgiveness in his late myth suggests a profound need to be forgiven.[55] We can only speculate why he longs for forgiveness, but as I have tried to suggest, Blake's trial for sedition forced him to resort in his defense to a benign sort of duplicity. In "The Grey Monk," a poem that Erdman identifies as having been written about the time of the indictment, Blake confesses, in the quiet of his notebook, that his prophetic vision is at odds with his worldly responsibilities:

> When God commanded this hand to write
> In the studious hours of deep midnight

> He told me the writing I wrote should prove
> The Bane of all that on Earth I lovd
>
> (489)

Blake deleted this stanza when he transferred the poem to the public arena of *Jerusalem*, where it functions as a lyrical epigraph to chapter 3. It comes as a bit of a surprise to find him so frankly describing the burden of vision and identifying himself with the passive suffering of a martyred monk. But in *Jerusalem* too he retreats from social action into a religious compensation.[56] The emphasis upon forgiveness and the internal dualism of mental fight are both a quietistic answer to public hostility, the fruits of trial and defense.

In another lyric Blake advances a conventionally Christian solution to human suffering:

> Seek Love in the Pity of others Woe
> In the gentle relief of anothers care
> In the darkness of night & the winters snow
> In the naked & outcast Seek Love there
>
> (498)

It would be easy to purge the implied passivity of these lines by referring them to Blake's myth. They would then become the sentiments of Beulah, seductive in their appeal for pity. But this appeal is in the spirit of much in *Jerusalem*. The celebration of forgiveness that runs through the poem, from Blake's request that his readers forgive what they do not approve (plate 3) to his own final forgiveness of Bacon, Newton, and Locke (plate 98), amounts finally to a psychologically serviceable quietism. Blake transforms his own political impotence into spiritual strength in a manner resembling Nietzsche's analysis of the powerless purveyors of *ressentiment*. Although Blake avoids the emptiness of a slave morality in his lasting devotion to the Human Form Divine, his insistence upon the Forgiveness of Sins allows him that psychological comfort characteristic, to quote Nietzsche, of "the weak and oppressed of every kind, the sublime self-deception that interprets weakness as freedom, and their being thus-and-thus as *merit*."[57]

Blake's late myth functions, at least in part, as a psychic defense against the despair that menaces a prophet among the deaf. The madness of the Spectre could easily have been Blake's own, had it not taken a functional form through the therapeutics of his art. Los's great chant acquires a profound psychological urgency when we recognize the therapeutic function of Blake's myth:

> I must Create a System, or be enslav'd by another Mans
> I will not Reason & Compare: my business is to Create
> (J, 10:20-21)

Los labors to master his Spectre, whose "howlings terrify the night" (J, 10:23). By means of his poetry, Blake likewise works to defeat the threat of madness, which persecution makes all the more real. Hence the systematic character of his late myth.

Blake's compensatory recourse to the religion of Jesus shows how necessary it is for the visionary to position himself in a viable cultural context, even at the risk of political quietism. For without such a context, which the Hebrew prophets found in the tradition of Moses, visionary experience has no authority and cannot be distinguished from delusion: even to the visionary! Blake situates his late myth in this context, as much to preserve *his* health as that of his people. His greatness as a poet is a deeply human greatness: the courage to confront that in all men and women most hostile to their full humanity. Blake declares the victory for which we must honor him in the closing vision of *Jerusalem*, which more than justifies his anguished struggle as "the Laborer of Ages in the valley of Despair" (J, 83:53).

Reading Blake, we must remember that his visionary art has its origin in visionary experience, which by contemporary standards would be considered at least potentially pathological. The use Blake made of such experience, turning it toward healthy ends through artistic activity, makes his work of supreme importance to an understanding of the full range of human being. For madness confronts our humanity with a profound challenge. Blake answers this challenge with a myth that defends against the suffering it depicts. "Were it not better," he writes in his last engraved work, "to believe Vision / With all our might & strength tho we are fallen & lost[?]" (271). As an epic poet of the human mind, Blake labors ever to secure its health.

Notes

Introduction

1. See Michel Foucault, *Madness and Civilization*, trans. Richard Howard (New York: Vintage, 1975).
2. For a psychological investigation of this norm from a phenomenological point of view, see the work of Erwin W. Straus, especially *Phenomenological Psychology* (New York: Basic Books, 1966). Much of my thinking derives from Straus's important work.
3. *Blake Records*, ed. G. E. Bentley (Oxford: Clarendon, 1969), 221. The details of my sketch are distilled from the many biographical and historical sources available to students of Blake, especially Alexander Gilchrist, *The Life of William Blake, Pictor Ignotus*, 2 vols. (1863; New York: Phaeton, 1969); Mona Wilson, *The Life of William Blake*, ed. Geoffrey Keynes, 3d ed. (London: Oxford University Press, 1971); Michael Davis, *William Blake: A New Kind of Man* (Berkeley: University of California Press, 1977); and *Blake Records Supplement*, ed. G. E. Bentley, Jr. (Oxford: Clarendon, 1988).
4. Gilchrist, 1:32.
5. For a transcript of Schofield's complaint, see *The Letters of William Blake*, ed. Geoffrey Keynes, 3d ed. (Oxford: Clarendon, 1980), 61-2.
6. See Leopold Damrosch, *Symbol and Truth in Blake's Myth* (Princeton: Princeton University Press, 1980), 144: "It is just this principle of *otherness* that Blake balks at."
7. *The Complete Poetry and Prose of William Blake*, ed. David V. Erdman, newly rev. ed. (Berkeley: University of California Press, 1982), 38. All references to Blake's poetry and prose will be to this edition.
8. Straus for one defines hallucination thus. See his penetrating article, "Phenomenology of Hallucinations," *Phenomenological Psychology*, 277-89.
9. Percy Bysshe Shelley, "A Defence of Poetry," *Shelley's Poetry and Prose*, ed. Donald H. Reiman and Sharon B. Powers (New York: Norton, 1977), 478-508, 503.

Chapter 1

1. Gilchrist, 1:7.
2. It is worth remembering that James Blake, the poet's father, was a hosier by trade.
3. See the accounts G. E. Bentley, Jr., presents in *William Blake: The Critical Heritage* (London: Routledge and Kegan Paul, 1975). Southey met Blake at his exhibition and had this reaction: "You could not have delighted in him—his madness was too evident. It gave his eyes an expression such as you would expect to see in one who was possessed" (41). Lamb never met Blake, but took an interest in his work, dubbing him "the mad Wordsworth" (247). Landor also sensed Blake's affinity with Wordsworth: "he protested that Blake had been Wordsworth's prototype, and wished they could have divided his madness between them; for that some accession of it in the one case, and something of a diminution of it in the other, would very greatly have improved both" (48).
4. Harold Bloom, *Blake's Apocalypse* (1963; Ithaca: Cornell University Press, 1970), 442.
5. Northrop Frye, "The Keys to the Gates," *Romanticism and Consciousness*, ed. Harold Bloom (New York: Norton, 1970), 233. Frye is similarly absolute in *Fearful Symmetry*: "A modern writer on Blake is not required to discuss his sanity, for which I am grateful: I could not do so without being haunted by one of his own epigrams: 'the man who pretends to be a modest inquirer into the truth of a self-evident thing is a knave'" (12). At the risk of sounding knavish, I would only suggest that such statements as Frye's and Bloom's are impediments to modest inquiry conducted without pretense.
6. T. S. Eliot, "William Blake," *Selected Essays* (New York: Harcourt, Brace and World, 1964), 275.
7. S. Foster Damon enumerates these accounts and works hard to purge them of any pathological taint in *William Blake: His Philosophy and Symbols* (Gloucester: Peter Smith, 1958), 196–211.
8. Excerpts from Robinson's diary are quoted from *Blake Records*. This passage occurs on page 311.
9. All these anecdotes were told by people who knew Blake personally: Henry Fuseli, Crabb Robinson, Thomas Phillips, and John Varley, respectively. Fuseli, Phillips, and Varley were all fellow painters, the first two of Royal Academy distinction, the last, one of the early innovative landscape artists. There's also the odd account, mentioned by Thomas Taylor, of Blake's frequent proximity to "the vast and luminous orb of the moon": "I have felt an almost irresistable desire," Blake confessed, "to throw myself into it headlong." See *Blake Records Supplement*, 95.
10. As he did Robinson (*Blake Records*, 547) and his patron Thomas Butts, in a letter (25 April 1803).
11. So reports J. T. Smith, Blake's acquaintance and casual biographer. See *Blake Records*, 459–60.
12. Jean Hagstrum suggests a less fantastic origin for Blake's printing method: it derives apparently from Alexander Browne's *Ars Pictoria*, published in the seventeenth century. See *William Blake: Poet and Painter* (Chicago: University of Chicago Press, 1964), 5. Samuel Palmer, however, took Blake's vision seriously: "Don't think I am laughing: I am not yet shrunk to such inspissated idiotcy as grins at every thing beyond its own tether," *Blake Records Supplement*, 9.

13. For all of the books about Blake whose titles include the words "vision" or "visionary" (I count 9 just from memory), none raises the basic issue of what vision *is* and where it fits in the modern world.
14. *Fearful Symmetry*, 8.
15. Frye's assurance on this point, however, is suspect: "Spirits of all kinds," he writes, "appeared to Blake, but only as unpaid models; they were forced to stand around and pose, open their mouths to display their teeth better, and were not allowed to depart before he had finished with them on any such thin excuse as the necessity of getting away at cockcrow" (78). The truth about Blake's visionary experience is quite otherwise. In sketching the notorious visionary heads for Varley, Blake often quit when his "unpaid model" moved or vanished, as when he left unfinished for some time a portrait of King Saul, or when the spirit of Edward I discourteously stepped in front of that of William Wallace. In his later years, Blake is said to have concluded that, at Felpham, the visions were angry with him.
16. See Morton Paley, *Energy and the Imagination* (Oxford: Clarendon, 1970), 201-6.
17. Critics who take Blake seriously as a visionary are few, but include Mark Schorer, *William Blake: The Politics of Vision* (New York: Henry Holt, 1946), and Leopold Damrosch, *Symbol and Truth in Blake's Myth*. Schorer examines Blake's visionary capacity in a social context and measures its personal cost, for Blake's "temperamental dilemma" was "to synthesize a visionary and a social experience of life" (392). Damrosch interprets Blake's visionary experience with the help of diverse theories of perception and symbol and stresses "the immediacy with which he perceived his visions.... Blake's visions were actual experiences" (47, 49). Damrosch leaves unanswered, however, the question of the psychological and social status of vision in the modern world.
18. On the status of vision in the Middle Ages, see Barbara Nolan, *The Gothic Visionary Perspective* (Princeton: Princeton University Press, 1977).
19. Harold Bloom, *The Visionary Company* (1961; Ithaca: Cornell University Press, 1971), 19.
20. Gilchrist, 1:369.
21. *Boswell's Life of Johnson*, ed. G. B. Hill, revised L. F. Powell, 6 vols. (Oxford: Oxford University Press, 1934-50), 1:397.
22. See Foucault, *Madness and Civilization*, xii.
23. It is interesting to note that Smart came to inhabit both of these institutions. After release from confinement in the madhouse, he became more and more destitute, until he was arrested for debt and put in prison, where he died.
24. Alexander Pope, *Selected Poetry of Alexander Pope*, ed. Aubrey Williams (Boston: Houghton Mifflin, 1969), 308, ll. 29, 34-5.
25. Keynes includes this letter in his edition of Blake's, 118. The italics are Hayley's.
26. Northrop Frye, "Toward Defining an Age of Sensibility," *English Literary History*, 22 (1955): 144-152.
27. See Max Byrd, *Visits to Bedlam* (Columbia: University of South Carolina Press, 1974).
28. *The Critical Heritage*, 66.
29. The Parisian *Revue Britannique* even published an account (July, 1833) of a meeting with the incarcerated Blake, "surnommé le Voyannt." For a full transcription of this strange piece, see Mona Wilson, 384-85. Thomas J. J. Altizer sums up the point nicely: "any visionary must live and create in a world of Vision, a world that must appear to

be madness to the rational mind," *The New Apocalypse: The Radical Christian Vision of William Blake* (Michigan State University Press, 1967), 33.
30. For an illuminating discussion of the way myth makes a symbolic language meaningful by organizing it, see Damrosch, "Symbolic Seeing," 38–44.
31. W. B. Yeats, "William Blake and his Illustrations to the *Divine Comedy*," *Essays and Introductions* (New York: Macmillan, 1961), 116–45, 128.
32. Yeats, "Introduction," *Essays and Introductions*, x.
33. Johann Wolfgang von Goethe, *Faust*, trans. Alice Raphael (New York: Holt, Rinehart and Winston, 1955), I.ii.306–11.
34. On Los and his function in Blake's myth, see Frye, 251–54.
35. See, for instance, Frye, 77.
36. Frye, "Sensibility," 151.
37. Friedrich Nietzsche, "Ecce Homo," *On the Genealogy of Morals and Ecce Homo*, trans. Walter Kaufman (New York: Vintage, 1967), 300.
38. Nietzsche, "The Birth of Tragedy," *The Birth of Tragedy and The Case of Wagner*, trans. Walter Kaufman (New York: Vintage, 1967), 37.
39. Bloom, *Apocalypse*, 17.
40. It is worth comparing Kierkegaard's vision of the psychogenesis of the self with Blake's. *The Sickness Unto Death* throws much light on Blake's later prophecies.
41. Others have made this observation, but gone no further. See, for example, R. D. Laing, *The Divided Self* (Middlesex: Penguin, 1969), 162. Laing's discussion of schizophrenia, though compassionate, remains limited by his own strange blend of existentialism and clinical relativism. For a comprehensive summary of Blake's "anticipations" of modern psychology, see Jerry Caris Godard, *Mental Forms Creating: William Blake Anticipates Freud, Jung, and Rank* (Lanham, MD: University Press of America, 1985).
42. I quote here from the second edition of the *Diagnostic and Statistical Manual* (Washington, DC: American Psychiatric Association, 1968), 33, because it provides a clearer general description of schizophrenia than the more recent third edition.
43. See for instance Irving S. Gottesmann, *Schizophrenia: The Epigenetic Puzzle* (Cambridge: Cambridge University Press, 1980); John M. Neale and Thomas F. Oltmanns, *Schizophrenia* (New York: John Wiley, 1980); Theodore Lidz, *The Origin and Treatment of Schizophrenic Disorders* (New York: Basic Books, 1973); Sigmund Freud, "The Case of Schreber," *The Complete Psychological Works of Sigmund Freud*, trans. James Strachey (London: Hogarth, 1958), 12:3–82, and "On Narcissism," 14:67–103; Julian Jaynes, *The Origins of Consciousness in the Breakdown of the Bicameral Mind* (Boston: Houghton Mifflin, 1976), especially Book III, "Vestiges of the Bicameral Mind in the Modern World." The most convincing and coherent explanation of schizophrenia's etiology is called the "diathesis-stressor" theory and unites a genetic predisposition with environmental influences to account for development of the disease. A genetic predisposition must be activated by situations that induce stress, thereby altering the chemical balance of the brain in such a way as to promote the development of schizophrenia.
44. Eugene Bleuler, *Dementia Praecox, or the Group of Schizophrenias*, trans. Joseph Zinkin (New York: International Universities Press, 1952), 8. See also the other classic investigation of the disease, Emil Kraeplin, *Dementia Praecox*, trans. R. Mary Barclay (1919; New York: Krieger, 1971).
45. Schorer approaches this position when he admits the strain of Blake's prophetic

vocation: "Certainly his mind was not deranged, yet finally his sensibilities were. They were deranged in a curious way by the violence of his own unchallenged response to the leading ideas of his time" (49).
46. Cf. Schorer's comment: Blake " 'used' his art now in the way that all poets who attempt to substitute it for religion do 'use' it, for solace and purgation, in an interchange as direct as the confessional" (346). The neurologist Oliver Sacks is one of the few writers actually to study the effects of mental suffering upon creativity: "there is often a struggle, and sometimes, more interestingly, a collusion between the powers of pathology and creation." See his delightful collection of clinical tales, *The Man Who Mistook His Wife for a Hat* (New York: Summit, 1985), 16.

Chapter 2

1. The details of this paragraph and the next are distilled from Erdman's *Prophet against Empire*, 3d. ed. (Princeton: Princeton University Press, 1977), 3–29. See also Jacob Bronowski, *William Blake in the Age of Revolution* (New York: Harper and Row, 1964).
2. Frye has shown how the divine order of Christian tradition becomes a human one in Romantic tradition. See *A Study of English Romanticism* (1968; Chicago: University of Chicago Press, 1982), 14. Along similar lines, Owen Barfield argues that Romanticism internalizes the inspiring godhead through its concept of the imagination. See "The Psychology of Inspiration and Imagination," *Speaker's Meaning* (Middleton: Wesleyan University Press, 1967), 68–91.
3. Frye emphasizes the "imaginative animism" of the Age of Sensibility, which is characterized by "treating everything in nature as though it had human feelings or qualities" and which includes a "curiously intense awareness of the animal world." See "Toward Defining an Age of Sensibility," 150.
4. A. E. Housman, *The Name and Nature of Poetry* (New York: Macmillan, 1933), 37.
5. Housman, 37. See Plato, "Phaedrus," *Phaedrus and Letters VII and VIII*, trans. Walter Hamilton (Middlesex: Penguin, 1973), especially "Socrates' Second Speech: Types of Divine Madness," 46–49. For a sweeping survey of madness as a literary theme, see Lillian Feder, *Madness in Literature* (Princeton: Princeton University Press, 1980).
6. For details of these afflictions, see the Oxford edition introductions to the poetry of Collins, Smart, and Cowper. Collins was clearly a depressive, and a severe enough case to warrant the label "mad" in his day. Cowper and Smart both required care, Cowper by friends and Smart by an asylum. See Max Byrd, *Visits to Bedlam*.
7. William Collins, "Ode on the Poetical Character," *Thomas Gray and William Collins*, ed. Roger Lonsdale (Oxford: Oxford University Press, 1977), 144, ll. 39–40.
8. William Cowper, "Lines Written during a Period of Insanity," *Cowper: Poetical Works*, ed. H. S. Milford (London: Oxford University Press, 1977), 298–90, ll. 17–20. See also Cowper's haunting autobiographical *Memoir* (New York: Taylor and Gould, 1835).
9. So Morton D. Paley relates in *The Continuing City: William Blake's Jerusalem* (Oxford: Clarendon, 1983), 47. Apparently Hayley hoped to gain some insight into Cowper's insanity by studying the poem that Smart wrote when mad.
10. Christopher Smart, "A Song to David," *The Poetical Works of Christopher Smart*, ed. Karina Williamson, 2 vols. (Oxford: Clarendon, 1980), 2:127–47, ll. 103–5.

11. A working definition of madness in psychoanalysis is the usurpation of conscious functions by the unconscious. Smart would fit such a definition.
12. Wallace Stevens, "The Figure of the Youth as Virile Poet," *The Necessary Angel* (New York: Vintage, 1951), 52.
13. For a suggestive discussion of Blake's relation to other sensibility bards and the "progress of poetry" motif, see Geoffrey Hartman, "Blake and the 'Progress of Poetry'," *Essays for S. Foster Damon,* ed. Alvin H. Rosenfeld (Providence: Brown University Press, 1969), 57–68.
14. Algernon Swinburne describes Blake's lyricism as "an inexhaustible, equable gift ... the lyric faculty had gained and kept a preponderance over all others visible in every scrap of his work," *William Blake* (1868; New York: Benjamin Bloom, 1967), 132, 188. Mark Schorer argues for the hardening of this gift in *The Politics of Vision.*
15. Percy Bysshe Shelley, "A Defence of Poetry," *Shelley's Poetry and Prose,* 480–508, 505–6.
16. Nietzsche, *Birth of Tragedy,* 48.
17. The best discussion of the importance of perspective in Blake's *Songs* is Robert Gleckner's essay, "Point of View and Context in Blake's Songs," *Bulletin of the New York Public Library,* 11 (1957): 531–38.
18. In this he anticipates Browning and other practitioners of the dramatic monologue. For the relation between dramatic and lyric elements in post-enlightenment poetry, see *The Poetry of Experience* by Robert Langbaum (New York: Norton, 1957), especially chapter 6 and the conclusion, 182–235. See also David Wagenknecht's discussion of the poem "Spring" in *Blake's Night: William Blake and the Idea of Pastoral* (Cambridge: Harvard University Press, 1973), 24–25. Wagenknecht notes the emergence of a dramatic quality from the poem's lyrical opening.
19. See Nietzsche, 49–50.
20. See Robert Gleckner, *Blake's Prelude* (Baltimore: Johns Hopkins University Press, 1982). Gleckner reviews these theories in his introduction, 1–15. His own theory of an antithetical structure is interesting for what it tells us of early experimentation in dialectic, but does little to illuminate either the poetry or the psychological problems it undertakes to solve.
21. For a perceptive discussion of the role of perception in Blake's poems, see Thomas Frosch, *The Awakening of Albion* (Ithaca: Cornell University Press, 1974), esp. 103–35.
22. J. T. Smith, whose memory on such matters is admittedly suspect, reports hearing Blake sing his poems to exquisite melodies of his own composing at the home of Mrs. Mathews, where Blake and other young artists gathered for amusement. See *Blake Records,* 457. Recent corroboration of Blake's musical talents has surfaced in the letters of Edward Garrard Marsh, a friend of Hayley's. See *Blake Records Supplement,* 17–20.
23. Nietzsche, 64.
24. *Blake Records,* 517. Blake made this claim to the ubiquitous Crabb Robinson.
25. Leopold Damrosch makes a running comparison of Blake and Hegel on this point throughout *Symbol and Truth in Blake's Myth,* as does Thomas J. J. Altizer in *The New Apocalypse.* See also David Punter, *Blake, Hegel, and Dialectic* (Amsterdam: Rodopi, 1982).
26. As does Harold Bloom in *Blake's Apocalypse.*
27. As Schorer remarks, "Myth is fundamental, the dramatic representation of our deepest instinctual life" (36).
28. Bloom argues similarly in "The Internalization of the Quest Romance": "It is within

the ego itself that the quest must turn, to engage the antagonist proper, and to clarify the imaginative component in the ego by its strife of contraries with its dark brother." Bloom errs, it seems to me, in locating the imagination *wholly within* the ego. This mistake significantly tames Blake's project—and the danger that attends it—which seeks human order that transcends the ego. For Bloom's argument, see *Romanticism and Consciousness*, ed. Harold Bloom (New York: Norton, 1970), 3–24.

29. Damrosch is skeptical of Blake's attempt to transcend the ego: "it is just this principle of *otherness* that Blake balks at. What he seems to want—whether it is symbolized in Albion or in Jesus the divine body—is a whole whose parts are not parts, in which individuality can be preserved without concession to otherness" (144). Damrosch fails to consider fully the implications of the dissolution of the ego in Blake's psychology.
30. For Freud psychosis results when unconscious excitations gain control of conscious functions that guide speech and action. See "The Interpretation of Dreams," *Standard Edition*, 5:567–68.
31. For a description of this phenomenon, see Erwin Straus, "Phenomenology of Hallucination," *Phenomenological Psychology*.
32. There are many biographical accounts of schizophrenic breakdown, but the most faithful and sympathetic is Susan Sheehan, *Is There No Place on Earth for Me?* (Boston: Houghton Mifflin, 1982). See also Eugene Bleuler's careful observations in *Dementia Praecox, or the Group of Schizophrenias* and the section entitled "Diagnosis" in John M. Neale and Thomas F. Oltmanns, *Schizophrenia*, 21–38.
33. Cf. Bloom's comment: "Schizophrenia is bad poetry," *Anxiety of Influence* (London: Oxford University Press, 1973), 95.
34. R. D. Laing is the foremost of these, arguing that schizophrenia is a journey through that "inner world" that includes the whole experience of mankind. See *The Politics of Experience* (New York: Vintage, 1976), 126.
35. See Foucault's *Madness and Civilization* and Laing's *The Politics of Experience*.
36. Laing, 67.
37. For a discussion of Blake's use of the Persephone myth throughout his poetry, see Kathleen Raine, *Blake and Tradition* (London: Routledge and Kegan Paul, 1979), 33–50.
38. See Freud, "On the Universal Tendency to Debasement in the Sphere of Love," *Standard Edition*, 11:177–89.

Chapter 3

1. See David V. Erdman, *Blake: Prophet against Empire*, 130–38.
2. Quoted in Manfred Guttmacher, *America's Last King* (New York: Scribner's, 1941), 199.
3. Guttmacher, 200. In its context, an interesting allusion to *King Lear*.
4. Quoted in Ida Macalpine and Richard Hunter, *George III and the Mad Business* (New York: Pantheon, 1969), 68.
5. See Guttmacher, 227, 231.
6. Quoted in Macalpine and Hunter, 29.
7. Percy Bysshe Shelley, "England in 1819," *Shelley's Poetry and Prose*, 311. Byron, in his inimitable way, called King George "the raving bedlam bigot." Although the origin of

the King's madness is still debated, many investigators believe it to have been caused by severe porphyria, an inherited metabolic disorder characterized by a debilitating buildup of porphyrins that causes symptoms typical of psychosis.

8. Damrosch's attitude is representative: "It would be hard to prove that, apart from incidental allusions, Shakespeare makes any significant contribution to the great myth," *Symbol and Truth,* 367 n. Damrosch and critics like him overlook the possibility that Shakespeare's contribution may have been negative.

9. Frye notes that *King Lear* and *Macbeth,* "especially the former, have left their mark on Blake's symbolism" (300). John Beer, in *Blake's Visionary Universe* (New York: Barnes and Noble, 1969), devotes an appendix to Blake's interpretation of Shakespeare (313–35). Beer notes many interesting parallels between specific passages in Shakespeare's plays and Blake's myth; regarding *King Lear,* see 319–26. His analysis suffers, however, from an easy revision of Shakespeare that translates themes and characters into Blakean ideas and symbols.

10. It is interesting to note that Blake alludes to *King Lear* in one of his last letters (12 April 1827, to Cumberland): "God keep me," he writes, "from the Divinity of Yes and No too" (*Letters,* 168). Shakespeare's play clearly had a firm hold over his imagination.

11. Aristotle, *The Poetics,* trans. S. H. Butcher (New York: Dover, 1951), 53. See also D. F. H. Kitto, *Greek Tragedy* (1936; London: Methuen, 1966).

12. In this Hegel concurs when he defines one sort of tragedy as "the collision of powers and individuals equally entitled to the ethical claim." Hegel emphasizes the contradictions that a strict adherence to the moral order can breed. Even so, that order is larger than humanity and ultimately limiting. See *Hegel on Tragedy,* ed. Anne and Henry Paolucci (Westport: Greenwood, 1978), 62–96, 68.

13. William Shakespeare, "King Lear," *The Riverside Shakespeare,* ed. G. Blackmore Evans et al. (Boston: Houghton Mifflin, 1974), IV.vi.100–105. All quotations refer by act, scene, and line to this edition.

14. Others have noticed Blake's allusions to *King Lear* in *Tiriel.* Jonathan Bate catalogues them in *Shakespeare and the Romantic Imagination* (Oxford: Clarendon, 1986), 135.

15. I am not arguing that Blake is a greater poet than Shakespeare, solving problems that the latter does not, rather that he sidesteps the strength of Shakespeare's tragic sense by inventing a mythological explanation for it. This strategy is at least in part an act of evasion.

16. See William F. Halloran, "Blake's *Tiriel:* Snakes, Curses, and a Blessing," *South Atlantic Quarterly,* 70 (1971): 161–79; Stephen C. Behrendt, "'The Worst Disease': Blake's *Tiriel,*" *Colby Library Quarterly,* 15 (1979): 175–87. Frye comes closer to the true effect of *Tiriel* by calling it a "tragedy of reason," *Fearful Symmetry,* 242.

17. These are the views respectively of Frye, 242; Bloom, *Blake's Apocalypse,* 31; Mark Schorer, *The Politics of Vision,* 197; and Erdman, 131. Bloom remarks that "In the mythic background of the poem *Tiriel* are the stories of Shakespeare's King Lear and Lear's friend Gloucester" (30). Schorer calls Tiriel "a kind of Lear reduced to his barest psychological essence" (195). Of related interest is the analysis of Blake's illustrations for the poem in *Tiriel,* ed. G. E. Bentley, Jr. (Oxford: Clarendon, 1967), 1–55.

18. For a full examination of the similarities and differences between Blake and Freud, see Diana Hume George, *Blake and Freud* (Ithaca: Cornell University Press, 1980). As George remarks, for Freud "psychic determinism is itself a category of natural determinism" (85). For Blake just the opposite is true, at least ideally. The problem

with approaching Blake from a Freudian perspective is that Freud's natural determinism falsifies the more radically psychological assumptions of Blake's mythology. George fails to remind her readers that to reduce Blake's myth to nature is to betray its whole program for mental healing.

19. As Bate remarks, "Blake, whose visionary imagination is fundamentally optimistic, often resists the tragic in his approaches to Shakespeare" (135).
20. Georges Bataille, *Literature and Evil*, trans. Alastair Hamilton (New York: Marion Boyars, 1985), 85.
21. Paul Ricoeur, *The Symbolism of Evil*, trans. Emerson Buchanan (Boston: Beacon, 1969), 237.
22. See Paul Cantor's thoroughgoing discussion of the poem in *Creature and Creator* (Cambridge: Cambridge University Press, 1983), 55–74.
23. Bloom, 164.
24. For a complete discussion of this strategy, see Bloom's *Map of Misreading* (New York: Oxford University Press, 1971), section 1, "Charting the Territory."
25. Leslie Tannenbaum, *Biblical Tradition in Blake's Early Prophecies* (Princeton: Princeton University Press, 1982), 222.
26. Søren Kierkegaard, *Fear and Trembling*, trans. Walter Lowry (Princeton: Princeton University Press, 1946), 38.
27. Kayla Bernheim and Richard Lewine maintain that schizophrenia is characterized primarily by these two divisions in the personality: self and reality, thought and feeling. For a full description, see their *Schizophrenia: Symptoms, Causes, Treatments* (New York: Norton, 1979), 9.
28. Bloom, commentary in *The Poetry and Prose of William Blake*, ed. David V. Erdman, 906.
29. See Frye, 254–59; Bloom, 164–75; Schorer, 232–35; Cantor, 29–54; Tannenbaum, 201–24; Clark Emery, "Introduction," *The Book of Urizen*, ed. Clark Emery (Miami: University of Miami Press, 1966), 1–47.
30. S. Foster Damon, *A Blake Dictionary* (1965; New York: Dutton, 1971), 419.
31. Tannenbaum, 204.
32. Morton Paley interprets *The Book of Urizen* as a history of the individual mind, the *principium individuationis* that supersedes the infant's oceanic consciousness. See *Energy and Imagination*, 67.
33. Bloom, commentary, 906.
34. For an intelligent description of this process, see Hazard Adams, "Blake, *Jerusalem*, and Symbolic Form," *Blake Studies*, 7 (1975): 143–65. Adams was the first to describe the dynamic of Blake's myth as a "dissociation of sensibility." As he points out, this dissociation is identical with the Fall.
35. For a general discussion of the problem that self-consciousness poses for Romantic thinkers, see Geoffrey Hartman, "Romanticism and 'Anti-Self-Consciousness,' " in *Romanticism and Consciousness*, 46–56.
36. Cantor, 38.
37. Tannenbaum, 204; Cantor, 45; Bloom, 170.
38. Cantor, 46.
39. R. D. Laing, *The Divided Self* (Middlesex: Penguin, 1965), 94–105.
40. Cf. Aristotle: "For the plot ought to be so constructed that even without the aid of the

eye, he who hears the tale told will thrill with horror and melt to pity at what takes place" (*Poetics,* 49).
41. Bloom, 175. For a discussion of Blake's relation to Urizen that focuses upon changes in his mythic role, see John Sutherland, "Blake and Urizen," *Blake's Visionary Forms Dramatic,* ed. David V. Erdman and John E. Grant (Princeton: Princeton University Press, 1970), 244–62.
42. Damrosch concurs: "There is surely a strong element of compensatory fantasy in the myth" (*Symbol and Truth,* 308). Freud argues that the delusional systems of paranoid schizophrenics are therapeutic insofar as they begin to reorient the patient toward reality. See "The Case of Schreber," *Standard Edition,* 12:9–82, 71.
43. Andrew Cooper also senses the therapeutic function of Blake's myth: "Blake's mythology is a compensation." See "Blake's Escape from Mythology: Self-Mastery in *Milton,*" *Doubt and Identity in Romantic Poetry* (New Haven: Yale University Press, 1988), 54–76. The problem with Cooper's generally astute analysis is that, in good Freudian style, it treats Blake's myth as a neurotic symptom of hidden anxieties. Far from being something to escape from, however, that myth is Blake's *means* of treatment, a defense against dissociation, not a projection of buried tensions. Cooper falls into the Freudian trap of reducing psychological phenomena to naturalistic antecedents. Blake's ultimate aim is not so much self-mastery as, to use his own term, self-annihilation.
44. Foucault, *Madness and Civilization,* 287.

Chapter 4

1. My use of the term "schizophrenia" is primarily descriptive, not clinically reductive, since the symptomology of madness varies with time and method of treatment. I take schizophrenia to be our best contemporary description of the phenomenon of madness.
2. *Blake Records,* 52.
3. Bloom maintains that in a limited sense Blake nearly went "mad" during his stay at Felpham with Hayley. See *Blake's Apocalypse,* 315.
4. In their full-length study of the poem, *Blake's Four Zoas: The Design of a Dream* (Cambridge: Harvard University Press, 1978), Brian Wilkie and Mary Lynn Johnson argue that "the entire poem reflects the universal, less strictly clinical, psychosis of mankind" (76).
5. Wilkie and Johnson note the public therapy of Blake's poem, but miss its private uses. They consider the epic "a mode of therapeutic public statement.... Man's spiritual sickness is treated by therapeutic art" (4, 166).
6. Frye set the precedent for this approach. See *Fearful Symmetry,* 269–309. See also Harold Bloom, *Blake's Apocalypse,* 189–284; Wilkie and Johnson, *Blake's Four Zoas.*
7. Donald Ault argues similarly in his monumental analysis of this monumental poem. See *Narrative Unbound: Re-visioning The Four Zoas* (Barrytown: Station Hill, 1987). Ault shows Blake working to free narrative from its traditional mimetic assumptions so that it can become a relational process that revises itself during the act of reading. Although Ault leaves very little room for serious consideration of the therapeutic uses to which Blake put his myth, he does isolate "narrative structures ... that could

function therapeutically to rehabilitate imaginations damaged by 'Single vision' " (3). Ault's emphasis upon Newton and "Newtonian narrative" throughout his argument is slightly anachronistic, since Blake never mentions Newton in *The Four Zoas.*

8. For an exhaustive study of *The Four Zoas* as a document of cultural and social history, see Jackie DiSalvo, *War of Titans* (Pittsburgh: University of Pittsburgh Press, 1983). DiSalvo describes the poem as containing "the entire social, cultural, and psychological history of the human race from its dim origins, recorded in ancient myth, to its present struggles and future possibilities" (14). This is a big claim, ultimately too big even for a poem as good and as big as *The Four Zoas* to live up to. DiSalvo runs into trouble when trying to argue that the poem renders cultural history literally. In fact, it examines the psychological assumptions of a variety of historical outlooks.

9. G. E. Bentley, Jr., notes that Blake's first allusion to the "four beasts" of Revelation, the Zoas (the anglicized plural is Blake's) comes in a letter to Ozias Humphrey written in 1808 and describing the design for *Vision of the Last Judgment.* See Bentley's facsimile edition, *Vala or The Four Zoas* (Oxford: Clarendon, 1963). Bentley dates the title-page revisions at 1807. By far the best facsimile of Blake's poem is the one recently edited by Cettina Tramontano Magno and David V. Erdman, *The Four Zoas by William Blake* (Lewisburg: Bucknell University Press, 1987); it is an indispensable tool for the serious study of Blake's greatest work.

10. Wilkie and Johnson note that Blake's method "has some affinity with dream narrative" (3). Their own practice militates against this assertion, however, as they pursue parallels and variations that no dream would produce spontaneously. In fact, because it is part of Blake's aim to show that what we take for waking consciousness is a collective nightmare, he depends less upon "dream logic" than the deluded logic of the unbalanced mind.

11. *William Blake's Vala,* ed. H. M. Margoliouth (Oxford: Clarendon, 1956). It should be noted that Margoliouth's reconstructed text is highly conjectural.

12. For a thorough discussion of this "romantic classicism" and Blake's endorsement of it, see Anne K. Mellor, *Blake's Human Form Divine* (Berkeley: University of California Press, 1974), 102-64. The idea that Blake, later a hater of the classics, ever espoused an admiration for classical beauty comes as a bit of a surprise. But as Mellor points out, his emphasis upon outline derives ultimately from the romantic classicism of Flaxman and Fuseli.

13. Margoliouth, 46.

14. See David V. Erdman, *Prophet against Empire:* "Blake did not shatter, he merely hid his heroic trumpet" (293).

15. Blake faced the same dilemma and sought the same solution in 1791, when he withheld publication of *The French Revolution,* even though Book I had been set in type.

16. Mark Schorer, *The Politics of Vision,* 165.

17. See Erdman, 301-2. It is interesting to note that Wordsworth too wrote—then withheld—a reply to the Bishop of Llandaff. What failure of nerve allows these poets of revolution to balk at taking a public stance?

18. Cf. Erdman's bewildered remark: "What sort of strategy can Blake's be that makes peace a prerequisite to the circulation of pleas for peace?" (302).

19. Erdman argues with some merit that the revisions of *The Four Zoas* were inspired by the fickle winds of war: "Never was a poem so bewilderingly attached to the shifting

fortunes of principalities and powers" (294). As Blake's invocation makes amply clear, however, those principalities and powers were *within*. His poem charts the fortunes of a highly personal psychological warfare.
20. See Leslie Brisman, *Romantic Origins* (Ithaca: Cornell University Press, 1978): "a story about origins becomes a story about original stories about origins—a story about originality" (255). This is an important point, but Blake has a greater confidence in origins—even of the divine—than Brisman suggests. See also Paul Cantor, *Creature and Creator*, 69–74.
21. Wilkie and Johnson characterize Tharmas as "the personality's unconscious knowledge of its own intactness" (20). See too Frye's fine discussion of the Zoas and their functions, *Fearful Symmetry*, 274.
22. His letters attest to the huge psychological swings from depression to exuberance that Blake experienced. It is worth remembering that Hayley, although a biased observer, wrote that Blake *"often appeared to me on the verge of insanity"* (*Letters*, 118), Hayley's italics.
23. As Brisman notes, the orthodox genealogical pattern of God-Satan-Man is internalized, becoming Man-Satan-God; in Blake's myth the human antedates the divine, not vice versa (251).
24. Bloom describes Albion with unsurpassable acumen: "Albion in his original form is a greater Adam, a man who contained all of reality within himself, and who is therefore human *and* divine, male *and* female, a fourfold balance of the faculties of intellect, imagination, emotion and instinct" (190). The fall scatters this original unity, as Leonard Deen notes when he argues that Blake's mature prophecies "imply a disintegrated community reflected in the parts of a single figure." See *Conversing in Paradise: Poetic Genius and Identity-As-Community in Blake's Los* (Columbia: University of Missouri Press, 1983), 1–20.
25. Søren Kierkegaard, *The Concept of Anxiety*, trans. Reidar Thompte with Albert B. Anderson (Princeton: Princeton University Press, 1980), 28.
26. See Wilkie and Johnson, 4; Frye, 274–78; Bloom, 190–91. Erdman takes a slightly different tack, closer to my own. Faced with the oppressions of Pitt's England, Blake separates the poet and the worker within him into Los and Urthona respectively. "His expedient is a split personality" (305). Erdman does not, however, pursue this illuminating idea very far.
27. Cf. Damrosch: "The Zoas are not faculties, and certainly not discrete beings; they are an ever shifting system of relationships within the self," *Symbol and Truth*, 128.
28. I have in mind here an understanding of identity similar to that presented in *Anti-Oedipus* by Giles Deleuze and Felix Guattari, trans. Robert Hurley, Mark Seem, and Helen R. Lane (New York: Viking, 1977). Like Blake, Deleuze and Guattari challenge our assumptions (which psychoanalysis has sanctified) about the integrity of the ego: "it is certain that neither men nor women are clearly defined personalities but rather vibrations, flows, schizzes, and 'knots.' The ego refers to personological co-ordinates from which it results, ... for everyone is a little group (*un groupuscule*) and must live as such" (362).
29. Although the psychological phenomenon of "multiple personalities" can be explained as the product of hysteria, Blake's myth, in its subtlety and sophistication, more closely resembles the severer disturbance of schizophrenia. Albion suffers not merely the proliferation of multiple personalities, but an extreme psychological depersonal-

ization (Blake calls it "death") that manifests itself as a withdrawal from reality accompanied by the dissociation of thought and feeling. His "dreams" are not temporary and intermittent trances but pathological hallucinations that presuppose a total usurpation of the outer world by the inner.

30. Contemporary criteria for diagnosing schizophrenia are too complex to be much use for literary analysis, though I believe Albion's symptoms would conform with them as well as with Bleuler's descriptions. See the *Diagnostic and Statistical Manual*, 3d edition, 181-94. The other great observer of schizophrenia besides Bleuler is Emil Kraeplin, whose *Dementia Praecox* (not to be confused with Bleuler's work of a similar title) details the affliction and its course with impressive completeness. The difference between Bleuler and Kraeplin concerns primarily prognosis: Bleuler holds out some hope for recovery, while Kraeplin, perhaps the more realistic observer, concedes almost universal decline into dementia, a grim prediction that neuroleptics have done much to alleviate. I have chosen to use Bleuler's standards and descriptions for their simplicity and compassion.
31. Eugene Bleuler, *Dementia Praecox, or the Group of Schizophrenias*, 460.
32. Most of today's clinicians have dismissed association disturbance as a major symptom of schizophrenia, believing that it belongs to an outdated understanding of how the mind works. I include it here simply to be true to Bleuler's standards.
33. E. D. Hirsch, Jr., *Innocence and Experience* (1964; Chicago: University of Chicago Press, 1975), vii.
34. Deleuze and Guattari again provide a parallel: "if schizophrenia is the universal, then the great artist is indeed the one who scales the schizophrenic walls and reaches the land of the unknown, he who no longer belongs to any time, any milieu, any school" (69).
35. Andrew Cooper takes a similar view, though for him Blake's myth masks a deeper anxiety. As I understand it, that myth is not something to escape from but to maintain, for it becomes a defense against the madness it dramatizes. See chapter 1 of Cooper's *Doubt and Identity in Romantic Poetry*.
36. See Paul Cantor, *Creature and Creator:* in the hands of the Zoas, myth becomes "a means of self-justification" (70).
37. In another context, Randel Helms compares Blake's prophetic ambitions with the symptomology of paranoid schizophrenia. See his "Blake at Felpham: a Study in the Psychology of Vision," *Literature and Psychology*, 22 (1970): 57-66.
38. Jean Hagstrum makes the shrewd observation that through Luvah's twisted reasoning Blake is confessing his own abuse of intellect in his impassioned naturalism of the early '90s. See "Babylon Revisited or the Story of Luvah and Vala," *Blake's Sublime Allegory*, ed. Stuart Curran and Joseph Anthony Wittreich, Jr. (Madison: University of Wisconsin Press, 1973), 101-18.
39. For a survey of the various accounts of the fall in the poem—fourteen in all!—see Wilkie and Johnson, 239-54.
40. Damrosch characterizes the emanation as the feminine aspect of the androgynous self, *Symbol and Truth*, 181. Cantor discusses the mechanism of projection that splits the psyche into hard and soft passions, *Creature and Creator*, 49-51. Wilkie and Johnson emphasize the narcissism that impels this dynamic, *Blake's Four Zoas*, 155. For an illuminating discussion of the development of the emanations during the course of

the poem, see Judith Lee, "Ways of Their Own: the Emanations of Blake's *Vala,*" *ELH* 50 (1983): 131-53.
41. See John Grant's investigation of Blake's preliminary sketches, "Visions in *Vala:* A Consideration of Some Pictures in the Manuscript," *Blake's Sublime Allegory,* 141-202, as well as the even clearer photographic reproductions in Magno and Erdman's facsimile of *The Four Zoas.* Infrared photography has revealed the pornographic character of many of these sketches. In one section of the poem, pages 38-42, Blake appears to have depicted scenes of oral and anal intercourse as well as sexual acts involving children.
42. As Damrosch remarks, independent will in the Zoas "is the expression of the insane desires of the fallen selfhood," *Symbol and Truth,* 135. Scattered individualities must will as one Man, Albion, to overcome this debilitating self-assertion.
43. Kierkegaard, *The Sickness unto Death,* 148.
44. R. D. Laing maintains that "schizophrenia cannot be understood without understanding despair" and alludes to *The Sickness unto Death* as one of the principal investigations of this condition. See *The Divided Self,* 38 n, 83 n.
45. Enion's existence "on the margin of Non-Entity" uncannily evokes more contemporary descriptions of modern marginality, our empty subsistence, in Heidegger's phrase, "on the fringe of being."
46. On the function of Los and Enitharmon in *The Four Zoas,* see Frye, *Fearful Symmetry,* 291-99; Wilkie and Johnson, *Blake's Four Zoas,* 34-35, 58-60; Paley, *Energy and Imagination,* 99-102; Deen, 123-165.
47. On the effects of schizophrenia upon sexuality, see Bleuler, 408-28.
48. See Frye's general discussion of the literature of this age, *Fearful Symmetry,* 161-77, as well as Cantor, *Creature and Creator,* 44-45.
49. Damrosch is best on the dubiousness of Los's creative undertaking: "Los's creative activity is significant for its fallenness" (317). See *Symbol and Truth,* "Blake and Los," 302-48.
50. *Blake Records,* 526 n.
51. We will have more to say about the Spectre in the next chapter. On his function in Blake's myth, see Frye, *Fearful Symmetry,* 292-93; Bloom, *Blake's Apocalypse,* 243-45; Wilkie and Johnson, *Blake's Four Zoas,* 90.
52. Freud examines this dynamic in "On Narcissism," his own exploration of the psychopathology of schizophrenia. Unlike Freud, Blake works to pass beyond narcissism to the reciprocal passion of universal brotherhood.
53. On the issue of Blake's conversion, see Hirsch, *Innocence and Experience,* 106-48; Jean Hagstrum, " 'The Wrath of the Lamb': A Study of William Blake's Conversions," *From Sensibility to Romanticism,* ed. Harold Bloom and Frederick Hilles (New York: Oxford University Press, 1965), 311-70; Paley, *Energy and Imagination,* 192-93; Mellor, *Blake's Human Form Divine,* 198; Altizer, *The New Apocalypse,* 34; Deen, 78.
54. See G. E. Bentley's thorough discussion of the history of *The Four Zoas* in his *Blake Books* (Oxford: Clarendon, 1977), 454-62.
55. I do not mean to suggest that religious conversion can be a cure for schizophrenia, just that, for a visionary personality like Blake's, such a conversion can provide context in which to situate and meaningfully interpret a potentially pathological mentality. Blake imposes this personal remedy on the more profound aberration dramatized in his myth.
56. William James, *The Varieties of Religious Experience* (Middlesex: Penguin, 1982), 196.

57. Damrosch describes Blake's renewed religious passion as an "allegiance to Christianity that is felt as a return from apostasy" (246).
58. As Diana Hume George remarks, "Christianity is the unifying principle of Blake's psychic mythology. In Christianity Blake saw the only possible vehicle for unification of mankind," *Blake and Freud*, 171. I would only add that Blake arrived at this position only after intense psychological struggle.

Chapter 5

1. See *Blake Records*, 122–49, and *Blake Records Supplement*, 24–28, for a factual account of the incident and ensuing trial. See too Mona Wilson, *The Life of William Blake*, 171–78; Alexander Gilchrist, *Life of William Blake*, 1:173–77.
2. See *Letters*, 61–62, for Schofield's complaint against Blake.
3. Of Blake's utterance, Erdman comments, "It is a common opinion that Blake is as unlikely to have said none of this as to have said all of it" (406). Erdman's analysis of the whole incident is scrupulous and informative. See *Prophet Against Empire*, 403–11. See also Jacob Bronowski, *Blake and the Age of Revolution*, 62–88. Bronowski hears the cadences of Blake's prophecy in parts of Schofield's complaint.
4. Cf. Erdman's remark that the effect of the trial upon Blake's prophetic vocation was "inevitably ... to intensify Blake's self-censorship and the tension between man and prophet.... How can a bard hiding from Satan's watch-fiends conduct intellectual war?" (412, 420).
5. Erdman sympathetically defends Blake's passivity as "a son of fire who did not know, in actual combat, how to wield his mental sword except by sheathing it in silence or in the privacy of his own manuscripts" (410). But would Ezekiel so silently have sheathed *his* mental sword?
6. Erdman argues suggestively that Blake found himself "frightened at his own republicanism" (413). Hence his turn inward: "Blake looked upon psychology as a phase of politics and politics as an acting out of mental strife" (422).
7. Erdman suggests that Blake resorts here to the quibble that, though he was *writing* seditiously (as Los), he was not *speaking* thus (as Blake), 410.
8. John Middleton Murry makes this dualism a central fact of Blake's poetry. See *William Blake* (1933; New York: McGraw-Hill, 1964), 32. Murry errs only in applying it to the whole of Blake's corpus, for it fits the late poems best.
9. Bloom relieves Blake of this tension and shifts the onus to his critics: "critics who ought to know better still mutter about Blake's paranoia," *Apocalypse*, 315. Bloom should have another look at the *Descriptive Catalogue* or "Public Address" before dismissing even the possibility that Blake struggled to maintain a psychic defense against the threat of persecution.
10. Damrosch alone among Blake's critics adequately stresses the importance of this function. See "Blake and the Spectre," *Symbol and Truth*, 307–17.
11. Bleuler, *Dementia Praecox, or the Group of Schizophrenias*, 135.
12. See Bleuler, 228–32; Neale and Oltmanns, *Schizophrenia*, 53–54; Bernheim and Lewine, *Schizophrenia: Symptoms, Causes, Treatments*, 40–41. For recent diagnostic criteria, see

the *Diagnostic and Statistical Manual*, 3d ed., 191. Paranoia usually sets in later in life than other mental disturbances.
13. Sigmund Freud, "The Case of Schreber," *Standard Edition*, 12:71.
14. Milton Percival points out the paradox of Blake's defensive system and the dualism that inspires it: "a hater of systems, he could not rest without one of his own. He was now Los, the inspired prophet, and now Urizen, the doubting spectre," *William Blake's Circle of Destiny* (1938; New York: Octagon, 1964), 90.
15. My position here opposes Frye, who sees Blake's system as operative from the beginning. Murry comes closer than Frye to the truth when he asserts that Blake's method was spontaneous: "His works were largely unforeseen, and grew into forms that were not consciously intended" (108). Except for the lyric, Blake never returns to a form he has previously used. Each poem is, in a sense, its own genre.
16. See Frye's suggestive discussion, *Fearful Symmetry*, 217-18.
17. For an extended treatment of Blake's vision of Brotherhood, see Michael Ferber, *The Social Vision of William Blake* (Princeton: Princeton University Press, 1985).
18. See Damrosch, 254. Damrosch stresses too the necessity to Blake's psychology of "a divine principle in which the individual is at once ratified and liberated from the isolation of the selfhood." In a similar vein, Murry dismisses Blake's recourse to a purely intellectual existence in *A Vision of the Last Judgment* as "wanton obscurantism" (355).
19. See Bloom's analysis of the final vision of *Jerusalem*, 431-33. Bloom anticipates a charge against Blake's sublimated idealism when he defends Los's turn to Jesus on plate 5: "to annihilate the selfhood is to emulate Blake's Milton by washing off the not human.... Many of Blake's best and most devoted critics have sought to mitigate the completeness of Blake's rejection here, but they ought to remain on their Beulah-couches without seeking to have their master join them in that soft repose" (371). Bloom underestimates the real difficulties Blake has in accounting for the "not human" in any other manner than a psychological dualism. If all of reality is human, then whence comes the not human?
20. See Damrosch's illuminating discussion of Blake, Los, and the Spectre, *Symbol and Truth*, 302-48.
21. R. D. Laing, *The Divided Self*, 80.
22. Although Frye and Bloom after him have made it unfashionable to associate Blake with mystical tradition, critics before them made this claim with some merit. Coleridge, upon reading *Songs of Innocence and Experience*, asserted with assurance that Blake "is a man of Genius — and I apprehend a Swedenborgian — certainly a mystic *emphatically*," *William Blake, the Critical Heritage*, 55. Ellis and Yeats, in their ground breaking three-volume edition of Blake's works, associate Blake with mystical tradition because "the creative mystic and the man of genius... live unenslaved by any 'reason' and pass at will into the universal life.... Blake's was a complex message — more adapted than any former mystical utterance to a highly complex age," *The Works of William Blake, Poetic, Symbolic, and Critical* (London: Bernard Quaritch, 1893), 243, xi. Percival argues that Blake "carries idealism to the point of mysticism," *Circle of Destiny*, 278. Murry maintains Blake to be "an authentic Mystic," a vocation that makes of him "a bruised and battered thing," *William Blake*, 17. Perhaps the best assessment of Blake's relation to mystical tradition is Frye's own appendix to *Fearful Symmetry*, "General Note: Blake's Mysticism," (431-32). Here Frye admits that there are some forms of mysticism

toward which Blake's vision is quite congenial. Finally, see Altizer's informed discussion of Blake as mystic in the section entitled "Mysticism and Eschatology," *The New Apocalypse*, 179–192.
23. Compare Blake's psychological dualism with that described by Aldous Huxley as belonging to the higher form of mysticism he calls "the perennial philosophy": "man's obsessive consciousness of, and insistence on being, a separate self is the final and most fundamental obstacle to the unitive knowledge of God. To be a self is... the original sin, and to die to self, in feeling, will, and intellect, is the final and all-inclusive virtue," *The Perennial Philosophy* (New York: Harper, 1945), 36.
24. As Damrosch argues: "profoundly aware of contradiction within himself and society, [Blake] seeks to define them as contraries and to imagine a realm of existence in which their activity can produce unity instead of division. He may claim to eschew mysticism and mystery, yet in the end he cannot avoid them" (240).
25. Frye insists that *Milton* and *Jerusalem* are "inseparable, and constitute a double epic" (323).
26. As Bloom might describe this passage, referring it to Satan's voyage through chaos in *Paradise Lost*. But texts do not always refer to other texts. Sometimes they refer to the pathological eruption in which they originate, even if condemned never quite to express its full horror. For Bloom's method of rhetorical (or antithetical) interpretation, see *Poetry and Repression*, chapter 1 (New Haven: Yale University Press, 1976). The passage I quote would, in Bloom's terms, constitute a classic example of *clinamen*, or turning away from the precursor.
27. Such visions are characteristic of dissociative disorders and sometimes even of schizophrenia, as Bleuler indicates when he asserts that "a combination of auditory and visual hallucinations permits the diagnosis of schizophrenia" (273). See also Kraeplin, *Dementia Praecox*, 7–17. Schorer is one of Blake's few critics to stress the real menace vision posed for Blake: "He was a slave to vision as other men are to cruelty or avarice or sensuality or opium, and the consequence for him was the same it was for them—a narrowing of individuality, and a final disregard for the order beyond one's own," *Politics of Vision*, 435. Blake's myth is in part an effort to make a profound autistic urge productive.
28. Foucault, *Madness and Civilization*, 288–89
29. Frye makes this observation about *Milton*, and then, rather desperately, adds a disclaimer: "the two great illuminations portrayed in that poem do not describe events in Blake's life" (327). How he knows this with certainty, Frye does not bother to tell.
30. For a reading of the Bard's Song openly hostile to any attempt to see it as compensatory, see James Rieger, "'The Hem of Their Garments': The Bard's Song in *Milton*," *Blake's Sublime Allegory*, 259–80. See, too, Frye's reading of the whole poem, "Notes for a Commentary on *Milton*," *The Divine Vision*, ed. Vivian de Sola Pinto (London: Victor Gollancz, 1957), 97–138.
31. Bloom rightly views Blake's Jesus as the agent of overcoming dualism: "To Blake all dualities are spectral, and Christ and the human imagination in the freedom of its power are as one" (364). But Blake's Jesus makes possible the unity *between* people that the individual gets glimpses of in moments of vision. He is Blake's hedge against solipsism. Blake does not so much identify Jesus with the imagination in his late works as the imagination with Jesus.
32. Frye, 292–93.

33. Bloom, 343, 345.
34. Bloom, "Blake's *Jerusalem:* The Bard of Sensibility and the Form of Prophecy," *The Ringers in the Tower: Studies in Romantic Tradition* (Chicago: University of Chicago Press, 1971), 65–80, 68.
35. Damrosch, 312, 314.
36. Morton D. Paley, *The Continuing City: William Blake's Jerusalem,* 250–51.
37. For a survey of Blake's visual representations of the Spectre, see Nelson Hilton, *Literal Imagination* (Berkeley: University of California Press, 1983). Hilton overlooks *The Ghost of a Flea.*
38. For a discussion of the Spectre in terms of the *doppelgänger* of later nineteenth-century Romanticism, see Edward J. Rose, "Blake and the Double: the Spectre as *Doppelgänger,*" *Colby Library Quarterly* 13 (1977): 127–39. Incidentally, and without developing the point, Rose suggests that Los and the Spectre exemplify a "healthy and prophetic schizophrenia" that contrasts with Albion's "pathological condition" (137).
39. Bleuler, 104.
40. See Janet Warner, "Blake's Figures of Despair: Man in his Spectre's Power" *William Blake: Essays in Honor of Sir Geoffrey Keynes,* ed. Morton D. Paley and Michael Phillips (Oxford: Clarendon, 1973), 208–24; Morton D. Paley, "Cowper as Blake's Spectre," *Eighteenth Century Studies,* 1 (1968): 236–52; Margaret Storch, "The 'Spectrous Fiend' Cast Out: Blake's Crisis at Felpham," *Modern Language Quarterly,* 44(1983): 115–35; and finally, Damrosch, 312–16.
41. Friedrich Nietzsche, "On the Genealogy of Morals," *On the Genealogy of Morals and Ecce Homo,* 93.
42. For the details of Cromek's opportunistic manipulations of Blake, see Mona Wilson, *Life,* 224–40. For a slightly more favorable view, see *Blake Records Supplement,* 45–53.
43. Cf. Bloom's remark, "The Spectre of Urthona is always right," *Ringers,* 74.
44. For a full discussion of this opposition and its importance to Romantic poetry, see Paul Cantor, *Creature and Creator,* especially chapter 4, "The Nightmare of Romantic Idealism."
45. Bloom writes of Blake that "it is his *own* Spectre of Urthona who must be overcome," *Ringers,* 74.
46. It should be clear that I am loosely applying the insights offered in Bloom's *Anxiety of Influence* (Oxford: Oxford University Press, 1973) to Blake's own career as a poet. Blake can recreate his precursors, as he clearly does in *Milton,* but thus to recreate his *own* earlier vision would mean openly to reject parts of it, resulting in a metaphysical dualism of the sort he works to avoid with his psychological alternative. Wordsworth is an example of a poet who, in outgrowing his past, lapses into a metaphysical dualism. Blake avoids this compromise by reducing the strength of his earlier vision through the benign violence of revision.
47. Paley calls this misreading the "anterior myth" (173) of *Jerusalem,* but fails to suggest why Blake accepts so simplistic a vision of beginnings after the subtlety of *The Four Zoas.*
48. This need would explain Blake's withholding in later years his early masterpiece, *The Marriage of Heaven and Hell,* when listing his saleable works for prospective buyers. See his letter to Dawson Turner of 9 June 1818 (*Letters,* 142), where he omits all reference to it.
49. *Blake Records,* 322.

50. Damrosch, 312.
51. The poems of the Pickering Manuscript, "The Crystal Cabinet" especially, also emphasize the fatality of fallen love. Damrosch contends that Blake is forced to capitulate the sado-masochistic tragedy of desire: "sex as we know it is incapable of being transformed" (201).
52. Foucault, 285.
53. Paley emphasizes the sexual origin of this resistance. The "anterior myth" of a primordial sexual encounter has Albion repressing his sexual impulses and suffering for feeling them, having "in effect programmed himself for guilt" (176). Such an interpretation does not explain, however, why Blake turns to Jesus to resolve an essentially sexual self-obsession. In *Jerusalem* Blake steps beyond a sexual therapy and embraces a religious one.
54. Bloom, 428.
55. Forgiveness is indeed, as critics usually contend, the imagination's means of annihilating restraint (see Frye, 259), but it is also a backhanded way of admitting guilt, which in Blake's case could refer to his repressed republicanism. Blake may have remained a republican, but not the outspoken one he was in his youth: "Come, O Lamb of God, and take away the remembrance of Sin" (*J*, 50:24).
56. As Schorer argues, "Insofar as the later poems are different in their content from the earlier poems, it is in their increased concern with a religious rather than a political solution" (384). Schorer wisely cautions against separating these alternatives except as variations on the same psychological theme.
57. Nietzsche, 46. Murry lodges a complaint against the bald "resentment" Blake reveals when he berates the work of more successful artists. See *William Blake*, 340.

Index

Adams, Hazard, 177 n. 34
Ahania, 116, 124
Albion. *See* Ancient Man
Albion Rose, 46
"All Pictures thats Panted," 30
Altizer, Thomas J. J., 171 n. 29, 174 n. 25, 182 n. 53, 186 n. 22
America, 7, 8, 59, 67–68, 73–74, 102, 138
Ancient Man, 38, 39, 41, 42, 86, 87, 96–97, 101, 103, 104, 105, 108–134, 148, 153, 154, 156, 162, 164, 165, 180 n. 24
"Annotations to *An Apology for the Bible*," 105, 106, 119
"Annotations to Bacon's *Essays*," 138
"Annotations to Spurzheim's *Observations on Insanity*," 24–25, 48
Aristotle, 75, 94, 176 n. 11, 177 n. 40
Art, ix, xi, xii, 6, 15, 18, 21, 22, 23, 24, 27, 28, 29, 30, 31, 33, 36, 39, 40, 41, 43, 53, 59, 60, 62, 98, 104, 126, 127, 128, 129, 130, 139, 142, 148, 167, 168
  and compensation, 35–36, 69, 155
  therapeutic function, 33, 39–40, 43, 60, 126, 147, 152, 167
"Auguries of Innocence," 40, 108
Ault, Donald, 178 n. 7
Autism, 23, 87, 90, 91, 92, 93, 95, 108, 111, 112, 113, 115, 117, 123, 126, 128, 131, 156

Bacon, Sir Francis, 24, 25, 138, 167
Barfield, Owen, 173 n. 2
Barlow, Joel, 8
Basire, James, 5–6
Bataille, Georges, 85–86, 177 n. 20
  Bate, Jonathan, 176 n. 14, 177 n. 19
Beer, John, 176 n. 9
Behrendt, Stephen C., 176 n. 16
Bentley, G. E., Jr., 169 n. 3, 170 n. 3, 176 n. 17, 179 n. 9, 182 n. 54
Bernheim, Kayla, and Richard Lewine, 177 n. 27, 183 n. 12
Beulah, 57, 128, 167
Blair, Thomas, 11, 157
Blake, Catherine, 5
Blake, Catherine Boucher, 6, 10, 12, 126, 127
Blake, James, 5, 170 n. 2
Blake, Robert, 6–7, 21–22
Blake, William
  biographical overview, 5–13
  engraver and designer, 5, 6, 8–9, 11, 12, 22, 102, 140
  human norm, 3–4, 14, 31, 33, 43
  mysticism, 145, 147, 150, 184 n. 22
  painter, 5, 7, 8, 9, 37, 140
  question of madness, ix, 42–43, 59, 69, 98, 108, 126, 127, 147, 153, 168
  quietism, 135, 143, 150, 156, 167, 168
  religious conversion, 128, 131–34, 144, 145, 165, 168

Blake, William (*continued*)
  reputation as madman, 3, 9, 13, 16, 20, 24, 27, 28–29, 112
  revolutionary, 7–8, 45–46, 61, 104–5, 138–40
  Schofield incident, 10–11, 137–38
  and sensibility bards, 47–48, 51–52, 145, 152, 159
  and Shakespeare, 74–84, 86–87
  trial for sedition, 11, 135, 139–40, 150, 154–55, 183 n. 1
  and tragedy, 57–58, 74–75, 78, 80–81, 82, 83–84, 85, 134
  and Urizen, 97–98
  visionary, xii, 5, 6, 7, 11, 14–15, 17–18, 20–22, 23, 30, 32–36, 42–43, 97, 102–3, 126, 131, 133, 135, 147, 148, 149, 151, 154, 155, 157, 168
Bleuler, Eugene, 42, 110, 111, 112, 113, 114, 115, 118, 123, 127, 131, 154, 172 n. 44, 175 n. 32, 181 nn. 30, 31, 182 n. 47, 183 nn. 10, 12, 185 n. 27, 186 n. 39
Bloom, Harold, 18, 19, 24, 38, 84, 86, 88, 89, 97, 114, 131–32, 144, 151, 170 n. 4, 171 n. 19, 172 n. 39, 174 nn. 26, 28, 175 n. 33, 176 n. 17, 177 nn. 23, 24, 28, 29, 33, 37, 178 nn. 3, 6, 41, 180 nn. 24, 26, 182 n. 51, 183 n. 9, 184 nn. 19, 22, 185 nn. 26, 31, 186 nn. 33, 34, 43, 45, 46, 187 n. 54
Boehme, Jakob, 145
The Book of Ahania, 7
The Book of Job engravings, 12
The Book of Los, 7
The Book of Thel, 7, 58, 90, 128
The Book of Urizen, 7, 74, 85–96, 97, 98, 103, 104, 109, 112, 113, 121, 124, 146
Borges, Jorge Luis, 94
Brisman, Leslie, 180 nn. 20, 23
Bromion, 63–66
Bronowski, Jacob, 173 n. 1, 183 n. 3
Bulwer Lytton, Edward, 9
Bunyan, John, 15
Burney, Fanny, 71
Butts, Thomas, 9, 11, 26, 31, 42, 98, 102, 127, 135, 170 n. 10
Byrd, Max, 171 n. 27
Byron, George Gordon, Lord, 18, 75, 175 n. 7

Calvert, Edward, 12
Camus, Albert, 94
Cantor, Paul, 91, 93–94, 177 nn. 22, 29, 36, 40, 182 n. 48, 186 n. 44
Chatterton, 47
Coleridge, Samuel Taylor, ix, 29, 32, 184 n. 22
  "Kubla Khan," ix, x
Collins, William, 27, 47, 48, 49, 50, 51, 52, 53, 57, 69, 173 nn. 6, 7
  "Ode on the Poetical Character," 48–49
Cooper, Andrew, 178 n. 43, 181 n. 35
Cowper, William, 9, 10, 24–25, 27, 47, 48, 49, 50, 52, 53, 57, 69, 159, 173 nn. 6, 8, 9
  "Lines Written during a Period of Insanity," 49
Cromek, Robert, 11, 157
Cumberland, George, 102, 104

Damon, S. Foster, 170 n. 7, 177 n. 30
Damrosch, Leopold, 144, 152, 169 n. 6, 171 n. 17, 172 n. 30, 174 n. 25, 175 n. 29, 176 n. 8, 178 n. 42, 180 n. 27, 181 n. 40, 182 nn. 41, 49, 183 nn. 10, 57, 184 nn. 18, 20, 185 n. 24, 186 nn. 35, 40, 187 nn. 50, 51
Dante, 20, 43
Davis, Michael, 169 n. 3
Deen, Leonard, 180 n. 24, 182 nn. 46, 53
Deleuze, Giles, and Felix Guattari, 180 n. 28, 181 n. 34
De Quincey, Thomas, 24
Descartes, René, 4
Descriptive Catalogue, 11, 21, 107
Diagnostic and Statistical Manual, 2, 41, 172 n. 42, 181 n. 30, 184 n. 12
DiSalvo, Jackie, 179 n. 8
Dissociation of sensibility, 87, 91, 92, 94, 177 n. 34. *See also* psychic dissociation

"The Ecchoing Green," 58
Edwards, Richard, 8
Eliot, T. S., 19, 170 n. 6
  The Waste Land, 43
Emanation, 106, 116, 117, 118, 156, 162, 181 n. 40
Emery, Clark, 177 n. 29
Enion, 106, 116–21, 124, 160, 180 n. 45

Index

Enitharmon, 57, 94–95, 98, 121–31, 161, 182 n. 46
Erdman, David V., 166, 169 n. 7, 173 n. 1, 175 n. 1, 176 n. 17, 177 n. 28, 197 nn. 14, 17, 18, 19, 180 n. 26, 183 nn. 3, 4, 5, 6, 7
Erin, 157
Europe, 7, 8, 22, 67, 68–69, 102, 146
Experience, human norm, 3–4, 33, 43

Fall, 21, 39
  as psychological phenomenon, 38–39, 69, 107–8, 110, 134
  as social phenomenon, 26, 28
Feder, Lillian, 173 n. 5
Feber, Michael, 184 n. 17
Flaxman, John, 9, 12, 74, 102, 103, 104, 179 n. 12
Foucault, Michel, 1, 19, 25, 26, 27, 40, 60, 98, 148, 164, 169 n. 1, 171 n. 22, 175 n. 35, 178 n. 44, 185 n. 28, 185 n. 52
  madness as linguistic phenomenon, 29–33
  madness as social phenomenon, 25–28
The Four Zoas, 55, 57, 62, 66, 84, 87, 97, 99, 101, 103, 105–34, 139, 142, 143, 144, 145, 148, 149, 150, 152, 155, 157, 159, 160, 161, 162, 164, 165
The French Revolution, 7, 8, 61, 179 n. 15
Freud, Sigmund, 42, 66, 83, 110, 142, 157, 163, 172 n. 43, 175 nn. 30, 38, 176 n. 18, 178 n. 42, 182 n. 52, 184 n. 13
Frosch, Thomas, 174 n. 21
Frye, Northrop, x, 13, 19, 23, 27, 36, 85, 106, 118, 151, 170 n. 5, 171 nn. 15, 26, 172 nn. 34, 35, 36, 173 nn. 2, 3, 176 nn. 9, 16, 17, 177 n. 29, 178 n. 6, 180 nn. 21, 26, 182 nn. 46, 48, 51, 184 nn. 15, 16, 22, 185 nn. 25, 29, 30, 32, 187 n. 55
Fuseli, Henry, 8, 102, 104, 170 n. 9, 179 n. 12

The Gates of Paradise, 7, 39
George III, 71–74, 76, 78, 81, 82, 175 n. 7
George, Diana Hume, 176 n. 18, 183 n. 58
The Ghost of Abel, 168
The Ghost of a Flea, 153
Gilchrist, Alexander, 23, 169 nn. 3, 4, 170 n. 1, 171 n. 20, 183 n. 1
Gleckner, Robert, 174 nn. 17, 20
Godard, Jerry Caris, 172 n. 41
Godwin, William, 8
Goethe, Johann Wolfgang von, 31, 172 n. 33
  Faust, 31
Golgonooza, 142, 145, 158
Gottesman, Irving, 172 n. 43
Grant, John, 182 n. 41
Gray, Thomas, 27, 47
  "The Bard," 47
"The Grey Monk," 166–67
Guttmacher, Manfred, 175 nn. 2, 3, 5

Hagstrum, Jean, 170 n. 12, 181 n. 38, 182 n. 53
Halloran, William F., 176 n. 16
Hartman, Geoffrey, 174 n. 13, 177 n. 35
Hayley, William, 9–11, 14, 22, 26–27, 43, 49, 102, 132, 138, 140, 150, 171 n. 25, 173 n. 9, 174 n. 22, 178 n. 3, 180 n. 22
  Little Tom the Sailor, 10
  Triumphs of Temper, 26
Hegel, G. W. F., 57, 174 n. 25, 176 n. 12
Helms, Randel, 181 n. 37
Hesketh, Lady Harriet, 27
Hilton, Nelson, 186 n. 37
Hirsch, E. D., 112, 181 n. 33, 182 n. 53
"Holy Thursday," 63
Homer, 43
  The Iliad, 104
On Homers Poetry, 75
Housman, A. E., 47, 53, 173 nn. 4, 5
"The Human Abstract," 26
Humphrey, Ozias, 179 n. 9
Hunt, Robert, 28
Huxley, Aldous, 185 n. 23

"Infant Sorrow," 122
"Introduction" to *Songs of Innocence*, 55–56
An Island in the Moon, 61–63, 88

James, William, 133, 183 n. 56
Jaynes, Julian, 172 n. 43
Jerusalem, x, 11, 49, 55, 103, 134, 140, 142, 143, 144, 145, 146, 151–68
Jerusalem, 106, 139, 165

192 Index

Jesus, 131, 132, 133, 134, 148, 150, 151, 161, 165, 167, 185 n. 31
Johnson, Joseph, 7-8, 102
Johnson, Samuel, 25

Kafka, Franz, 94, 101, 105, 113
Keynes, Geoffrey, 169 nn. 3, 5, 171 n. 25
Kierkegaard, Søren, 1, 86, 108, 120, 172 n. 40, 177 n. 26, 180 n. 25, 181 n. 43
Kitto, D. F. H., 176 n. 11
Kraeplin, Emil, 172 n. 44, 181 n. 30, 185 n. 27

Laing, R. D., 60, 61, 88, 94, 144-45, 172 n. 41, 175 nn. 34, 35, 36, 177 n. 39, 181 n. 44, 184 n. 21
Lamb, Charles, 170 n. 3
Landor, Walter Savage, 170 n. 3
Langbaum, Robert, 174 n. 18
Langland, William, 23
Laocoön, 25, 112
The Last Judgment, 40, 143
Lee, Judith, 182 n. 40
Lidz, Theodore, 172 n. 43
Linnell, John, 12, 26
Locke, John, 4, 24, 25, 91, 167
Los, 31, 32, 34, 55, 87, 89, 92-95, 97, 98, 121-31, 144, 145, 147, 150, 151, 164, 165, 166, 167, 168, 172 n. 34, 182 n. 46
Luvah, 109, 113-15, 132, 160
Lyric, 46-47, 50, 52-53, 55

Macalpine, Ida, and Richard Hunter, 175 nn. 4, 6
Madness, xii, 9, 13, 18, 19, 22, 24, 31, 46, 60, 65, 89, 93, 96, 108, 111, 114, 118, 120, 121, 125, 130, 132, 138, 142, 152, 154, 155, 159, 164, 165, 167
  clinically understood, 1-2, 40-42, 59, 87
  and George III, 71-74
  historically understood, 1-2, 24-31, 60-63
  and human norm, 3, 36
  and *King Lear*, 76-78, 83-84
  and lyric, 48-50, 53
  metaphysically understood, 76-77
  and poetic inspiration, 18, 27, 37, 47, 53, 126

and religion, 24, 25, 48-51, 96, 116, 132, 145, 147, 150, 165
and the sensibility bards, 47-52, 54, 69
as subject for myth, x, 16, 18, 40, 42, 55, 59, 69, 85, 87, 88, 89, 98, 101, 103, 107, 108, 110, 112, 126, 144, 168
and Urizen, 88-96
"Mad Song," 52, 55, 152
Margoliouth, H. M., 104, 179 nn. 11, 13
The Marriage of Heaven and Hell, x, 7, 14-15, 58, 105, 140, 143, 152, 160, 163, 165, 166, 167, 186 n. 48
Marsh, Edward Garrard, 174 n. 22
Masturbation, 65, 128
Mellor, Anne K., 179 n. 12, 183 n. 53
Milton, 11, 102, 103, 134, 140, 142, 144, 145, 146-51, 153, 154, 160
Milton, John, 20, 50, 51, 52, 85, 88, 92, 97, 142, 149, 150, 153
  Paradise Lost, 85, 89
Murry, John Middleton, 183 n. 8, 184 nn. 15, 18, 184 n. 22, 187 n. 57
"My Spectre around me night and day," 117
Myth, xii, 19, 22, 58, 97, 114, 122, 132, 134, 138, 148, 153, 160, 161, 167
  and compensation, 98, 125, 135, 140, 150, 155, 166, 167
  and dramatic form, 38, 53, 58
  and history, 66-69, 73-74
  and language, 29
  and lyric, 38, 52-53, 58, 66
  and psychic dissociation, 38, 41, 55, 66, 85, 86, 89, 109
  and religious conversion, 133
  as representation of madness, x, 16, 40, 55, 85, 101, 103, 107, 108, 109, 110, 111, 112, 115, 131, 144, 164-65, 180 n. 29
  and schizophrenia, 110-12, 115
  and symbol, 55, 58, 133
  therapeutic function, x, 15, 18, 33, 37-40, 43, 59, 63, 69, 86, 96, 98, 101, 103, 108, 112, 121, 126, 129, 131, 142, 146, 164, 167, 168
  and vision, xi, 13-15, 20-22, 31, 33, 35, 37, 59, 146, 148

Narcissism, 52, 62, 64, 66, 95, 163
Neale, John M., and Thomas F. Oltmanns, 172 n. 43, 175 n. 32, 183 n. 12
Newton, Sir Isaac, 24, 25, 91, 167
Nietzsche, Friedrich, 19, 36, 41, 55, 58, 59, 84, 155, 167, 172 nn. 37, 38, 174 nn. 16, 19, 23, 186 n. 41, 187 n. 57
  The Birth of Tragedy, 18, 37, 38, 53, 54
  Ecce Homo, 36–37
  On the Genealogy of Morals, 155, 167
  Apollinian and Dionysian elements in art, 37–40, 53–54, 57, 58, 60
  therapeutic function of art, 38–39, 54, 58
Nolan, Barbara, 171 n. 17

Ololon, 149
Oothoon, 63–66, 67
Orc, 58, 74, 95, 98, 133, 160, 161
Ovid, 63

Paine, Thomas, 7, 8, 105
Palamabron, 133, 149
Paley, Morton, 23, 152, 171 n. 16, 173 n. 9, 177 n. 32, 182 nn. 46, 53, 186 nn. 36, 40, 47, 187 n. 53
Palmer, Samuel, 12, 170 n. 12
Paranoia, 114, 141–42, 151, 157
Percival, Milton, 184 nn. 14, 22
Phillips, Thomas, 170 n. 9
Plato, 27, 47, 88, 144, 173 n. 5
Poetical Sketches, 6, 9, 51, 55
Pope, Alexander, 26, 171 n. 24
  The Dunciad, 26
Priestly, Joseph, 8
Psychic dissociation, 18, 37–39, 41, 42, 66, 67, 68, 83, 84, 85, 86, 89, 96, 107, 109, 110–11, 113, 115, 117, 126, 129, 130, 132, 144, 150, 151, 152, 154, 155, 157, 161, 162, 165
Psychoanalysis, xi, xii, 50, 59, 83, 174 n. 11
"Public Address," 98, 141, 143
Punter, David, 174 n. 25

Rahab, 131, 163
Raine, Kathleen, 175 n. 37
Reynolds, Sir Joshua, 97
Richmond, George, 12
Ricoeur, Paul, 86, 177 n. 21

Rieger, James, 185 n. 30
Rintrah, 133, 149
Robinson, Henry Crabb, 20, 162, 170 nn. 8, 9, 10, 174 n. 24
Rose, Edward, 186 n. 38
Rose, Samuel, 11, 139, 140
Rousseau, Jean-Jaques, 29, 163

Sacks, Oliver, 173 n. 46
Sade, Marquis de, 163, 164
Sartre, Jean-Paul, 94
Satan, 133, 146, 150
Schizoid experience, 144–45, 151, 154, 155, 157, 158, 163, 164, 167
Schizophrenia, xii, 2, 40–42, 60, 61, 87, 88, 94, 101, 103, 107, 108, 109, 110–11, 113, 115, 116, 117, 131, 141–42, 164, 165, 172 n. 43, 175 n. 32, 177 n. 27, 178 n. 1, 180 n. 29, 181 n. 30
Schofield, John, 10, 11, 137–38, 154, 169 n. 5, 183 n. 2
Schopenhauer, Arthur, 55
Schorer, Mark, 105, 171 n. 17, 172 n. 45, 173 n. 46, 174 nn. 14, 27, 176 n. 17, 177 n. 29, 179 n. 16, 185 n. 27, 187 n. 56
Scott, Sir Walter, 18
Sensibility bards, x, 27, 46–51, 52, 54, 56, 59, 60, 66, 67, 68, 69, 101, 126, 145, 152, 159
Sexuality, 63–66, 90, 116–20, 122–24, 127–29, 162–64
Shakespeare, William, 20, 74, 176 nn. 9, 10, 13, 15
  King Lear, 19, 74, 76–78, 79, 80, 81, 82, 83, 87, 91, 143
  MacBeth, 57
Sheehan, Susan, 175 n. 32
Shelley, Mary, 158, 159
  Frankenstein, 158, 159
Shelley, Percy Bysshe, ix, 15, 53, 169 n. 9, 174 n. 15, 175 n. 7
  A Defence of Poetry, 15, 53
  Prometheus Unbound, 75
  "England in 1819," 73
  "Julian and Maddalo," ix, x
Smart, Christopher, 25, 47, 48, 49, 53, 60, 69, 171 n. 23, 173 nn. 6, 9, 10

Smart, Christopher (*continued*)
  Jubilate Agno, 27, 49, 50
  "A Song to David," 49–50
Smith, J. T., 170 n. 11, 174 n. 22
The Song of Los, 7, 29
Songs of Innocence and of Experience, 7, 17, 55, 152
Southey, Robert, 170 n. 3
Spectre, 125, 126, 127, 128–37, 132, 144, 145, 151–64, 166, 167, 168, 182 n. 51
Spurzheim, Johann, 24, 48
Stevens, Wallace, 45, 51, 67, 69, 174 n. 12
Storch, Margaret, 186 n. 40
Stothard, Thomas, 11
Straus, Erwin, 169 nn. 2, 8, 175 n. 31
"To Summer," 51–52
Sutherland, John, 178 n. 41
Swinburne, Algernon, 174 n. 14
Symbol, 55, 58
  and fantasy, 65
  and psychic dissociation, 38, 55, 112
  and obscurantism, 8, 133, 156
  and schizophrenia, 60
  and tragedy, 81, 82, 84
  and vision, 56–57
Swedenborg, Emanuel, 145

Tannenbaum, Leslie, 86, 89, 177 nn. 25, 31, 37
Taylor, Thomas, 170 n. 9
Tatham, Frederick, 12, 126, 127, 128
Tharmas, 106, 109, 116–21, 124, 125, 128, 154
Theotormon, 63–66
There is No Natural Religion, 141, 166
Tiriel, 74, 76, 77–84, 86, 93
Tirzah, 163
Tragedy, 37, 57, 74–75, 80, 82, 94, 134, 163
  Blake's revaluation, 78, 80–81, 87
  Greek, 37–38, 57, 58, 73
  Shakespearean, 75, 76, 77, 96

Ulro, 131
Urizen, 22, 38, 55, 58, 67, 87–96, 97, 98, 104, 109, 113, 114, 115, 116, 122, 123, 124, 125, 126, 146, 160

Vala, 103–5. *See also The Four Zoas*
Vala, 104, 114, 115, 160

Van Gogh, Vincent, 19
Varley, John, 12, 170 n. 9, 171 n. 15
Vision
  and empiricist philosophy, 25, 27, 30
  and hallucination, 15, 20–21, 23, 42–43, 147, 185 n. 27
  and human norm, xi, 33, 36, 59
  and imagination, xii
  and madness, xii, 16, 17–18, 23, 30, 32, 36, 46, 48–50, 59, 63, 103, 127, 134, 147, 148, 158, 168
  and religion, 18, 48–50, 132, 134, 146, 150, 166
Visionary experience, 5, 7, 11, 12, 14, 15–16, 20–22, 23, 32, 36, 37, 42–43, 58, 68, 69, 131, 134, 135, 144, 145, 146, 147, 148, 149, 156, 165, 168, 171 n. 15
Visionary heads, 12, 171 n. 15
Visions of the Daughters of Albion, 7, 61–67, 116, 128
Voltaire, François, 20

Wagenknecht, David, 174 n. 18
Wakefield, Gilbert, 105
Warner, Janet, 186 n. 40
Wedgewood, Josiah, 12
Wilkie, Brian, and Mary Lynn Johnson, 178 nn. 4, 5, 6, 179 n. 10, 180 nn. 21, 26, 181 nn. 39, 40, 182 nn. 46, 51
"William Bond," 167
Wilson, Mona, 169 n. 3, 171 n. 29, 183 n. 1, 186 n. 42
"With happiness stretch'd across the hills," 32–36
Wollstonecraft, Mary, 8
Wordsworth, Dorothy, 20, 53
Wordsworth, William, ix, 17–18, 29, 32, 33, 49, 53, 75, 149, 170 n. 3, 179 n. 17, 186 n. 46
  The Prelude, 134
  "Resolution and Independence," ix, x, 33
  "Tintern Abbey," 32

Yeats, William Butler, 21, 30, 124, 163, 172 nn. 31, 32, 184 n. 22
Young, Edward, 9
  Night Thoughts, 9, 102

Zoas, 39, 112, 113, 115, 116, 117, 121, 132, 160

www.ingramcontent.com/pod-product-compliance
Lightning Source LLC
Chambersburg PA
CBHW031551300426
44111CB00006BA/262